the Unofficial Guide™ to Homeschooling

Kathy Ishizuka

IDG Books Worldwide, Inc.
An International Data Group Company
Foster City, CA • Chicago, IL • Indianapolis, IN •
New York, NY

IDG Books Worldwide, Inc.
An International Data Group Company
919 E. Hillsdale Boulevard
Suite 400
Foster City, CA 94404

This publication contains the opinions and ideas of its author and is designed to provide useful advice to the reader on the subject matter covered. Any references to any products or services do not constitute or imply an endorsement or recommendation. The publisher and the author specifically disclaim any responsibility for any liability, loss or risk (financial, personal or otherwise) that may be claimed or incurred as a consequence, directly or indirectly, of the use and/or application of any of the contents of this publication.

Certain terms mentioned in this book that are known or claimed to be trademarks or service marks have been capitalized.

IDG Books Worldwide, Inc., does not attest to the validity, accuracy or completeness of this information. Use of a term in this book should not be regarded as affecting the validity of any trademark or service mark.

Unofficial Guides are a trademark of IDG Books Worldwide, Inc.

For general information on IDG Books Worldwide's books in the U.S., please call our Consumer Customer Service department at 800-762-2974. For reseller information, including discounts and previous sales, please call our Reseller Customer Service department at 800-434-3422.

ISBN: 0-02-863814-X

Manufactured in the United States of America

10 9 8 7 6 5 4 3 2 1

First edition

To Mom and Dad, my first teachers
To Keiji and Noah, who inspire me to continue learning
And to Tom, an extraordinary teacher

Acknowledgments

I wish to thank the many individuals who generously contributed to this book: Annette, Karen Andreola, Lorie Bacon, Pam Baker, Denise Banker, Sonja Becker-Bolter, Virginia Belknap, Amanda Bennett, Ann D. Bingham, Sherry Boas, Amber Brannon, Tammy Cardwell, the Caron Family, Cathy Carter, Barbara Cooper, Sarah Covington, Dorothy Davis, Kandie Demarest, Deborah Dow, Lynn Emerson, Richard C. Endsley, Georgette Evans, Janie Gilbert, Kysa Kohl Gilkerson, Tammy Glaser, Giovanna Gomez, Janet Griffin, Susan Groover, Lauren Gross, Micki Haas, Cheryl Hall, Anne Heerdt-Wingfield, Helen Hegener, Lisa M. Henderson, Stephanie Holland, Jan Hunt, Cecilia Hutchings, Christina Joyner, Beth Krolak, Beverly Krueger, Nancy Lande, David D. Lanier, Georgia Ana Larson, Sherry Linsenbach, Charity Lovelace, Susan Lynch, Susan Thogerson Maas, Heather Madrone, Lawrence J. Magid, Debra Marcotte, Beverly Mastroianni, Lin McBee, Melissa, Mary Anne Melloy, Elisa Mohrmann, April Morris, Teressa Morris, Carole Muncy, Anne Ohman, Jackie Orsi, Liz Pike, Nancy Pistorius, Wendy Priesnitz, Marsha Ransom, A. Reedy, Jole Reinhardt, Cheri Reynolds, Howard Richman, Kathleen Roberts, Dani M. Sanders, Margo Sanders, Pam Sautbine, Sophia Sayigh, Susan Schaeffer, Jamie Shafer, Cerelle Simmons, Pam Sorooshian, Joe Spartaro, Robin Stalte, Teri Stettnisch, Patty Tanner, Christy Taylor, Joanna Tenaglia, Lyn Turner, Vicki Van Camp, Cindy Wade, Barb Wagner, Ellen Walterscheid, Joanne Ward, Kathy Ward, Lisa Weirauch,

Cynthia G. Welch, Julie Woessner. Other members of the homeschooling community took the time to offer their thoughts and personal experiences. Your contributions enlightened this author, as well as the text—thank you all.

For assistance, Kim O'Hara, Jan Arrigo, and Wing San Ho.

Special thanks to my editors Kris Fehr, Lynn Northrup, Brice Gosnell, and Randy Ladenheim-Gil; my agent Bert Holtje.

Contents

The *Unofficial Guide* Reader's Bill of Rights

We give you more than the official line

Welcome to the *Unofficial Guide* series of Lifestyles titles—books that deliver critical, unbiased information that other books can't or won't reveal—*the inside scoop.* Our goal is to provide you with the *most accessible, useful* information and advice possible. The recommendations we offer in these pages are not influenced by the corporate line of any organization or industry; we give you the hard facts, whether those institutions like them or not. If something is ill-advised or will cause a loss of time and/or money, we'll give you ample warning. And if it's a worthwhile option, we'll let you know that, too.

Armed and ready

Our hand-picked authors confidently and critically report on a wide range of topics that matter to smart readers like you. Our authors are passionate about their subjects, but have distanced themselves enough from them to help you be armed and protected, and help you make educated decisions as you go through the process. It is our intent that, from having read this book, you will avoid the pitfalls everyone else falls into and get it right the first time.

Don't be fooled by cheap imitations; this is the genuine article *Unofficial Guide* series from IDG Books. You may be familiar with our proven track record of the travel *Unofficial Guides*, which have more than three million copies in print. Each year thousands of travelers—new and old—are armed with a brand-new, fully updated edition of the flagship *Unofficial Guide to Walt Disney World*, by Bob Sehlinger. It is our intention here to provide you with the same level of objective authority that Mr. Sehlinger does in his brainchild.

The unofficial panel of experts

Every work in the Lifestyle *Unofficial Guides* is intensively inspected by a team of three top professionals in their fields. These experts review the manuscript for factual accuracy, comprehensiveness, and an insider's determination as to whether the manuscript fulfills the credo in this Reader's Bill of rights. In other words, our panel ensures that you are, in fact, getting "the inside scoop."

Our pledge

The authors, the editorial staff, and the Unofficial Panel of Experts assembled for *Unofficial Guides* are determined to lay out the most valuable alternatives available for our readers. This dictum means that our writers must be explicit, prescriptive, and above all, direct. We strive to be thorough and complete, but our goal is not necessarily to have the "most" or "all" of the information on a topic; this is not, after all, an encyclopedia. Our objective is to help you narrow down your options to the best of what is available, unbiased by affiliation with any industry or organization.

In each *Unofficial Guide,* we give you:

- Comprehensive coverage of necessary and vital information
- Authoritative, rigidly fact-checked data
- The most up-to-date insights into trends
- Savvy, sophisticated writing that's also readable
- Sensible, applicable facts and secrets that only an insider knows

Special features

Every book in our series offers the following six special sidebars in the margins that were devised to help you get things done cheaply, efficiently, and smartly.

1. **Timesaver**—tips and shortcuts that save you time

2. **Moneysaver**—tips and shortcuts that save you money

3. **Watch Out!**—more serious cautions and warnings

4. **Bright Idea**—general tips and shortcuts to help you find an easier or smarter way to do something

5. **Quote**—statements from real people that are intended to be prescriptive and valuable to you

6. **Unofficially...**—an insider's fact or anecdote

We also recognize your need to have quick information at your fingertips, and have thus provided the following comprehensive sections at the back of the book:

1. **Glossary**—definitions of complicated terminology and jargon

2. **Resource Directory**—lists of relevant agencies, associations, institutions, Web sites, etc.

3. **Recommended Reading List**—suggested titles that can help you get more in-depth information on related topics

4. **Important Documents**—"official" pieces of information you need to refer to, such as government forms

5. **Important Statistics**—facts and numbers presented at-a-glance for easy reference

6. **Index**

Letters, comments, questions from readers

We strive to continually improve the *Unofficial* series, and input from our readers is a valuable way for us to do that.

Many of those who have used the *Unofficial Guide* travel books write to the authors to ask questions, make comments, or share their own discoveries and lessons. For Lifestyle *Unofficial Guides*, we would also appreciate all such correspondence—both positive and critical—and we will make best efforts to incorporate appropriate readers' feedback and comments in revised editions of this work.

How to write us:

Unofficial Guides
Lifestyle Guides
IDG Books
1633 Broadway
New York, NY 10019

Attention: Reader's Comments

About the Author

A freelance writer and mother of two, Kathy Ishizuka specializes in family and children's issues. She has published magazine articles on a variety of related subjects, from window falls and online educational programs to playdate issues and lead hazards in the home. Her books include *10,000 Names for Your Baby* (Dell, 1997) and a collective biography of Asian American authors for young people.

The *Unofficial Guide* Panel of Experts

The *Unofficial* editorial team recognizes that you've purchased this book with the expectation of getting the most authoritative, carefully inspected information currently available. Toward that end, on each and every title in this series, we have selected a minimum of two "official" experts comprising the Unofficial Panel who painstakingly review the manuscripts to ensure the following: factual accuracy of all data; inclusion of the most up-to-date and relevant information; and that, from an insider's perspective, the authors have armed you with all the necessary facts you need—but that the institutions don't want you to know.

For *The Unofficial Guide to Homeschooling*, we are proud to introduce the following panel of experts:

Maureen McCaffrey has been involved in the publishing world for almost 30 years. She started as a teenager part-time at the Conservative Book Club and Arlington House Publishers. After finishing her schooling in Westchester County, New York, and Florence,

Italy, she began working full-time, starting with clerical work and eventually becoming vice president of the Conservative Book Club. There she was responsible for discovering books, rights arrangements, and helping to market the monthly selections. Along the line she encouraged publishers to take homeschoolers into consideration in their lists.

Her interest in good wholesome children's books led her to develop the homeschool and children's market for the Conservative Book Club. She realized early on that homeschooling was the wave of the future in America. In April 1997, Maureen purchased a controlling interest in *Homeschooling Today* magazine, a publication that she had long admired.

Tamra Orr has taught about home education regionally and nationally and has had a homeschooling newspaper column in Indiana. She is the author of the forthcoming *101 Ways to Make Your Library Homeschooling Friendly* and writes for numerous magazines on homeschooling and other child-development issues. She is also the mother of four children, all unschooled from birth.

Brian D. Ray, Ph.D., is President of the National Home Education Research Institute (NHERI, www.nheri.org), a nonprofit research and educational organization dedicated to serving home, private, and public educators by conducting research on home-based education, developing a network of researchers, and educating the worldwide public about homeschooling. He has conducted numerous studies on homeschooling, founded and serves as editor of the academic, refereed journal *Home School Researcher,* spoken widely at professional and homeschool conferences and to the media, and provided expert testimony before many courts and legislatures. Dr. Ray earned his Ph.D. in science education from Oregon State University, has taught at the elementary-school through graduate-university levels, and has published many articles and books. He is author of *Strengths of Their Own—Home Schoolers Across America* and *Home Schooling on the Threshold: A Survey of Research at the Dawn of the New Millennium,* and is co-author of *Home Schooling: Parents as Educators.*

Introduction

I n 1990, a Department of Education study concluded that between 250,000 and 300,000
school-aged children were being educated at
home. Those numbers have skyrocketed: As many as
1.5 million youngsters are now being homeschooled, an estimated 2 percent of the total elementary and secondary students.

Individual homeschoolers are also making headlines. In the 1980s, the Colfax family of California
achieved celebrity when three of their four homeschooled sons were admitted to Harvard. More
recently, Rebecca Sealfon, a 13-year-old from
Brooklyn, New York, became the first homeschooled child to win the National Spelling Bee.
She was one of 17 homeschooled students among
the 245 competitors in the 1997 event. Homeschooler Rio Benin scored a perfect 1600 on the
SATs and won a $20,000 scholarship in the 1999
Intel Science Talent Search. Country singer LeAnn
Rimes was homeschooled, as was Jason Taylor, a
football player for the Miami Dolphins.

While homeschoolers have traditionally been characterized as either religious fundamentalists or leftist radicals, the burgeoning movement is seeing a broader range of parents choosing the option for more practical reasons—they want to provide a better education for their children. Today, homeschoolers "are often from the same American mainstream that once frowned on homeschooling," observes David Guterson, author of *Family Matters: Why Homeschooling Makes Sense* (see Appendix C), and the bestseller *Snow Falling on Cedars*.

Opting out of school

Increasing disenchantment with our public schools has caused many families to opt out of the institution. Overall, our public system is simply not making the grade, leaving many of our youngsters illiterate or without adequate skills. In a recent assessment of young people in 21 countries, American high school seniors placed second-to-last in advanced math. In science, only 18 percent of fourth-graders scored at the proficient level, and only 2 percent scored at the advanced level (NAEP).

Unwieldy class sizes, discipline problems, and weak academics were among the key reasons why two-thirds of parents interviewed for a recent Seattle schools survey considered pulling their children out of the public system. Nearly 60 percent stayed in the public system due to the expense of private alternatives. However, two-thirds of the parents interviewed said they attended those schools because they believed in the public system and appreciated its diversity.

Indeed, all the bad reports do not obviate what the good schools are doing, nor the commitment of the many dedicated teachers and administrators whose heroic efforts grace many of our classrooms nationwide.

However, good public education is not locally available to all. Impatient for reform, many parents are choosing to leave the system.

Diverse reasons for homeschooling

While many families cite ideological reasons for homeschooling, other factors are coming to the fore. In a recent survey in Florida, for example, dissatisfaction with public and private schools was the more common reason for homeschooling, moving ahead of religious reasons. Patricia Lines, a researcher at the U.S. Department of Education, believes this does not necessarily mean these are secular homeschoolers, but rather their primary motivation has shifted.

In addition to academic quality, parents also face personal issues related to school. The adverse effect of institutional schooling is reported by researchers Susan Groover and Richard Endsley in their 1989 report *Family Environment and Attitudes of Homeschoolers and Non-Homeschoolers:* "Some parents cited the change in their child's personality—from happy and eager to learn, to being depressed and resistant to learning, or developing a poor self-image, having daily headaches, becoming hyperactive, or simply being bored."

There are also the negative aspects of peer culture. In addition to sex, drug use, and alcohol consumption, the general social atmosphere of the schoolyard is often fiercely competitive, cruel, and exclusionary. As opposed to the generalized view of homeschooling as socially damaging, home educators maintain it is, in fact, school, and its same-age peer immersion, that causes emotional harm.

Recent concern for the self-esteem of adolescent girls inspired researcher and author Susannah Sheffer to evaluate their peers in the homeschool setting. Sheffer found that homeschooled adolescent girls did not typically "lose their voice" or lose confidence in themselves when their ideas and opinions weren't embraced by their friends. Still others homeschool to reclaim family closeness, or meet the special needs of their children who may be highly gifted or who have learning disabilities or emotional issues.

Recent incidents of school violence have also inspired many to consider homeschooling. In the weeks after a deadly school shooting spree in Littleton, Colorado, and the wave of bomb scares and threats of violence against schools that followed, homeschool leaders reported a spike in parent inquiries about home education.

For many, however, homeschooling remains based on their belief that parents should be the primary influence in their children's lives. This includes passing on their religious, moral, and other personal values as an essential aspect of their homeschooling.

An increasingly respected option

"Bumpkin goes to Harvard" is how the media originally viewed their story, says David Colfax, whose three homeschooled sons were admitted to Harvard, as we mentioned earlier. Today, however, homeschooling is no longer perceived as a fringe activity. Homeschooled students routinely gain admittance to some of the most competitive colleges and universities in the country. There are so many homeschooled applicants that Harvard University, among other schools, has assigned an admissions officer to review their applications. When examining the overall academic record, homeschooling appears to be successful. According to researcher Patricia Lines, "Virtually all the available data show that the group of homeschooled children who are tested is above average." Homeschoolers consistently score well on standardized tests.

According to recent nationwide statistics, homeschoolers placed well above their traditionally schooled peers on the ACT, a college admissions test. Homeschoolers posted an average score of 22.7 out of a possible 36, tying with students in Rhode Island, who had the highest ACT scores of teens in any state. Also noteworthy is the selection of 70 homeschooled students as semifinalists in the National Merit Scholarship competition in 1998.

The changing face of education
Technology is also playing a role in the growth of homeschooling. As a group, homeschoolers are more likely to own computers than other American families. An estimated 86 percent of homeschoolers own computers, and almost as many are using them to teach their children, according to a study by Brian Ray of the National Home Education Research Institute. By contrast, 24 percent of single-mother households and 58 percent of married-couple households with children own computers, according to the U. S. Department of Commerce.

Unlike slow-moving school districts, homeschoolers can keep up with the rapid advances in hardware, and many take full advantage of the very best in educational software and online resources.

Increasingly, though, technology is exerting a much larger impact on education across the board, with computer access now blurring the line between school-based and home-based education.

Public systems are also reaching out to home educators, allowing them access to facilities and extracurricular activities, as well as to programs specifically designed to serve homeschoolers.

Homeschooling families, in increasing numbers, participate in some form of assisted homeschooling. According to homeschool researcher Brian Ray, 76 percent of homeschooling parents in Washington, Utah, and Nevada said they wished to enroll their child part-time in public or private school courses.

The mixing of homeschool and public schools is quite controversial. Critics within the schools are concerned that families are being enticed to leave the system without, perhaps, fully realizing what they're taking on. On the other hand, some home-school advocates believe parents are being lured back into the traditional setting, which, they fear, may have the long-term effect of increasing regulation of all homeschoolers.

Still others feel that bridging the gap between homeschoolers and traditional education will benefit all. Mark Weston, state services coordinator for education in Denver, and a homeschooling parent, suggests school reformers could learn much from home educators. In *Education Week* magazine, Weston writes: "The home-school phenomenon provides an opportunity for [school] reformers to strengthen their case for greater parental involvement and the use of diverse schooling approaches matched with individual learning styles. With education rapidly being reshaped by technological advances and efforts to foster diverse and personalized approaches to schooling, schools of the future may look more like homeschool looks today." Thus, the homeschooling movement and its place in the greater educational arena will continue to evolve.

Persistent concerns

Despite its growing acceptance, homeschooling continues to illicit concern.

Many worry that homeschooled children do not acquire adequate social skills. Research in this area does not seem to support a deficiency. In the frequently cited Shyer study, trained observers of eight- to 10-year-olds could not distinguish between those who were schooled conventionally and those who were educated at home. The study also found no differences among the children in either self-concept or assertiveness, although the homeschoolers were found to have fewer behavior problems.

Other studies demonstrate that homeschoolers do in fact engage in a wide variety of social activities, including Scouting, 4-H, and church and special-interest groups.

Still, homeschooling is not for everyone. As even homeschool advocates will attest, it's hard work that requires incredible commitment on the part of both parents and children. "It is rewarding work when things go right," author David Guterson wrote in *Newsweek* magazine, "but like all teaching and learning, it makes a variety of demands and is freighted with difficulties."

Parental involvement is key

Given the necessary motivation and commitment, homeschooling can be a successful and rewarding endeavor. The individualized tutorial approach is optimal for learning. No matter what teaching methods are involved, homeschooled children benefit from the one-on-one involvement of their parents. Theodore Wagenaar of Miami University found that from an early age homeschooled children "are considerably more likely to experience someone in the family doing the following activities with them three or more times a week: tell a story, teach letters, teach songs, do arts and crafts, play with toys and games indoors, play games and sports outdoors, take child on errands, and involve child in household chores."

The implications are not lost on traditional educators. Commenting on a study of homeschoolers and their academic performance, Bruce S. Cooper, a professor of educational administration at Fordham University in New York, told *Education Week* magazine, "The message is: Small is better. Strong parent and community involvement is key. We've known that for a long time."

Why you need this book

If you are curious about homeschooling, or are considering this education option for your family, you'll need clear, thorough, and objective information. This is why we've created this book.

Unlike other homeschooling guides on the market, we don't assume that this is the right choice for every family. We'll address the issues you need to consider, with an emphasis on how they relate to your personal situation. As researcher Nola Kortner Aiex summarizes, "The success or failure of the homeschooling experience depends inevitably on the success or failure of the family's interpersonal relationships." At the outset, homeschooling is a very personal matter to be decided according to individual family needs, a point that we emphasize throughout the book.

If you peruse other homeschooling materials— books, magazines, Web sites, and catalogs—you'll find that most expound a specific point of view. You'll be told the reasons you should homeschool, what to teach, when and how, what curriculum or other products you need to buy, along with other directives. Sources, of course, conflict, with one declaring, "unschooling is the only way to go," while another says "buy structured, textbook-based curriculum brand X." Based largely on personal opinion, this information can be misleading and may discourage you from homeschooling altogether. We don't preach any specific philosophy or technique of homeschooling. Again, we believe that not everything will work for every parent and child.

What you'll find in this book is comprehensive, balanced information on all aspects of homeschooling. From teaching methods (structured or traditional homeschooling, unit studies, and different teaching models) to choosing or designing a curriculum, we provide complete coverage of various alternatives, including the relative pros and cons of each. Homeschoolers of every stage will find pertinent information, from guidance on preschool issues to the college admissions process and beyond.

Rather than lyrical musings on the wonders of home learning, *The Unofficial Guide to Homeschooling* concentrates on providing you with practical information you'll need for successful homeschooling. Concerned about complying with the law? We include detailed summaries of homeschooling regulations for every state, as well as the nuts and bolts on other important matters: record-keeping, assessment, scheduling, and much more. The costs of homeschooling are fully described, along with money-saving tips for creating your own learning materials and budget-wise shopping.

When it comes to "school," we'll take you through subject by subject, and show you how best to maximize your child's level of interest and support their learning. If you're concerned about difficult or specialized subjects, understand that you don't need to go it alone in homeschooling. We'll help you with resources for determining your curricular plan, as well as teaching assistance.

Unlike other books, our coverage of homeschooling encompasses more than academic matters. We acknowledge the fact that teaching your children at home must necessarily dovetail with other aspects of life. There are the bottom-line issues of balancing your work schedule and managing expenses, all described in this volume. With everyone living together 24 hours a day, seven days a week, you need to install some system of home management, or at the very least get your kids to help with the chores. We'll tell you how.

Then we'll step out into the community to explore opportunities for learning—such as volunteering and apprenticeships; valuable resources including libraries, local schools, and colleges; community organizations; and some others you might not have thought of as having educational value, such as a local business or your neighbor's expertise.

With the information at hand, we hope this book will enlighten your own experience as you begin to explore homeschooling. Good luck!

A Homeschooling Primer

PART I

GET THE SCOOP ON...
Who's homeschooling, and why?
- Key research on performance and socialization
  - The history of modern homeschooling
  - The pros and cons of homeschooling

The ABCs of Homeschooling

In 1990, there were about 300,000 homeschoolers nationwide. Many of these families were forced underground by punitive regulations, and they were largely stereotyped as being on the "fringe" of society. In the years since, homeschooling has gained recognition as a legitimate option in education—the U.S. Senate recently honored the contributions of homeschool families, passing a resolution declaring September 19–25 National Home Education Week.

Homeschooling has indeed experienced an explosion in popularity, as more and more parents are taking their children's education into their own hands; by current estimates as many as 1.5 million children are being educated at home. Motivations vary from a desire to pass on religious and moral beliefs to the quality of education, concern over the school environment, the strengthening of family bonds, or a combination of reasons. Altogether, homeschoolers view the endeavor as a natural extension of parenting and believe that they can do a better job than traditional schooling. This chapter examines homeschooling as a movement, from its historical roots to the latest research findings on academic performance and socialization. I'll discuss the personal issues involved in homeschooling, including the many benefits, and the potential challenges that families should consider before deciding on this education alternative.

What is homeschooling?

Modern homeschooling is an alternative form of education in which school-aged children primarily learn at home, under the supervision of their parents, rather than in traditional school.

In practice, homeschooling can mean many things, encompassing a broad range of methods and philosophies as diverse as the people who choose this alternative. For some, homeschooling means duplicating school at home, complete with textbooks, report cards, and standardized tests. At the opposite end of the spectrum, "unschoolers" take a less structured approach, allowing their children's interests to determine what they study, and letting them work at their own pace. Still others—eclectic homeschoolers—pick and choose according to their children's needs, as they change over time.

Homeschoolers can create a curriculum from scratch or choose from a rich variety of tools to help them in their task. They can pool teaching resources through a homeschool co-op, participate in a distance learning program, or apprentice with a local craftsperson, among a host of other choices.

Many see the world as their classroom. Practiced to its full potential, homeschooling offers the possibility of making learning an integral aspect of family life.

Is it legal?

Homeschooling is a legal option in all 50 U.S. states and every province in Canada. However, each state handles homeschooling quite differently within the governance of compulsory attendance laws, or in some cases, statutes specific to homeschooling. Requirements can run the gamut from quite restrictive to rather relaxed. I will cover the laws for each state in more detail in Appendix E.

The legalities often cause great anxiety for new or prospective homeschoolers, but today, compliance is usually a rather straightforward process. This contrasts to the 1970s and 80s when state and local governments, responding to the increasing numbers of families who sought to educate their children at home, enacted punitive laws threatening parents who did not comply with the local codes of compulsory attendance. Hence, many homeschoolers chose to "go underground."

Legal challenges to the law include a 1985 case in which six homeschooling families, led by Gary and Cheryl Leeper, filed a class action suit against the Arlington, Texas, school district and all other Texas school districts, seeking a ruling that homeschooling meet the statutory definition of a private school. The case eventually made its way to the Texas Court of Appeals, which described the school district's actions as "harassment." In 1994, the Texas Supreme Court backed the lower court rulings, stating definitively that the homeschoolers were exempt from the compulsory attendance law. Today, Texas home educators may establish and operate a homeschool as a private school, which exempts them from any state or local oversight.

Many states began to formally recognize homeschooling as a legal practice during the 1980s and early 1990s. Although legal issues do arise, they are rare and generally concern the regulation of homeschooling, rather than a parent's right to homeschool.

If you're considering the homeschooling option, you'll need to get information on the current laws in your state. You should also connect with other homeschoolers in your area—local or state homeschool groups have organized in practically every community. Not only are these groups the best source for informing you about the applicable education laws, they can also give you the rundown on compliance in your area. For more information on locating these groups, see Chapter 9.

Who is homeschooling?

The public may stereotype homeschoolers as either societal dropouts or those with religious or moral concerns trying to isolate their children from a culture that runs counter to their beliefs. While a great many do, in fact, homeschool for reasons of spiritual and moral values, homeschoolers represent a range of backgrounds, motivations, and family situations. Collectively, they tend to be very conscientious parents who are taking charge of their children's education.

Homeschoolers live in the suburbs, big cities, and in the farmlands. They come from every ethnicity and culture. They may be stay-at-home moms with husbands who work, or vice versa; they may be single parents or step-families; they may be parents with strong religious convictions, or non-believers. The children they teach range from preschoolers to teens.

The movement has become an international phenomenon, with families homeschooling in

66

I decided to homeschool for academic reasons. I am not one of those radical homeschoolers who thinks that all traditional schools should be abolished. There are good schools out there, but there are not enough of them.
—Dani M. Sanders, homeschooling parent

99

Australia, France, the United Kingdom, South Africa, Spain, Israel, and Japan, among other countries.

...And why?

In a recent analysis of 300 newspaper and magazine articles about homeschoolers, researcher Isabel Lyman found that "the top four reasons to homeschool were dissatisfaction with the public schools, the desire to freely impart religious values, academic excellence, and the building of strong family bonds."

In the midst of the growing diversity of homeschooler backgrounds, religious values remain an important factor. Parents consider religion, morals, and values training as crucial elements of curriculum content, according to June Hetzel, in her 1998 doctoral dissertation on homeschooling. Other surveys, including one in Florida, show the primary motivation for homeschooling changing from religious reasons to dissatisfaction with public schools. Despite the shift in motivation, these new homeschoolers are not necessarily secular, according to researcher Pat Lines.

There are, of course, many good public schools, and dedicated teachers and other professionals whose skilled and caring efforts serve many children. However, good schools may not be available to everyone.

Numerous statistics and studies point to declining educational standards in the United States, ineffective teaching methods, bloated bureaucracies, and a host of other ills that not only fail children, but also smother the joy of learning. Previously, parents had few alternatives, with private and religious schools prohibitively expensive for many families.

Other elements within public schools also cause concern. Parents resist sending their children into an environment they believe is filled with violence, negative peer influences, drugs, alcohol, and teen sex. Even the seemingly more benign but still harmful elements of schoolyard culture make parents leary. Homeschooler Julie Woessner cites the "simply bad behavior" at her eight-year-old daughter's school: "Cliques, unkind words, a willingness to exclude, a desire to feel good at someone else's expense—these were things that I was seeing firsthand." Parents are acutely concerned with school safety. In the immediate aftermath of recent school shootings, homeschool groups reported a surge in parent requests for information on homeschooling.

Their various motivations not withstanding, homeschoolers are united by a common belief in their ability to do a better job at home than a conventional school.

Homeschoolers also cite reasons particular to their situation, such as the desire to provide necessary care and attention to a child with special needs or one who learns differently. These children, so often stigmatized in an institutional setting, often bloom to their full potential at home. Gifted students, whose needs are often just as misunderstood, can thrive with a program tailored to their abilities. (I discuss gifted children in Chapter 3.)

When Heather Madrone started homeschooling her children, she discovered "family and work blending and spilling over into one another. It's a radical departure from the way we were raised," she says. "Garry [their father] has a closer relationship with the girls now. Our energy is focused on the family. We are a "homeschooling" family, all of us learning, all of us growing, all of us working

Unofficially...
In a 1998 study, the top factors that pushed parents out of the traditional school setting and into homeschooling were: "negative peer influences," "class size too large," "poor moral climate," and "children not learning enough."
—June Hetzel, doctoral dissertation, "Factors that Influence Parents to Homeschool"

together as a team. Post-industrial society, here we come!"

Other homeschoolers offer their experience:

■ "We decided to homeschool before we ever had children. We had been exposed by friends and had seen positive results. Our reason for homeschooling was we want to be the primary influence on our children."
—Margo Sanders, California

■ "My son, now homeschooling (first time) in fourth grade, used to say, 'I don't learn stuff at school—I learn from you and Dad, TV (PBS) and our trips [family day trips].' I never believed him, just thought he was the typical school-hating kid, but after a LONG final year of anxiety/grade troubles and having him evaluated for LDs [learning disabilities], we found that he was actually right! He is now making nearly straight A's, anxiety is gone, and my happy son is finally back!"
—Pam Baker, Maryland

■ "Homeschooling appears to have been the right decision for my son and his two younger sisters. All three have a great love of learning, and appreciate having been given the opportunity to stay at home all these years. My son is in his third year of college, working toward long-term goals he set for himself. My older daughter is applying to colleges now, though she is also considering apprenticing and other options; I have been most impressed at how she is looking at all her options and working through this transition time. My younger daughter started ninth grade this fall in public school at the local arts magnet school. This is

66
Overall, many parents complained about 'busy work' [in school] and the lack of individualized instruction, and for every parent who claimed his/her child was not being challenged by the curriculum, there was one who said their child was being overwhelmed by it.
—Susan Varner Groover and Richard C. Endsley, on parent dissatisfaction with schools
99

Unofficially...
In the 1996 Third nternational Math and Science Study, an assessment of young people in 21 countries, American high school seniors came in dead last in physics, and second-to-last in advanced math.

her first experience with school...Even though she is happy at school now, she says she is very glad for the years she had at home, and all that she gained from her homeschooling experience. I'm not going to say there weren't times when I was ready to throw in the towel on homeschooling, but we worked through those difficulties as a family, and the end result has been very positive."

—Susan Schaeffer, North Carolina

Why homeschooling isn't for everyone

While the educational option holds many benefits, a decision to homeschool should not be entered into lightly. Homeschooling is difficult work, requiring an extraordinary level of commitment on the part of the parents.

Physical, emotional, financial, and other demands may tax the family, and some find that homeschooling isn't the right option for them.

A primary consideration involves an honest appraisal of your family relationships. Ask yourself and your family members the following questions:

- Do you really want to spend this amount of time together? In the wry words of one homeschooler: "The children never go away."

- Can you cope with the loss of the built-in babysitting that school provides? You may be surprised by how much you were relying on it once you give it up.

- Are you willing to dedicate additional time to plan lessons and obtain appropriate materials? Depending on the methods you choose, preparations can be time-consuming and require a certain degree of organization and scheduling.

- Can everyone handle you being both parent and teacher? Both children and adults may have difficulties with a shift in family dynamics.

- Do you have relatives to provide backup childcare? If you have a partner, is that person supportive of the enterprise? Many homeschoolers point to the support of family and others as being critical to the success of their program.

Homeschooling takes time and energy. Recently, Margaret Martin, an educator, conducted a small survey of homeschoolers within the New York metropolitan area. When asked about any disadvantages to homeschooling, the respondents unanimously cited the degree of work involved. Martin wrote: "Women especially complained of this because they were the ones who usually did most of the homeschooling."

Homeschooling also raises financial issues, primarily an adjustment to one or perhaps both parents' work status. Living on one income can cause an adjustment in lifestyle that has many homeschoolers squeezing into their budget a subscription to *Cheapskate Monthly* or the *Tightwad Gazette*! For more on financial issues see Chapter 4.

Finally, the inevitable moments of doubt and frustration that plague any parent take on new dimensions when you homeschool. Parents may fear a subject that they don't feel qualified to teach, in which case there are other options, including private tutoring, team teaching, or enrolling in a school course.

It's critical to seek help when you need it. Even the most seasoned homeschoolers experience difficulties as their children's needs and levels of motivation change over time. Chapter 14 provides details on accessing support.

Homeschoolers must continually assess their situation: How do my children learn best? What methods really work for them? How can I resolve my child's lack of motivation? What about future plans for college and a career? How does our homeschooling affect everyone, and the family as a whole?

Successful homeschooling requires a unique capacity for reflection, self-motivation, flexibility, organization, patience, and stamina. It adds a whole new dimension to the already challenging job of being a parent and should never be considered "the easy way out." And, of course, it must be in the best interest of your child.

Homeschooled children: How do they fare?

Any consideration of homeschooling inspires two lines of questioning:

- How well do these children perform academically?

- Can they gain necessary social skills?

In the sections below, I'll explore each of these concerns.

Academic achievement

How well do homeschooled children perform academically? Here's an overview of some of the research:

- In their analysis of the SAT scores of home-schooled children in Washington state since 1985, the Washington Homeschool Research Project found that those children consistently scored above average.

- In a 1990 study of homeschooled children in West Virginia, Mark Tipton compared their test scores against those of conventionally schooled students. On the Comprehensive Test of Basic Skills (CTBS), he found that homeschooled children scored higher across a range of subjects, except for homeschooled ninth graders, who scored lower in math. Additionally, Tipton found that the longer families intended to homeschool, the better their children's scores were.

▪ Robert Calvery and others compared the scores of Arkansas homeschoolers with their public school counterparts in grades 4, 7, and 10. According to the 1992 report, homeschoolers outscored public school students in reading, mathematics, language, total basic battery, science and social studies at grades 4 and 7. At grade 10, homeschoolers posted significantly higher scores in these same subjects except language, in which the homeschoolers scored significantly below the public school mean.

▪ Researcher Gary Knowles conducted a 1993 survey of adults who were home-educated as young people. Forty-two percent had attended a college or university, with 12 percent attaining undergraduate degrees, and another 16 percent going on to graduate work. (By comparison, 31.9 percent of high school graduates attended college in 1993.) None in the survey were unemployed or on public assistance, and nearly two-thirds were self-employed. (In the 1999 Rudner study, cited below, the median income for homeschoolers surveyed was $52,000 in 1997 compared to $36,000 for all U.S. families with children in 1995—only 1995 figures are available.)

When asked if they would do it all over again, 96 percent answered yes, they would choose to be home-educated, citing the development of self-reliance and resourcefulness, together with the study skills employed in their college experience.

▪ In a 1997 study of 5,403 homeschool students, Dr. Brian Ray of the National Home Education Research Institute also reported exceptionally high average achievement levels.

▪ On the ACT college entrance examination, homeschoolers in 1998 had an average composite score of 22.8, compared to the national ACT average of 21.0.

▪ Based on a March 1999 nationwide study of 20,760 homeschool students who took the Iowa Test of Basic Skills or the Tests of Achievement and Proficiency, researcher Lawrence Rudner found that the median scores of this group were typically in the 70th to 80th percentiles. The report further demonstrates that the median scores for homeschool students are well above their public/private school counterparts in every subject and in every grade. For example, homeschool students in grade 3 had a median score of 207, which corresponds to the 81st percentile nationwide. (The national median for grade 3 is 168.) Moreover, starting from grade 5, this achievement test score gap starts to widen. The Rudner study also found that 25 percent of homeschooled students were studying at a level one or more grades above normal for their age. While there are no comparable figures nationally, the Rudner study cites the case of one large school district that estimates that less than 5 percent of their students are enrolled above grade level.

However, because this was not a controlled experiment, these results should be interpreted with caution, according to Rudner, who also directs the federally-funded Educational Resources Information Center Clearinghouse on Assessment and Evaluation at the University of Maryland College Park. "The study does not demonstrate that homeschooling is superior to public or private schools," Rudner writes. "The report clearly suggests, however, that home school students do quite well in that educational environment."

The caveats on homeschool research

While these and other findings are quite impressive, other issues must factor into a full consideration of homeschool research. Critics cite:

- **The limited make-up and size of sample populations in existing research.** If only a limited population is studied, results could be skewed by other factors, such as socioeconomic status or the parents' level of education. At present, however, a representative sample is unattainable; some states do not require homeschoolers to register, and many homeschoolers remain underground.

- **The drawbacks of traditional outcome-based analysis.** Existing studies have measured homeschooling using the traditional yardstick of standardized test results, which are rejected by many homeschoolers as an inaccurate measure of learning. Moreover, these records are unavailable for those homeschoolers who do not administer tests.

Unofficially...
Homeschooler Hall of Fame: Pearl S. Buck, Andrew Carnegie, Agatha Christie, Thomas Edison, Thomas Jefferson, Abraham Lincoln, Margaret Mead, Sandra Day O'Connor, Booker T. Washington, George Washington, and the Wright Brothers were all schooled at home.

■ **The lack of funding for homeschool research.**
Thus far, serious study into homeschooling has
garnered limited interest and funding support
from scholarly journals. Expectations are that
this will change with the burgeoning growth of
homeschooling.

For now, research seems to establish that those
who commit to homeschooling perform very well.
Experts will not say, however, that these same children would do better or worse in a public or private
school.

The "s-word": Socialization

By far, the most common concern surrounding
homeschooling is the issue of socialization. Many
assume that homeschooled children are isolated
and that without the fellowship of a traditional classroom, they will fail to develop social skills.

Homeschoolers counter the "s-word" with two
main arguments.

First, homeschoolers claim that if their children
were in traditional schools, they would learn a
negative kind of socialization. They maintain that
navigating the cliques, endless gossip, and sudden
betrayals that make up the average school's terrain
can cause children to be preoccupied with peer
acceptance and materialism. They also say that the
school environment—public or private—estranges
young people from people outside their age group.

Second, argue homeschoolers, socialization
skills actually form much earlier, in children's interactions with their parents beginning in infancy.
They view homeschooling as a natural extension of
this process. In addition, they believe that the self-
esteem and independence fostered in the home
environment better prepares children for the peer

66

Would you rather
your child take
her cues from
the librarian, the
kids in Sunday
school, and the
woman at the
museum, or from
a group of
twenty same-age
peers?
—The Caron
Family Web
site, caronfam/
index.htm/

99

pressure and conflicting values they may face in the outside world.

Moreover, most homeschoolers provide their children with rich and varied social opportunities, including homeschool networking groups, Scouting, special classes through museums and other organizations, churches, and more. In fact, the typical homeschooled child is involved in 5.2 social activities outside the home each week, according to Brian Ray of the National Home Education Research Institute.

"School is not the only place to meet people," comments Christy Taylor, a homeschooler now attending college. Like other homeschoolers, Taylor believes that overall she may have fewer friends, but more close friends than most kids in school. During the course of her homeschooling, Taylor interacted with others of different ages, particularly through drama classes and other activities.

Other research regarding socialization includes the following:

▪ In his 1992 dissertation, Edward Shyers of the University of Florida found homeschooled children between ages eight and 10 to have significantly fewer problem behaviors as measured by the Child Observation Checklist's Direct Observation Form, than traditionally schooled children of the same age.

▪ Thirty West Virginia homeschooling families were compared with 32 conventionally schooling families by Lee Stough in 1992. According to the findings, the homeschooled children developed the skills, knowledge, and attitudes needed to function in society at approximately the same rate as conventionally schooled children.

■ A 1989 study by Julie Webb examined adults who had been wholly or partly home-educated and found that all who had gone on to college had been successful and that their socialization was often better than that of their schooled peers.

Unofficially...
A distinct side benefit of home-schooling—an improvement on school lunches!

■ Other research points to the negative socialization of the school environment. A 1998 Johns Hopkins University study found that a disorderly first-grade classroom may well be a training ground for boys who become troublemakers in middle school.

A homeschooling chronology

Following American independence, the Founding Fathers recognized the need for a unified system of instilling knowledge and instruction to the youth of the nation. By the 1800s, industrialization demanded a foundational education for the growing labor force. Education reformers Horace Mann, Henry Barnard, and James G. Carter responded with a plan for a conformed secular curriculum, which became known as the common-school. However, free public education was not a universally popular new concept, the opposition citing taxpayer expense, religious conviction, and parental rights.

Nevertheless, the common-school movement began to take hold, and together with the institution of compulsory attendance, ultimately became our public school system. Following is a brief timeline of recent key events that have shaped homeschooling as a movement.

1969: Dr. Raymond S. Moore, a former U.S. Department of Education employee, initiates his inquiry into the institutionalizing of young children in schools, and the best timing for school entrance. After consulting more than 100 child development experts who supported limiting young children's daily contact with institutionalized settings, Moore, together with his wife, Dorothy, also an educator, advocates educating children at home.

1970: Compulsory attendance laws are enacted in every state of the the union save Mississippi, which follows suit in 1983.

Early 1970s: It is estimated that 10,000 to 15,000 children are being schooled at home.

1977: Education reformer John Holt launches *Growing Without Schooling* magazine to help support homeschooling families and provide a forum for them to communicate with one another. Other home school journals, such as *Home Education Magazine,* follow.

1978: In a landmark case, Perchemlides v. Frizzle, the Massachusetts court upholds the right of the Perchemlides family to homeschool their young son.

1981: John Holt's ground-breaking book *Teach Your Own* is published. Shortly after, the number of homeschooled children in the United States is estimated at 60,000 to 125,000.

1983: Michael Farris and Michael Smith found the Home School Legal Defense Association.

1986: All 50 states, in one form or another, allow home instruction.

Moneysaver
Homeschooling can help you save on a school wardrobe, school lunches, transportation, and childcare expenses.

Unofficially...
Homeschooler David Biehl won the 1999 National Geography Bee by correctly answering this question: The condition characterized by unusually cold ocean temperature in the equatorial region of the eastern Pacific Ocean is known by what Spanish name? (Answer: La Niña.)

1988: With their book *Homeschooling for Excellence,* David and Micki Colfax achieve celebrity status when three of their four homeschooled sons are admitted to Harvard University; also, publication of the *Big Book of Home Learning,* by Mary Pride (Crossway Books). Close to a quarter million copies have been sold.

1991: *Dumbing Us Down: The Hidden Curriculum of Compulsory Schooling* by John Taylor Gatto is published. A New York City public school teacher for 35 years, and former Teacher of the Year, Gatto becomes an outspoken advocate of home education.

1992: Larry Shyers of the University of Florida releases a study measuring the self-esteem of eight- to 10-year-olds, finding no difference between homeschooled and regularly schooled children. The Shyers study and other research answer critics' concerns about the emotional well-being of homeschooled children.

1994: "The Dawn of Online Home Schooling" appears in *Newsweek* magazine. The article describes how homeschoolers employ advanced technology.

1995: *The Manufactured Crisis: Myths, Fraud, and the Attack on America's Public Schools* by David C. Berliner, Bruce J. Biddle, and James Bell is published. This book made national news with its debunking of popularly accepted myths about the dire state of public education in America. The authors proved that SAT scores are rising for many groups, among other findings.

1996: Homeschoolers lobby Capitol Hill, reversing a move by Congress to require homeschooling parents to possess teaching certificates.

1997: The National Education Association (NEA) adopts a resolution, which states that homeschooling "cannot provide the student with a comprehensive education experience"; also, thirteen-year-old Rebecca Sealfon of Brooklyn, New York becomes the first homeschooled child to win the Scripps Howard National Spelling Bee, held in May.

1998: More than 70 homeschooled children are selected as semifinalists for National Merit Scholarships; also, Dr. Raymond Moore, widely considered to be the grandfather of modern homeschooling, publishes, "The Ravage of Home Education Through Exclusion By Religion," which illuminates growing divisions among homeschoolers.

1999: In the weeks following a deadly shooting spree at Littleton, Colorado's Columbine High School, national homeschool leaders report a spike in parent inquiries into homeschooling.

1999: Thirteen-year-old homeschooler David Biehl wins the National Geography Bee.

Advantages of homeschooling

When families consider homeschooling their children, several aspects tend to appeal to them. In fact, a recent study of homeschooling families revealed that these attractive aspects were more influential in a decision to homeschool than the negative features of traditional school. These benefits include:

Home, sweet home

For many children, the optimal setting for learning is the home. Foremost is the understanding and love of parents, who can respond to and nurture their child's individual strengths and interests. At home, children may be allowed to act on their natural curiosity, as they engage in real-life activities, such as learning about plant life cycles by tending a garden.

A program tailored to your child's individual needs

> **"** Let your child be herself. Teach her to love that self and to be compassionate to others. Those, in my mind, are the only two social skills you need. Everything else comes with that.
> —Christy Taylor, homeschool student **"**

Unlike school curriculum, which is limited in how far it can stretch to cover the needs of all students, homeschooling provides parents the opportunity to individualize their child's course of study.

In addition, the growth of homeschooling has enriched the options available to home educators. New curriculum suppliers and correspondence schools stimulate an ever-burgeoning market. The Internet has enabled access to lesson plans, teaching ideas, current events databases, museum collections, and a variety of other resources, all of which can be adapted to serve individual interests. I will cover this in more detail in Chapter 10.

Flexibility

Home education allows families to work at their own pace. Without a preconceived schedule or class periods, children can take more time to master the material, jump ahead, or move on to another subject, as they wish. Freed from a district calendar, field trips and other travel can be planned according to the family's schedule. If a particular teaching method or curriculum is found to be ineffective, you have the freedom to try something else. Home educators can also keep up with the rapid advances of computing technology—unlike schools, which are often left saddled with outdated equipment and software.

Real world 101

"The world is our classroom," is the tenet of unschoolers, whose philosophy expands the boundaries of traditional education (for more on unschooling, see Chapter 7). But in fact, every home educator has as vast a resource. Freed from the confines of a designated "school," learning can take place anywhere, becoming an active adventure. Homeschooling parent Heather Madrone says, "We're out and about, involved in activities of our choosing and engaged in our community. Garry and I do volunteer work and participate in the life of our town. I think this is a valuable social education for our children. They learn that we care about the community and that we feel it's important to contribute to the well-being of the community as a whole."

Goodbye, school bureaucracy

Homeschoolers happily shed the top-heavy bureaucracy inherent in the public school system and all of its effects, arbitrary regulation, tracking, mandatory tests, outmoded teaching techniques, and so forth.

An improved student-teacher ratio

In a typical public school classroom, there is one teacher to 25 pupils. Homeschooling features a one-on-one (or one-to-three or slightly more) tutorial. The ratio is hard to beat.

Reduced cost

Private school tuition can cost over $10,000 a year. The most expensive homeschool curriculum package costs 10 percent of that amount. Many homeschoolers create their own curriculum and use free

"
We have used the community quite a bit. Our oldest son did volunteer work for a local mechanic. He also worked as a volunteer docent for the Maritime Museum, for his speech credit. Our second son volunteered for the Department of Natural Resources, monitoring bluebird nesting patterns on a local walking trail.
—Marsha Ransom, homeschooling parent in Michigan
"

educational tools such as the Internet and public library, further reducing the expense.

Maximizing "on task" time

Public school students spend about six hours a day at school, and their teachers spend much of that time dealing with organizational routines, discipline problems and other crowd control issues. Although the time required for homeschooling depends on various factors—the methods used, the ages of the children, and the number of children being taught—by and large, homeschooling is much more efficient. According to one source, a homeschool child only spends two hours a day, seven days a week studying each year. Without the time spent on institutional issues, the homeschooler logs more than three times as many hours devoted to learning in a year than a public school counterpart.

Spiritual and moral development

Whether you homeschool specifically for religious reasons or not, this option allows greater opportunity for parents to impart spiritual and moral values to their children.

"I made a deliberate choice to have a curriculum permeated with the Catholic faith," says Joanna Tenaglia, who homeschools in Wisconsin. "I didn't want my kids to have the religious upbringing I did. I went to a 'progressive' Catholic school—very little Catholicism and much error." Beyond the prohibitive tuition of private school, Joanna states, "I don't trust anyone else with the religious education of my children."

While Cathy Carter, a homeschooling mom in Georgia, doesn't use a Christian curriculum, she says, "Our world view touches and shapes how we interpret everything we study." Similarly, Jan Hunt, director of The Natural Child Project, wasn't motivated to homeschool for religious reasons, but she says, "We have always welcomed the time available to explore questions of personal ethics, and to encourage such qualities as kindness, honesty, trust, cooperation, creative solutions to problems, and compassion for others. This is a significant part of our 'curriculum.'"

Learning together

Homeschooling allows a more integrated family life, promoting unity and a depth of understanding that is difficult to attain in today's world, where family members are so often pulled in separate directions. In fact, one study found that a "desire for more family time" was the factor most associated with longevity in homeschooling.

Homeschooling provides a nurturing atmosphere, so vital to a child's early development, which can also strengthen family bonds in the challenging teen years. Learning and growing becomes a shared experience, treasured by all homeschoolers.

Cathy Carter, a homeschooling mom, describes what this decision has meant to her. "When my children accuse someone of acting like J. Thaddeus Toad or Puddleglum, or say some ramshackle house reminds them of the Radley place, I know what they're talking about, because we've read those books together," she says. "Having common daily experiences and delighting in the sharing of those experiences is, I believe, one of the best things about homeschooling."

Bright Idea
Homeschooled children experience lasting friendships by coming together with others based on common interests, such as 4-H, Scouts, or the Amateur Athletic Union.

Just the facts

- All 50 states allow homeschooling, but procedures vary widely, so find out what's required in your area. Contact your regional homeschool organization.

- Homeschooling families are a diverse group with many different motivations, and they are successfully educating their children in a range of family circumstances.

- Various studies indicate that homeschoolers excel academically and engage in a rich social life.

- Home can be an ideal educational setting, with an individualized program enhanced by a rich variety of community and online resources, and optimal tutorial teaching.

- Although homeschooling offers many advantages, it is a major undertaking that requires careful consideration of a number of factors, including an honest look at whether your family relationships would facilitate such a choice.

GET THE SCOOP ON...
The attributes and skills you'll need
■ Finding support and handling family
opposition ■ How to homeschool one, two,
three, or more children ■ How different kinds of
families manage homeschooling

Making the Decision

Some people try homeschooling and quit. While a statistical dropout rate is unavailable, the anecdotal evidence points to a variety of reasons for this to occur. Some fail to get enough support from their spouses, others can't find a learning method that will motivate their children, and some give up for health reasons. Still others find the financial constraints too rough, and others need more time for themselves.

Even homeschooling advocates agree that it isn't for everyone. If you are considering this option yourself, this chapter explores the personal issues involved in the decision, from what it takes to be a parent/teacher to facing the opinions of others.

I'll also show you how homeschooling works for different families. Homeschoolers are a varied bunch, with different issues and motivations. Single parents, working parents, minority families, families in urban and rural settings, and military families have all successfully adapted homeschooling into their lives, and you can, too.

27

Is homeschooling really right for your family?

Like any decision that can influence your child's future, making a choice about education requires careful consideration of multiple factors. A plethora of books and other resources can inform you about every aspect of homeschooling, but only you and your family can decide if it's right for you.

In Chapter 1, I discussed some of the considerations you need to make before you decide if your family is emotionally ready for homeschooling. But before you jump ahead to the nuts and bolts of working out your learning plan and teaching method, do the following:

- Consider carefully your personal motivations for homeschooling. What are your goals for you and your child? Are you prepared to make the commitment in time and resources?

- Evaluate your child's current school situation. Is your child engaged, enthusiastic, and appropriately challenged? Are there particular issues involved that make the classroom setting difficult for your child, or does your child have needs that aren't being met? Have you examined all your education options, both public and private?

- Read everything about homeschooling that you can, including books, magazines, and research on the Web (see Appendix C for a list of recommended readings). While many sources provide helpful, balanced information, others are based largely on personal opinion—particularly in online sources—and you're also likely to encounter conflicting philosophies. If you keep your personal situation in mind, it will be easier to view such opinions with a critical eye and take away what is useful to you.

- Attend a homeschooling support group meeting or a homeschool conference, and talk to homeschoolers about what has worked for them and what has challenged them. Many experienced homeschooling families got started by connecting with like-minded homeschoolers. See Chapter 9 for in-depth coverage of homeschool support groups.

For most, the decision to homeschool does not occur overnight. Many have had specific problems with the school, the teachers, or the administration that they found could not be resolved; others saw a gradual deterioration in their situation that eventually became intolerable. Still others had philosophical or spiritual reasons, a desire for a more integrated family life, or a combination of several factors that eventually led them to choose homeschooling. Many parents planned to homeschool all along. Whatever your motivation, make sure you are homeschooling because it's the best option for your child, and not because of an emotional response to a situation or a whim.

Whatever your decision, it isn't necessarily a permanent one. If you find that homeschooling isn't appropriate for you right now, table it as one more option available to you. It might fulfill your needs at a later time.

If you would like to homeschool, consider giving it a trial period, or, for an older student, try out a correspondence course. Before implementing any plan, consult with your family, allowing them to voice any concerns or ideas.

Unofficially... A 1998 study concluded that "the attractive features of the homeschool setting have greater weight in deciding to homeschool than the negative factors of the traditional school setting." —June Hetzel, doctoral dissertation, "Factors That Influence Parents to Homeschool"

Do you have what it takes?

This intriguing question inspires many different responses among homeschoolers, all of whom, at one time, have probably asked this of themselves. On the one hand, certain requirements must be met to ensure that your child receives a well-rounded, quality education; on the other hand, you have a great deal of freedom to determine how to fulfill these requirements.

Experienced homeschoolers say that your job will be easier if you possess certain attributes, such as the following:

- An eagerness to learn that includes a sense of wonder and an excitement for discovery

- A love of books on a wide variety of subjects

- Flexibility

- Focus and determination

- Confidence

- An enthusiasm for spending lots of time with your children

The bottom line is that as a parent, you know your children best; you know how they learn and what their relative strong points and interests are. Implementing this on a practical level and learning to trust your instincts to help guide your teaching are key, according to experienced homeschoolers.

On the practical side, successful homeschooling involves a certain capacity for organization and, at the same time, a willingness to change what isn't working. One parent, for example, tried the whole desk and blackboard arrangement, but she found it didn't work for her children. Others have started with a radical unschooling approach and drawn back, seeking more structure. Still other parents find that certain aspects don't work for them personally. Keep in mind that homeschooling needs to fit everyone involved, children and parents alike.

Do you need teacher training?

Successful homeschoolers come from varied educational backgrounds, and most have no formal teacher training. In a recent survey, researcher Lawrence Rudner found that homeschool parents had more formal education than parents in the general population: 88 percent continued their education beyond high school compared to 50 percent for the nation as a whole. Rudner also found that while nearly 20 percent of homeschool mothers in his survey were certified teachers, no significant differences emerged between the academic achievement of homeschool students whose parents are certified and those that are not. Many homeschool parents don't attempt formal teaching at all, but instead facilitate their children's learning by taking on the role of tutor, or by providing the tools for their children to learn independently.

Because your background is probably rooted in traditional schooling, you may find it difficult to conceive of a different mode of education, which in turn may lead you to doubt your abilities. To consider homeschooling is to challenge traditional learning models.

Put simply, traditional learning models are, for the most part, based on the idea that teaching leads to learning. The teacher teaches, the student learns. Critics charge that this model pays little attention to the individual learning styles of students and leaves little room for the development of curiosity or creativity. Education becomes little more than a

Unofficially...
"An analysis of 300 articles about homeschoolers revealed that the top four reasons to homeschool were dissatisfaction with the public schools, the desire to freely impart religious values, academic excellence, and the building of stronger family bonds."
—Isabel Lyman, "Homeschooling: Back to the Future?"

meaningless drill that fails to produce people who love to learn.

The learning process is further hampered, according to many homeschoolers, by requiring teachers to address large groups of children in an institutional setting. Because of this environment, subjects must be taught in isolation rather than in a more multidisciplinary approach that would allow students to explore how history relates to art, which relates to math, which relates to science, and so on.

Homeschoolers tend to believe in the natural curiosity of children. They believe that if children are given opportunities to fully engage the world, and receive encouragement and guidance from loving adults, it will lead to learning.

They further tend to believe that if teachers spend most of their training time preparing to manage large numbers of children in institutional settings, then homeschoolers need to worry less about becoming trained teachers and prepare themselves for one-on-one or small group tutorials.

For unfamiliar subjects and advanced coursework, parents can learn alongside their children, or they can enlist help from a number of sources, including private tutoring, correspondence courses, part-time enrollment in a traditional school, or apprenticeship. It's important for parents to recognize when they need help, and then seek out appropriate options.

> My husband and I went to a state conference together, and that was what convinced him that this would work...seeing all those great families under one roof, and the "graduating seniors" made him realize that the socialization problems he imagined were expectations based on his own schooling.
> —Beth Krolak

When your spouse objects to homeschooling

If your partner objects to homeschooling, this presents a major conflict. As I've mentioned, successful homeschooling depends on the cooperation of the entire family. Experienced homeschoolers suggest the following strategies for handling this situation:

- Read as many books about homeschooling as possible, and discuss the pros and cons of what you read.

- Talk to as many homeschoolers as you can find. Be sure that you don't take over the conversation in a way that keeps your partner from voicing his or her concerns.

- Attend a state or national homeschooling conference together to meet and observe successful homeschooling families.

- Discuss with your partner all of the potential negatives and positives and make a plan for overcoming them.

- Homeschool on a trial basis—perhaps a half year, September to December, or other defined period—and evaluate the experience before the school year is scheduled to begin.

- Throughout your discussions, keep the needs of your child in mind. When you're ready to make your decision, list your child's needs and discuss which setting would be best suited to meet each of them: public school, private school, or homeschooling. Be open to the possibility that your partner may be right.

Bright Idea
If you're pondering the decision, take your spouse along and sit in on a meeting of your local homeschooling support group.

What will my mother-in-law say? Telling others about homeschooling

Whether pro or con, your decision to homeschool is guaranteed to draw strong reactions. Relatives and friends, and even complete strangers, will undoubtedly voice their opinions.

You may find it easiest to create and distribute a homeschooling fact sheet to provide answers to the basic questions such as "Is this legal?" and "What about socialization?" It's a good way to inform someone, particularly if you anticipate a hostile reaction, which may draw an emotional response from you.

Beyond that, you'll have to decide who is entitled to more information, such as specifics about your program, and further debate. Consider whose opinion really matters and their relationship to the kids. In the case of grandparents and other close relatives, appreciate that they have a genuine concern for your child's welfare. Your patient indulgence may bring them around to supporting your efforts, making your home education experience all the richer.

To keep your children from being confronted by opposing views, try to do the explaining yourself when dealing with teachers, relatives, and others. (Older children may be capable of articulating their own knowledge of homeschooling. See bulleted tip below.)

If someone does confront your children, follow these tips:

- Prepare your kids by having an honest conversation about what they might hear. Depending on the child's maturity, help them develop answers to any comments that you anticipate.

- Be clear and firm with grandparents and others who confront the child directly, with comments such as, "You don't really want to leave school, do you?" State that you do not want them undermining your authority, and if they have concerns to please direct them to you and

Bright Idea
Take your home-schooled children to observe the school they would otherwise be attending. One mother who did said that her children saw that they were learning the same things but in less time, so that they could concentrate on other activities.

not your child. Explain that those kinds of comments only confuse your child.

■ In addition to providing information, you might try involving grandparents or other concerned relatives. Invite them to your local support group meeting, take them on a field trip, or incorporate their participation in some aspect of your homeschooling.

■ Enlist your spouse's help, particularly with your in-laws. It always helps to present a united front.

Of course, some people will never be won over. Through your reaction to these people, you can model the kind of behavior you want your children to learn. Finding a homeschool support group will also help balance out unfavorable opinions.

Preparing the kids

How your children adjust to homeschooling will depend largely on their experiences with school, if they're old enough to have attended. With that in mind, here are some general suggestions for preparing your children to homeschool:

■ **Let them take part in some of the decision-making.** Allowing them some measure of control from the beginning might help smooth the way, as well as enhance a successful program in the long-term. If they're interested in space exploration, for example, consider using that subject as a springboard for study.

■ **Communicate.** Tell them of your wishes to help them learn and grow. Without getting into value judgments (such as "school is bad"), explain that you believe that this is the best environment for learning. Inspire them to feel

> 66
> I worked 20 hours a week the first two years we home-schooled. I have to say, if I had to do it all over again, I would have quit work sooner. I'm not saying home-schooling and working can't work, but it is a struggle...
> —Cynthia G. Welch
> 99

especially fortunate for this experience. Sit down and brainstorm together, writing down your plans for the future.

∎ **Remain open to feedback.** Your children may miss school, friends, the bus ride, and other related activities. Don't get defensive. Appreciate their feelings and concerns. September, in particular, may be a difficult time for them. Take positive steps to offset any disappointments. Schedule dates with friends from school, arranging to meet regularly through church activities or the soccer league, or schedule a special field trip. Shopping for new "school" clothes and materials might also get them enthused.

∎ **Take a break.** Allow some time for your children to adjust if they're coming out of traditional school. Such a process even has a name: deschooling. Most closely associated with the unschooling approach, deschooling may be appropriate for all beginning homeschoolers.

Consider giving your children a total break from formal methods. Take your cues from them about when to start. Some homeschoolers report having taken a year before they found a comfortable routine.

∎ **Connect with other homeschoolers.** In the midst of your own networking, encourage your child to make new friends. Most support groups provide opportunities in the form of playgroups, events, social gatherings, and other activities.

∎ **Visit the library.** Let your kids become accustomed to following their own interests, checking out a book and taking it from there. Get to know the reference librarian, and learn to use the computerized catalog.

■ **Take time to find what will work with your kids.** Perhaps a structured start may be more familiar in the beginning. For others, a child-directed approach is immediately comfortable. Finding out your child's learning style and creating a rhythm to your program may be achieved in stops and starts. Conversely, your child may initially need more direct guidance from you.

If your child is starting right from preschool age, you will, most likely, not be coping with a mindset conditioned to school (outside of your own). Here are some ideas for preschoolers:

■ **Avoid formal curricula.** There are packaged curriculums aimed at preschoolers, but such formal teaching may turn off a child this young. Save your money. Simply providing an engaging environment and remaining receptive to their questions will stimulate their curiosity and a love of learning, the most important things you can "teach."

■ **Read, read, read.** Reading to your children will further their language development. Books should be a featured element in your home environment, and make sure sturdy, appropriate choices are easily accessible to your young one. Make a trip to the library a regular outing.

■ **Engage in a variety of activities each day.** There's a richness of learning opportunities available, even in what may seem just a mundane trip to the store. A tour of the grocery store can exercise your child's senses, introduce your child to math and science, and more.

Your schedule will also be influenced by the number of children you have to homeschool.

Homeschooling an only child

Many families successfully homeschool a single child, or in some cases, a child whose siblings attend traditional school.

Inevitably, this situation reintroduces the question of socialization. The advantages of one-on-one nurturing not withstanding, parents must be proactive in finding opportunities for cooperative and social learning, as many homeschoolers do (as I discuss a little later in this chapter). Participation in support groups is an especially good way for your child to get together with homeschoolers of all ages.

Homeschooling one child has its advantages. With no conflicting agendas, you can freely pursue your child's interests, and getting about and utilizing other resources is logistically less complicated.

Homeschooling with siblings

Homeschooling a houseful of kids can be a rich and rewarding experience. Siblings can actually ease the way, helping each other's transition to homeschooling. Or an older child can help a younger one, and both will benefit from the experience. Then, of course, there are the built-in opportunities for cooperative and social activities.

The approach you use will depend on the ages of your children. For preschoolers, you may wish to avoid formal methods altogether, and simply allow them to explore alongside their siblings.

Many parents recommend unit studies as a method in which multiple ages can investigate one subject, varying the activities according to each

Unofficially...
Joyce Swann, a single mother with a high school education, homeschooled her 10 children, nine of whom went on to earn master's degrees.

child's level. Other large families unschool, encouraging independent work in older children, and trying to allow each child some time to themselves (with adequate supervision, of course).

Organization can be critical. Some families find it necessary to lay out a plan for each child, scheduling time to work with each one individually. Other time management tricks can help you keep on track:

- Have older children take some responsibility for managing their own time. Have them schedule study sessions at a time when they are most alert and prepared to concentrate.

- Employ creative organizational tools, such as color-coded folders for each child.

- Use a central calendar to help coordinate your projected schedule.

- Review a daily log to assess how time was used, and whether the schedule needs revision.

Experienced families report that the intensity of teaching multiple children eases over time. Here are some other recommendations:

- Many realize that actual "teaching" is accomplished in just a few hours each week, particularly for young ones. "If I had to do it all over I would probably do more unschooling at those early grades," reflects April Morris, a homeschooling mother of four. "I would have relaxed more and just enjoyed the ages."

- A rigid schedule may be impossible. Elisa Mohrmann, mother of six girls, set up "school" for her four year old. "I was trying to do this with a two year old and a newborn to care for!" she says. "We didn't finish the year and I felt like a failure. We continued this pattern for

several more years before I learned that I
didn't have to do 'school' at home."

■ Team teaching and other cooperative methods
are available options. For more information,
see Chapter 9.

How homeschooling works for different families

While homeschoolers share many similarities,
including a desire to be the primary influence
in their children's lives, they also differ in many significant ways. In this section, I'll show you a spectrum of family situations and how they integrate
homeschooling.

Working parents

Though certainly a challenge, many parents find
ways to balance work and homeschooling. How can
you do this successfully? "Scheduling, scheduling,
scheduling," according to one experienced mother.
Indeed, working parents require a high degree of
organization, budgeting the time to plan lessons,
commute, review "homework," and manage the
house—all in addition to working a job.

Another factor is the maturity of the child.
While younger children present a higher logistical
challenge, homeschooling older children may actually require just a few hours of one-on-one teaching,
with "homework" and other assignments managed
independently.

Many parents successfully—and creatively—
adjust their work schedules to accommodate homeschooling.

For information on alternative work arrangements, see Chapter 4.

In addition, spouses can work together, negotiating personal schedules to accomplish their

Unofficially...
According to
current forecasts,
there will be
more than
50 million
telecommuters
in the U.S. by
the year 2030.
—JALA
International,
Inc.

homeschooling goals. One mother, a public school teacher, wished to continue her fulltime position while homeschooling. With her husband's more flexible job and willingness to take on some of the home teaching, they were able to accommodate homeschooling.

Involve your child in the plan

When both parents work, and scheduling sometimes is down to the minute, letting the kids participate in scheduling will optimize its success. Allowing them some control will also instill a sense of responsibility. You'll need to make other considerations as well, such as the following:

- Make sure your child is "covered" during the day. In addition to confirming any childcare arrangements, schedule activities (such as practicing music or doing chores) and assignments (such as reading or writing a paper) and stipulate when they should be completed.

- Review with your child what you will work on together during your teaching time.

- If your older child will be alone in the house, establish clear rules, such as not allowing anyone in the house while you're away. Connect with a neighbor, whom your child can go to for help, and perhaps ask them to check in periodically.

- Establish a clear line of communication. Inform your child or babysitter where you can be reached at all times, and prearrange a time for at least one daily phone call, when you can discuss the child's progress. If you regularly change locations during the day, carry a cell phone or pager.

Timesaver
When you approach your boss about a change in your work schedule, have in hand a clear, written proposal. It will reassure your boss that you've covered all the bases, and increase your chances of coming to an agreement.

▪ Consider trading work time with other homeschoolers. If your job requires you to be gone only for a short time, see if you can find another homeschooler who would be willing to oversee your children's study time.

Single parents

Homeschooling almost always requires single parents to reconfigure their work situations. Some job-share or work shifts; others return to school for additional training or to embark on a different career path.

Still others make arrangements to bring children to work with them. On certain days, for example, Sherri Linsenbach, a single mom and editor of *Homeschool Fun Online Magazine,* took her son to work after his lessons, where he would help out at the office. "This was a very important part of his education and training," says Linsenbach. "Other days I'd bring work home from the office, so we'd have more time together."

A major issue for single parents is childcare, which requires a proactive effort to arrange. Express your needs to relatives and friends, who may help you out or provide a backup if regular plans fall through.

You can arrange cooperative babysitting with friends or among your homeschool support group. Such an arrangement could involve just two families, with one supervising or teaching the kids for certain hours while the other works, and vice versa. Consider your child's schedule when making such arrangements. One work-at-home mother, for example, opted to homeschool in the morning hours, when her children were "fresher." During hours when someone else is covering, have the kids work on independent assignments.

If your schedule prevents you from fulfilling your end of a babysitting trade, consider offering your services instead. You can exchange word-processing, consultation, carpooling, or other services. Also consider your personal interests, which may enable you to offer such things as sports instruction, music lessons, sewing, or baking.

Single parents may also have to take extra steps to assure their children are provided with regular and varied social opportunities. Participating in support groups and homeschool co-ops (discussed in Chapter 9) are good ways to get involved.

Moneysaver
How about no-cost childcare? Consider forming a babysitting co-op, where member families trade babysitting, using a system of points, which can be cashed in for equivalent hours of babysitting. Check out co-op sites on the Web for more information.

Singles and support groups

Homeschool groups are a great source of support and companionship, but single parents may feel they are in the minority. Miki Haas used to belong to three homeschool support groups, but found her work schedule conflicted with their field trips and activities. "I really liked the educational aspect and the socialization, but then again, I was the only single parent," she says. "This posed a problem when fathers were needed for special activities." Eventually, Haas dropped out.

If things don't work out with one group, try another, where you might meet other single home-schoolers. Perhaps you can arrange your own babysitting or home-teaching cooperative, independent of the larger organization. Remember, it only takes two of you to form a support group that caters to your needs.

When a former spouse opposes homeschooling

Homeschooling has become an issue in divorce situations. If a former spouse disapproves of the educational program for his or her child, he or she may use homeschooling as a tool in negotiating child support payments or even custody. In some cases, a judge's personal opinion of homeschooling—usually negative—may influence a legal decision, which may involve returning the child to school.

According to Jackie Orsi, former legal chair of the California Homeschool Network and author of *Homeschooling the Child of a Divorce* (California Homeschool Network), "In these situations, the homeschooling parent is almost always at great disadvantage. Family courts have displayed little or no understanding of homeschooling, much less approval of it. In truth, homeschooling is going to court probably as often as once a week in California, and it is losing badly there. This is especially tragic because homeschooling is an effective way for children who have been badly traumatized by the divorce to take time away from stress and to heal in the nurturing environment of home."

If you find yourself in a similar legal conflict, it is recommended that you take the following steps:

- Make sure you are in compliance with your state education statutes.

- Provide those involved with your case information about homeschooling, including research studies, statistics, and other material that explain its benefits.

- Contact your state homeschool network for guidance.

Homeschooling dads

In most households, mom carries the responsibility for homeschooling, often forgoing paid work to remain at home.

Homeschoolers come in a variety of family situations, with both mom and dad juggling work schedules and sharing in the homeschooling, or maybe it's dad who stays at home or does most of the teaching. In these cases, the father may set aside a lesser-paying job, or perhaps he may have the more flexible schedule.

Whatever your situation, plenty of support is available for men to participate in homeschooling. Fathers have a big presence in the community, leading activities in support groups and exchanging ideas on the Internet; there's even an online magazine devoted to homeschooling dads.

There persists a general impression that dads occupy a lesser role in homeschooling. Expanding your concept beyond the traditional model of "teacher" will help you realize the contribution that he can make. Dads "teach" by example, supporting an optimal environment for learning, involving their child in their personal interests, and numerous other ways.

Here are a few suggestions that are especially helpful for dads:

- Be involved from the beginning. Take an active part in setting up your homeschool program.

- Support your wife's efforts.

- Decide together how you will share in your child's learning and schedule your participation.

- Take part in a support group by leading a field trip or other activity.

- Find creative ways to teach your kids, involving them in your work or hobby. Share activities around your home, such as building a birdhouse or planning a garden.

Ethnic and religious minorities

Minority families are teaching at home for the same reasons as non-minority parents. Concern for academic excellence, self-esteem, religious and cultural training, and family life are among the priorities. "Homeschooling allows you to spend plenty of time teaching your kids things about your culture and history that may not be covered in public school," says Dani M. Sanders, an African American homeschooler.

In addition to participating in other homeschool groups, minority homeschoolers have organized their own networks to provide support, particularly for those families who are at some geographic distance from their community. As the Muslim Home School Network's mission states, "No matter where a Muslim homeschooling family resides, we want to insure that they never feel alone." (Muslim Home School Network Web site: http://islam.org/MHSNR/)

A variety of approaches are used. Jewish parents may teach the Torah themselves, or hire a tutor. Homeschooling offers the opportunity, according to the Jewish Home Educator's Network, "to teach the Torah as it arises in daily life, rather than a 'subject' apart from living."

In an effort to recover a culture lost through assimilation, Native American families can impart their languages, religion, history, songs, and crafts to their children—and to succeeding generations, as well—through homeschooling.

Parents choose from available teaching resources. Those desiring non-Christian-based curricula can consider Oak Meadow, among others. Other options are becoming increasingly available, such as Al-Hadi Curriculum or ArabesQ Islamic

Academy, designed specifically for Muslim home-schoolers. I will discuss curricula in greater detail in Chapter 8.

Location, location

Where you live is a function of the individual circumstances of your family, your job or career, proximity to relatives, and the community in which you choose to raise your kids. Successful home-schoolers maximize their available resources wherever they reside, as you'll see in the following examples.

Homeschooling in the city

Urban home educators have a wealth of cultural opportunities, a diverse population, and other valuable resources. On the other hand, the stresses of city living provide equally unique challenges to any parent raising children there.

Homeschoolers should fully exploit various city resources. Look beyond the obvious—large museums and the like. Most urban areas feature at least one major university or college. These institutions may provide access to scholarly libraries, with specialized collections and other services; lectures; and theatre and other performance events. Check into ethnic organizations, which sponsor events and workshops through which you can explore diverse cultures.

Rural homeschoolers

Many families homeschool in rural or isolated areas. A big challenge here is the lack of readily available resources, including cultural institutions such as museums and comprehensive libraries.

On the plus side, homeschooling families in rural areas can take advantage of the outdoors and

The kind of things home-schoolers are doing may be the saving grace of the nation.
—Martin Luther King III

study nature firsthand. Many rural homeschoolers also take full advantage of the Internet and computer technology, which they use to access online courses, information databases, and library catalogs from across the country and beyond. Even the smallest community libraries offer interlibrary loan services, which permit you to borrow materials from other institutions.

While a support group may not be convenient to your location, contact a state network, which may be able to connect you with other homeschoolers living nearby. You can also connect with homeschoolers across the country (and beyond) via electronic communication. Homeschool mailing lists, newsgroups, and message boards function as mini-communities offering fellowship and support, no matter where you live.

An overseas homeschooling adventure

American families homeschool all over the world, including those in the military and on foreign assignment. Some educational resources are hard to come by—families may not have access to an English library, and they may have to purchase their curriculum materials on return trips to the States. However, especially in larger cities, homeschool support groups are strong and offer many activities for children. Denise Banker, who is homeschooling her five children in Beijing, China, where her husband's job took them, said, "One of the nicest things about being here and homeschooling is that if we want to travel we can go at any time." Her children, who have seen "more of Asia than they have the United States," have benefited from the educational experience of travel.

If you would like to homeschool your children while living in a foreign country, consider the following:

- Advanced planning is critical. Make sure you're covered regarding any applicable laws and obtain the homeschooling materials you'll need—well before you're due to leave.

- If you are on active duty in the military, you may not be required to file paperwork for homeschooling, but it's a good idea to inform the base or your unit commander.

- Civilians are generally subject to the local education laws. Some countries allow home-schooling, as in France, where the law states specifically that education (compulsory for children age six and up) can take place at public or private schools, or at home. (Assessment is required at ages 8, 10, and 12.) The situation in Germany, however, is much more difficult. Prospective homeschoolers must request permission from the local school board and submit a curriculum for the year. Even then, homeschooling may not be permitted. For information and assistance, civilians should consult their employer.

- Consider the resources and materials that you will need. Is there a library, or other resources, convenient to your location? What is the availability of English-language materials? Shipping homeschool supplies can be quite costly and may take months to arrive. Plan your state-side purchases accordingly.

- Contact a homeschooling support group, or other homeschoolers in your area. International homeschooling organizations include

Education Otherwise in the United Kingdom, and the Misawa Home Educators Support Group in Japan, which welcomes both civilian and military homeschoolers. Most of these groups have Web sites and electronic mailing lists, which can provide helpful information.

Just the facts

- While your personal program will most likely involve some degree of trial and error, homeschooling generally requires organization, flexibility, and a united commitment on the part of both parents.

- Some parents are teaching professionals; however, successful homeschooling is not dependent on teacher training.

- Consider how your child will adjust to homeschooling, particularly if they're making the transition from traditional school. Make sure to accommodate their needs, personal as well as academic, and remain open to their feedback. At the outset, your children should be involved in their homeschooling, including having a part in the decision-making and helping determine their course of learning.

- Homeschooling seems to draw emotional responses from practitioners and observers alike. With those whose opinions matter most, help bridge the gap of understanding by providing information on homeschooling and being open to thoughtful discussion.

- Homeschooling works for a variety of families, from those who juggle work and single parenting, to large families or those with one child.

GET THE SCOOP ON...
Homeschooling gifted and learning
disabled children ▪ Meeting your child's needs
through homeschooling ▪ The ins and outs of
testing for a learning disability ▪ How to access
public services

Homeschooling Children with Special Needs

Chapter 3

In the 1800s, an energetic youngster having trouble in school was yanked out of the institution by his mother, who decided to homeschool him. Given the historical record and anecdotal evidence, the boy, Thomas Alva Edison, fit modern criteria for Attention Deficit Hyperactivity Disorder (ADHD).

After meeting with his teacher, Nancy Edison was angered by his rigid ways, and she dedicated herself to nurturing her son's interests. Having no formal credentials, Mrs. Edison began by instilling in young Thomas a love of reading. Before he was 12, he had read works by Shakespeare and Dickens, and Edward Gibbon's *Decline and Fall of the Roman Empire,* among other titles. Responding to his enthusiasms, she gave him a book on the physical sciences, *R.G. Parker's School of Natural Philosophy,* which explained how to perform chemistry experiments at home. From that point on he devoured books on electricity, mechanics, and manufacturing technology.

51

Looking back, Edison, America's most prolific inventor, said, "My mother was the making of me. She understood me; she let me follow my bent."

Today, many parents of special learners, the gifted, those with particular talents, and other exceptional children are turning to homeschooling. In this section I will describe the advantages and disadvantages of home education for these children. I will also give you information on support groups and other resources to help you explore this option.

Special children in public school

Schools can provide valuable special needs services, but in some cases, a student who doesn't fit neatly into the system can fall through the cracks. Traditional school may not fit a range of children, such as the gifted, high achievers, second-language learners, and those with ADHD or other learning disabilities.

In fact, many children pegged as learning disabled due to inattentiveness, "acting out" in class, delayed reading, or other issues, are simply bored, under- or over-stimulated by the environment, or ill-served by conventional teaching methods. If these needs are appropriately addressed—which may be achieved when the child is educated at home—these children can go on to experience personal, social, and academic success.

Gifted children—an estimated 10 to 15 percent of the student population—may likewise find themselves at odds with the school environment. Students with exceptional talent or ability may challenge their teachers, become bored, or engage in delinquent or impulsive behavior. Services to the gifted vary, and participation in a program requires that the student be recognized by the school, as well as meet certain criteria. In some areas, gifted education may not be available at all.

By law, schools are obliged to evaluate special needs children and provide free, appropriate education and needed services. But problems can occur with assessment, an inappropriate educational program, uncaring or uninformed staff, and other issues that can deny a child's individual needs and affect his or her academic future and overall well-being. Consider the following potential problem areas:

- **Mainstreaming.** With learning disabilities, for example, a school may place the child in a regular class, and supplement with special education offerings. This may be convenient for the school, but it may not be in the best interests of your child. Mainstreaming also presents an added burden to teachers, who may not have appropriate experience. A survey of teachers revealed that 85 percent had taught children with ADHD, but the majority had received no related training.

  A large classroom is noisy and distracting for a child with ADD, for instance, who may have trouble concentrating. Traditional techniques also involve too much listening and sitting still, with infrequent breaks. In order to maximize success at learning, ADD students require specially modified lessons, presentation techniques, and appropriate behavior management.

- **An inappropriate classroom.** Overcrowded, traditional classes neglect individual needs of the overall population, but special kids are particularly at risk. For example, those with

Unofficially...
As a child, Albert Einstein was so slow to speak, his parents feared he was retarded. He was a lackluster student, who disliked organized education. Einstein said it is "nothing short of a miracle that the modern methods of instruction have not yet entirely strangled the holy curiosity of inquiry."

dyslexia—which is believed to affect 2 to 8 percent of elementary school children—respond best to one-on-one therapy. Moreover, the highly structured, passive learning environment is not optimal for restless ADHD youngsters, whose impulsive behavior often gets them pegged as "bad" or "lazy"—labels that can stick for life.

■ *Lack of resources.* The local school may simply not have the professional staff or resources specific to your child's needs. As previously mentioned, children of exceptional ability and their families may find themselves in a school district without a mandated enrichment program or other services for the gifted.

■ *Social issues.* Special students may suffer emotional abuse from their peers and teachers, who may not fully understand their needs. Exclusionary social groups, so common in traditional schools, may target ADHD youngsters, who tend to lack social skills.

■ *Medication.* While teachers or school administrators cannot prescribe Ritalin or any other drug, the school may try to influence your decision to medicate your child. Keep in mind that teachers may simply want active children medicated so that they will be easier to control.

Bright Idea
If there is a university medical school in your area, you might consult them regarding assessment of a suspected learning disability.

What is a Learning Disability? LD is defined as a disorder that affects a person's ability to either interpret what they see and hear or to link information from different parts of the brain. These difficulties, which can impede a child's ability to read and write, among other skills, fall into three broad categories: developmental speech and language disorders, academic skills disorders (including dyslexia), and other handicaps, which include coordination disorders. Attention Deficit Disorder (ADD) and Attention Deficit/Hyperactivity Disorder (ADHD) are diagnoses applied to children and adults who consistently display certain characteristics over a period of time, most commonly, inattention, hyperactivity, and impulsive behavior.

Advantages of homeschooling differently-abled children

In homeschooling, you can design an educational program based on your child's individual strengths, weaknesses, preferences, and learning style. Students may be auditory, visual or kinesthetic (hands-on) learners, who best receive information when it is presented according to their learning style. For instance, spoken instructions may work well with auditory learners. Home education can also bolster self-esteem, which may be difficult to maintain in a school environment.

Homeschooling students frequently shed diagnostic labels—"Learning Disabled" or "ADD" (Attention Deficit Disorder)—and the stigma that goes along with them. LD labeling is assigned based on demonstrated symptoms, which in the case of ADD and ADHD is particularly controversial. Kids classified as "ADD" or "ADHD" may simply be bright children who are bored within a classroom or just plain fidgety people! Providing the child with a positive environment, daily structure, and consistent and appropriate feedback from caring parents very often ameliorates the very behavior that caused their ADD diagnosis.

Likewise, gifted youngsters may thrive within a homeschool program. Unlike schools, which may provide limited enrichment, or refuse to allow acceleration, the flexibility of homeschooling allows the student to proceed at their own pace, and engage in mentorships, internships, college and other programs that will help them achieve their full potential.

The U.S. Department of Education makes recommendations for teaching different types of students. Listed below are its suggested strategies for teaching students with ADD. As you read the list, consider which setting—a traditional classroom or a homeschool situation—would be more likely to be able to carry out these guidelines:

- Repeated and simplified instructions
- Supplementing verbal instructions with visual
- One-on-one tutorials
- Clear expectations and immediate feedback
- Student-centered curriculum
- Frequent breaks

Likewise, consider the recommendations for gifted children by The Council for Exceptional Children:

- A curriculum and instruction tailored to the student's individual needs and paced according to his/her learning rate
- Content that involves the use of more advanced or complex concepts, abstractions, and materials
- Extending the depth and breadth of study, and allowing time for in-depth exploration
- A learning climate that encourages him/her to question, exercise independence, and use their creativity
- Including opportunities for interest groups, clubs, science fairs, or internships

" Part of the misfit between schools and at-risk children may result from mixing economics and education—using free market values of competition and survival of the fittest to achieve the mutually exclusive goal of universal excellence. —LD Online: the interactive guide to learning disabilities for parents, teachers, and children (www.ldonline. org) **"**

Should you homeschool your LD child?

The love and understanding that only parents can provide their children has enabled many families to successfully homeschool their special needs children. (Homeschooling gifted children is described more in-depth later in this chapter.)

Research findings confirm the considerable anecdotal evidence regarding homeschooling and special needs. In a 1994 study, Dr. Steven Duvall compared the academically engaged time (AET) and basic skill development of learning disabled students who were homeschooled to those in special education programs. The home-educated students demonstrated higher rates of AET and made greater academic progress. Parents—even without credentials and special education training—provided effective instructional environments at home that positively influenced the academic growth of their children.

"I think that the most important thing is to really know your child as well as you can," says Lisa Weirauch, who homeschools her three children, including a son and daughter who were diagnosed ADHD/combined and ADHD/inattentive, respectively. Weirauch also has the support of their special education teacher, who happens to be a good friend and neighbor. "She has encouraged me as I homeschool these children and has helped immensely in the evaluation process."

"Relax," advises Tammy Glaser, who homeschools her two children, one of whom is autistic. "You are going to make mistakes like all homeschoolers do. Every year, you will continue to find more effective ways to teach your children. Do not compare yourself to the perfect families described in some homeschooling books." Glaser has dedicated herself to learning as much as possible about her daughter's needs. She has read extensively on the subject, attends conferences on education and autism, and has explored related issues of diet and supplements, as well as the chronic illnesses, which can affect children with autism. Her daughter, for example, has been diagnosed with "incurable eczema." After a special diet and supplements, Glaser reports that the eczema has been in remission for years.

When selecting your teaching materials, keep the following guidelines in mind:

- Although some specialized material may be in order, choose most of your material according to your child's learning style.

- Focus on what works for your child instead of on the latest prescriptive therapeutic formula.

- Read extensively about other factors that may be contributing to your child's learning difficulties, such as physiological causes (i.e., vision or hearing problems), diet, chronic illness, and allergies.

Special needs homeschooling is challenging and requires particular dedication on the part of the family.

You may want to consider alternatives to homeschooling if:

- You don't feel you have the patience to teach your child.

- You are, by nature, a perfectionist.

- Your home environment may not be optimal for learning (having younger children at home, for instance, might be too distracting).

- Your family is coping with other stresses, such as financial pressures or health problems.
- Your family relationships would become adversely affected.

Parents must continually assess their child's needs—as well as the needs of siblings—and seek professional help when necessary. Experienced parents also recommend that you:

- Garner support from family, friends, and other homeschoolers. Seek out those who homeschool in a similar situation.
- Find professional resources, public or otherwise, that offer support for your educational choice.
- Take care of yourself. Access any personal services that you need, such as counseling or regularly scheduled childcare.

Professional evaluation and testing

Some developmental delays and disabilities only become apparent when a child begins school. Parents and others may observe immature or unusual behaviors or an inability to keep up with others.

Parents should keep in mind, however, that youngsters, and people in general, learn and acquire skills at different rates. This is evident in language skills, for example, where children can begin to read as young as three or as late as nine or ten.

A formal diagnosis can be a helpful tool in accessing services and information specific to your child's needs. Within the school environment, labels can represent limited goals, but parents have a fuller perception of their child's potential. "Don't be afraid of labels," said one homeschooling parent, "they will get you the help that you need."

Also, if you are seeking access to special services through your school, you will need to undergo a school evaluation in order to qualify for these services. This procedure involves the development of an Individualized Education Plan (IEP) for your child, which is discussed in the following section. In some areas, you may elect to receive some services from the school, while you assume responsibility for some stipulations of the IEP at home. Laws vary, so make sure to check with your local or state homeschooling organization to confirm the regulations in your region.

Still, many homeschoolers caution against testing, citing the following drawbacks:

- The potential for school officials to influence or exert control over your child's education

- The possibility of further testing

- The risk that screening methods may be inaccurate and unfair (some critics, for example, cite a bias against boys)

- The possible undermining of confidence for both parent and child

Alternatives to testing

If you wish to avoid testing and are not planning to go the special education route, there are many ways in which you can help your child.

They include:

- **Observing your child.** By spending time together, parents can understand a great deal about their child's abilities, talents, and personal style that enable them to optimize learning. It is helpful to keep a log or other record of your child's difficulties or behavior patterns, which may then be related to specific hours or foods consumed.

■ **Considering other causes.** Parents are also likely to be aware of a hearing or vision problem, for example, which they could then follow up with a healthcare provider. Parents may also consider homeopathy and other alternative therapies.

■ **Trusting your instincts.** As parent, you will sense what is right for your child. This applies to the most appropriate educational setting, and whether or not traditional school will best serve your interests.

■ **Educating yourself.** Parents can derive greater understanding by reading appropriate literature on child development and related issues. Other parents in the same situation can also provide valuable insight and advice.

Learning difficulties can occur with reading, mathematics, comprehension, writing, spoken language, or reasoning abilities. Determine whether the problems are chronic or represent a genuine developmental delay. It's important to keep in mind that all children learn in highly individual ways, and some—labeled LD—simply process information differently.

What to expect in an evaluation

A thorough evaluation is necessary to determine a child's qualification for services to the handicapped under the Individuals With Disabilities Education Act (IDEA, or Section 504 of the Rehabilitation Act of 1973).

An evaluation cannot take place without written permission from the parents. School personnel

Timesaver
If your child is under school age, they may not be eligible for evaluation by the public school. However, you can seek testing from other available sources, whose independent recommendations may offer options outside the school system. Still, know that you are entitled to an evaluation by law.

must also inform you in writing about specific tests that will be administered and the professionals who will be evaluating your child.

Assessment is conducted by a multidisciplinary team, which may include a psychologist, speech pathologist, social workers, and medical personnel. Psychological and educational assessments will help determine if a child needs special services and the specific areas in which your child qualifies for assistance.

When the evaluation is completed, the team meets to discuss the individual assessments with you. As parent, you are considered a member of the team. In order to fully understand the findings of an evaluation and help design your child's educational program, do your homework, learning as much as you can about the disability, including terminology; what you can expect in testing, and your rights during the procedure. When meeting with professionals, be prepared with notes about your child's behavior, medical history, and educational background.

Also, make sure to talk to your child and respond to any questions he or she may have about assessment.

If the school does not feel that the child has a disability, or you are otherwise dissatisfied with the judgment, you may request a second opinion. A school may also refuse to test a child, but they must inform parents of this decision in writing. Parents are then entitled to appeal the decision in a due process hearing.

The IDEA dictates specific requirements for local education agencies to provide such impartial hearings for parents who disagree with the identification, evaluation, or placement of a child.

The Individualized Education Plan (IEP)

If an assessment determines that your child has a specific disability, the team, including the parents, develops an Individualized Education Plan (IEP). The IEP contains:

- A statement of the child's present level of educational performance

- A statement of annual goals

- Appropriate procedures for determining whether the short-term objectives are being achieved

- A statement of specific educational and related services to be provided to the child

- Identification of the providers of the various services

- Dates for initiation and expected duration of services

- Evaluation procedures and schedules for determining whether objectives are being met on an annual basis

IDEA guidelines govern the procedures involved in the IEP development process, including your rights as parent. Again, get some background before attending the formal IEP meeting; contact other parents who have been through a similar experience, as well as trusted professionals. You are entitled to bring one or more individuals with you to an IEP meeting, such as a friend, a professional who is familiar with your child, or a representative of an advocacy or support group.

Accessing public services while homeschooling

Many parents take advantage of the special services of their local school as a supplement to

Unofficially...
Children covered under the Individuals With Disabilities Education Act (IDEA) must have an Individualized Education Plan (IEP). Students covered under Section 504 of the Rehabilitation Act of 1973 require a less formal arrangement.

homeschooling, benefiting from helpful programs, and dedicated and caring professionals. (Again, you will have to undergo a school evaluation in order to qualify.) If the parents decide to provide these services at home, they may have the option of amending their IEP and specialists will provide training or materials for them to work with at home.

But for some, using free services of the state has been problematic. One mother had trouble with a special education program that refused to release her child to be homeschooled. Although families are not obligated to accept such services, the school has a vested interest in keeping students, or they risk losing funding.

Again, consult your local homeschoolers for advice. You can also try making exploratory contact with the school. You can get an idea of what's available, as well as gauge the school's willingness to work with homeschoolers.

Don't forget other sources to supplement your homeschooling. One mother contacted her local college and met a student majoring in speech pathology, whom the family hired to work with their autistic child. Through their support group, another special needs family found a speech language pathologist, who works with the local school district and also homeschools her own children.

Appropriate state agencies you can contact include the Developmental Disabilities Planning Council and your state Departments of Mental Health, Mental Retardation, Health, and Human Services. Also try local chapters of national organizations such as the National Academy for Child Development and the Learning Disabilities Association of America. They may be able to advise you on the availability and quality of local services.

Home-teaching special children

Once you make the decision to educate your child with learning disabilities at home, consider incorporating the following suggestions:

- Provide an appropriate environment. Avoid distracting clutter and excessive noise.

- Keep a schedule to encourage organization skills. Set up specific times for schoolwork, chores, meals, rest, and bedtime.

- Base teaching on your child's learning style (not yours). Visual learners, for example, prefer charts and diagrams. Be prepared to keep changing the curriculum to find one that works.

- Prioritize your child's talents or interests. Successful home teachers of ADD or LD tend to use the child-centered approach, in which learning is tailored around a child's interests.

- Break down assignments into smaller units. ADD students may need more time than other students. Start a lesson with questions or activities that you know your child can successfully accomplish.

- Establish clear rules for appropriate behavior. To be effective, consequences must be immediate and consistent. Reward good behavior. Professionals can advise you on specific strategies for dealing with problem behavior.

- Keep a record of your child's progress, and continue to document other aspects, such as medication and diet.

- Provide regular breaks and opportunities for physical activity.

Watch Out!
Some parents may not be effective teachers of children with ADD, particularly those who are perfectionists or have unreasonable standards. As one parent suggested, "It takes extraordinary patience to teach a child who can't sit still."

Unofficially...
Computer
instruction has
been shown
to increase
attention in
students with
ADHD. Computers
also allow
individuals to
work at their
own pace,
provide immedi-
ate feedback,
and help develop
problem-solving
skills.

- If required, administer tests in alternative formats (computer, oral exams, handwritten) and combine both auditory and visual stimuli whenever possible.

- Follow your child's pace, and provide for lots of practice or review, and positive reinforcement.

Gifted education

As with other special children, the needs of highly gifted or specially talented children may not be met by a traditional institution.

What determines giftedness? Following are general characteristics (although no child will excell in every area):

1. Shows superior reasoning powers and outstanding problem-solving ability

2. Demonstrates persistent intellectual curiosity

3. Engages a wide range of interests, often of an intellectual kind; develops one or more interests to considerable depth

4. A demonstrated command and sophisticated use of written and/or spoken vocabulary

5. Exceptional reading ability; reads and comprehends books well beyond his or her age

6. Learns quickly and easily, and is able to recall important details, concepts, and principles

7. Demonstrates particular ability in music, art, dance, drama, or other creative expression

A one-size-fits-all curriculum is undoubtedly inappropriate for these children, who require different teaching methods, which the school staff may not be able to provide.

Highly gifted children may occupy several levels simultaneously. A gifted individual, for example, may be several years ahead in reading and below grade level in math. Therefore, gifted children may not fit neatly into level grades.

Traditional schools may shortchange gifted and talented students by:

- Fostering anti-intellectual attitudes. High achievers and those who enjoy learning are frequently ostracized

- Not allowing students to study interests beyond basic curriculum

- Not encouraging abstract concepts that require more than simple thinking

- A lack of enrichment or Advanced Placement programs

These recommendations for gifted programs can be achieved at home:

- An individualized, challenging curriculum

- A flexible schedule

- Active support by parents

- The incorporation of life experiences and the child's interests

Teaching a gifted child may present a particular challenge to a parent, who may feel less able to manage the child's education. Outside resources are available, including tutors or a mentor in that child's area of interest. Distance learning programs, which enable participation in specialized high school or college level courses electronically, also offer unique learning opportunities for gifted children, and some of these are listed in Appendix B.

Bright Idea
Mentorships enable gifted students to pair with an adult or student who is an expert in their field of interest.

Unofficially...
The education of political philosopher John Stuart Mill was overseen by his father, James Mill, who believed that ordinary schooling fails to develop a child's intellectual capacities early enough. John Stuart Mill believed that his intense learning as a young boy gave him a 25-year head start over his contemporaries.

Moneysaver
Certain private, nonprofit organizations offer financial assistance to people with disabilities. Other agencies, such as the Muscular Dystrophy Association, may provide specialized services.

Special needs support groups

Homeschooling veterans recommend that anyone considering this education option first contact a support group. Those organizations that address homeschooling within the context of special needs may be particularly helpful. Beyond general assistance with homeschooling, these groups provide invaluable support across the range of special needs. They offer:

- Information on recent medical and special education news, including alternative therapies, gifted education, and more

- Advice on curriculum and testing

- Help in negotiating the public school system

- Other local support services

- Sharing of materials and programs

- Encouragement

If there are no special needs groups in your area, there are many e-mail lists and other online groups, which you can find through the Web sites listed in Appendix B. You also can get a referral to a local group, and other valuable information, through national organizations. These include: NATHHAN (National Challenged Homeschoolers), a Christian support network that offers a newsletter, lending library and other resources to members; and for talented and gifted children, the TAG Family Network. Other informative sources include LD Online.

Just the facts

- If your public school system lacks resources or does not provide an appropriate setting for your special youngster, homeschooling is a viable option that enables individualized attention.

- Parents who homeschool special needs children must be proactive in seeking information and securing services. Ideally, they should have the support of family, friends, and caring professionals.

- To qualify for school services, a child must undergo a formal assessment through the local district. Parents should take an active role in the IEP process to help determine their child's education.

- In addition to the public school, consider other helpful resources, such as private therapy, nonprofit organizations, and special needs support groups.

- At home, gifted children are free to pursue in-depth study and advanced coursework. Outside the confines of school, vast resources await them that can nurture and challenge their intellectual abilities.

- Support groups have organized to provide assistance to special-needs homeschoolers. There are mailing lists, bulletin boards, and organizations dedicated to specific challenges, from blindness and physical impairments to Downs syndrome and autism.

Getting Ready for Homeschooling

PART II

GET THE SCOOP ON...
Homeschooling expenses and savings ▪ Tips for
economizing ▪ Working and homeschooling
under one roof ▪ Launching a home business

The Financial Picture

Chapter 4

Homeschool families span all income levels, according to a 1998 survey by Lawrence Rudner. Their expenditures for education—including textbooks and other materials, tutoring, and enrichment services—were just as wide-ranging: anywhere from less than $200 to more than $2,000 in one year.

Rudner also found that, compared to the nation, a much larger percentage of homeschool mothers stay at home—76.9 percent do not work for pay, and the 86.3 percent who do work do so part time.

So how do they do it?

In this chapter I'll guide you through homeschool finances, with a look at a homeschool shopping list, alternatives to full-time traditional work, and tips for scaling back your lifestyle.

How much does homeschooling cost?

Depending on your homeschooling program and whether you create your own curriculum or buy a packaged one, you can spend a little or a lot. Complete curriculum packages are relatively expensive, anywhere between $200 to $500, but many

Unofficially...
The total tax expenditure per pupil in public elementary and secondary schools for the 1996–97 school year was $7,371.
—National Center for Education Statistics

homeschoolers—perhaps concerned over what to cover—choose this option for their first year.

Your budget will also be shaped by your need to make any big-ticket investments, such as a home computer. Your expenditures will also vary from year to year.

A sample homeschool shopping list

I'm including a list of the more common purchases made by homeschoolers, which you can photocopy, use to check off what you anticipate for your own needs, and use to sketch out a thumbnail budget.

Keep in mind that as you get more involved in homeschooling, you'll refine your needs and find ways of reducing your expenses.

Homeschool Supplies	Estimated Cost
☐ Curricula (approximate range: $20–500):	_____
☐ Correspondence program (approximate range: $100–500):	_____
☐ Manipulatives (commercially available sets of rods, blocks or other hands-on tools used to learn counting and other math concepts):	_____
☐ Books:	_____
☐ Magazines:	_____
☐ Basic supplies (paper, pencils, etc.):	_____
☐ Art supplies:	_____
☐ Computer software:	_____
☐ Online service:	_____
☐ Videos, audio cassettes, CDs:	_____
☐ Travel and field trips:	_____
☐ Homeschool conferences (approximate range: $30–100):	_____
☐ Homeschool magazines and newsletters (approximate range: $15–26):	_____
☐ Institutional fees (ISPs (independent study programs), private school programs):	_____

Homeschool Supplies	Estimated Cost
☐ Private fees (classes, tutors):	_____
☐ Membership dues (state and local homeschooling orgs. approximate range:$12–$35.):	_____
☐ Other memberships (museum, clubs, etc.):	_____
Total:	_____

❝
How many
things can I
live without.
—Socrates
❞

Optional purchases

You will also want to have a computer and printer. Choose wisely, since you'll most likely have to live with your system for at least a couple of years. Key factors in deciding on a family computer should be reliability and ease of use. You want all family members to be comfortable with the computer, so they'll want to use it.

To ensure reliability, always choose a computer manufactured by a reputable company. Consider all aspects of the computer package—hardware, software, and service. The cheapest package may not provide the best service. Major manufacturers generally provide a three-year warranty, with a one-year on-site warranty in which the technician comes to your house to fix your machine if anything goes wrong.

Families should look at a system's multimedia capabilities (sound and video) that can make the most of educational software. Another important feature, of course, is a modem. A modem enables you to connect to the Internet and online services; modem speed is a consideration. Available for less than $100, color ink-jet or bubble-jet printers are a bargain.

In addition to a computer and printer, you may wish to purchase some of these items, depending on your interests:

- Scanner

- Copy machine

- Portable tape recorder

- File cabinets

- High-quality pencil sharpener

- Reference works (encyclopedias, dictionaries—CD-ROM or hard volume)

- CD or cassette player

- VCR

- Geography items (globe, atlas, and maps)

- Science items (Binoculars, microscope, scale and weights, other lab equipment, aquarium, field guides)

- Educational games and kits

- Camera (video, digital)

- Musical instruments

- Cuisenaire rods (colorful sets of plastic or wooden rods that teach basic math principles)

- Kitchen timer (for timing tests, time-outs, games)

Watch Out!
One of the most common mistakes attributed to newcomers is overexpenditure in the first year of homeschooling. If possible, borrow before you buy. Check out magazines from the library, for example, to save on subscriptions.

How to keep a lid on your expenses

Walk into almost any school supply store or look at one of their catalogs, and you'll see the most wonderful, colorful, must-have items imaginable. In the midst of such incredible purchase opportunities, it can be easy to lose sight of your educational goals. But if you're trying to keep your expenses within reason, you'll need to figure out if anything that you already have around the house will accomplish the same educational objectives.

Take, for example, those tiny plastic math manipulatives that come in different colors and fun shapes. You could buy them, but as homeschooling mother Cerelle Simmons points out, "If you want to give your kids something to count and sort, how about SOCKS?! Or leaves? Or acorns? Good grief, everyone's house and yard is already bursting with things to count. Why would we think we needed to buy a bunch of little plastic teddy bears to teach our kids math!"

The freedom of choice in homeschooling expands educational opportunities but can also lead to overspending, if you aren't careful. Here's how to keep your costs down:

- **Do your research.** Joining a support group and communicating with other homeschoolers, studying catalogs, and comparison shopping online will help guide you to the best, most cost-efficient sources, and save you from making mistake purchases in the first place.

- **Consider used materials.** Shop at flea markets, garage sales, and used book stores. Used or outdated textbooks are often available through college and university bookstores. Numerous resale outlets carry items specifically for homeschoolers. Local homeschool groups frequently host used material sales.

- **Shop creatively and examine all your alternatives.** Locate community resources and events, overstocks at the local printer, readings at the local bookstore, teaching kits from the museum, and other activities and items in the area. Follow your children's interests and allow them to have a say in what you buy. That way you'll be less likely to buy something that won't work with them.

- **Create a homeschool budget and stick to it.**
Consider establishing a separate checking account for homeschooling. Give yourself a spending limit at curriculum fairs. To avoid impulse buying, place a desired item on a three-month list, and, after three months have passed, if you still think the item is essential, you can make the purchase.

- **Exploit freebies (and the nearly-free).**
Numerous sources abound. For example, some school districts make extra or used books available on a first-come, first-served basis. Public libraries always have a sale shelf with 25- or 50-cent books. You can also find free Internet access, free government publications, free downloadable materials, and more.

Watch Out!
Combing yard sales and used book stores can yield bargains, but also involves an investment of your time.

Throughout the rest of this book, I'll share some effective, practical teaching methods and tools that are also easy on your wallet.

How much can you save?

Conversely, you can think of homeschooling as an opportunity to save money. Here's what you could be spending if you sent your kids to traditional school:

- Private school tuition (according to the Bureau of Census, Current Population Survey, 1997: preschool:$3,636; secondary: $9,374)

- Childcare (Of families with income of $54,000 or more, 6 percent of their income was spent on preschool childcare. Fees for school-age children vary: $2.41 per hour in Minnesota to $4.70 in New Jersey according to the Census bureau, 1995.)

■ School wardrobe. It's true that homeschoolers still need to wear clothes; however, this expense can be greatly reduced within homeschooling. For example, on most school campuses today, a great deal of emphasis is placed on fashionable clothing, where the upkeep on a wardrobe may be quite costly.

We have two mottos: 'Use it up, wear it out, make do, or do without,' and 'Learn to admire without having to acquire.'
—Amber Brannon, homeschooling mom

Maximizing your income options

For many, the family budget is less affected by homeschooling expenditures than by the related decision of how to balance the demands of homeschooling with earning a living. Many parents who wish to homeschool must make some adjustments in their work schedules.

Fortunately, the world of work is changing, and more options are available for people to integrate the needs of their families. Telecommuting and flextime options can allow parents to remain in their current jobs, or an interest or hobby can lead parents into an entrepreneurial venture.

Successful implementation of any alternative work option involves careful planning. Consider how these changes will affect your family. Apply homeschool ingenuity to your own life: Evaluate your skills, consider additional training or returning to school, and with every endeavor, from finding childcare to connecting with other work-at-home parents, build a network.

Alternative work options

Reconfiguring an existing job is a practical option for many. The feasibility of such an arrangement, however, depends on your particular industry and the flexibility of your employer. Consider the following options:

Unofficially...
In a recent study, 57 percent of companies permitted workers to move from full-time to part-time status while in the same position or level. Thirty-eight percent allowed job-sharing.
—National Study of the Changing Workforce

- *Flextime.* A popular alternative that continues to gain acceptance among employers, flextime involves an alternate starting and quitting time, while maintaining a full-time schedule.

- *Telecommuting.* This option allows you to work at home during part of your scheduled hours. It saves you the time and expense of commuting and is popular among employers as well. According to recent estimates, there are 15 million telecommuters in the U.S., and this figure is expected to increase each year by 20 percent. All the considerations of working at home apply (see "Working at home," below).

- *Compressed work week.* This option has you working 40 hours in fewer than five days. Choosing to work 10 hours for four days a week can gain you a day, but it can leave you feeling drained.

- *Job sharing.* A form of part-time work, two people share the responsibilities of one full-time position. Success hinges on finding a flexible partner who shares your need for part-time hours and has good communication skills.

- *Other part-time options.* Many parents wish to remain in a job, but cut back on their hours, as in a shortened work week. Part-time arrangements require careful consideration from the employer's perspective, as well as the financial implications for the family.

How to approach your boss about an alternative arrangement

While you may be tempted to fly into your boss's office and announce your brilliant plan, taking time to prepare your case will optimize your chances for success.

First, draw up a written proposal, explaining your desire for this alternative; the advantages to your employer, including any savings to the company; a detailed explanation of how the work will be accomplished; any revision to your salary and benefits; and a proposed trial period.

Anticipate any comments or questions from your boss, such as, "This isn't company policy," or, "Your job can't be turned into part-time." Rehearse your responses, then arrange a meeting to discuss your proposal.

If your boss says no, look for an alternative position elsewhere. Just as you would for any job, consider your needs and those of your family, refine your resume, and prepare to interview. Seek out companies that have a policy of alternative work options.

Bright Idea
Many employers agree to a well-thought-out work-at-home proposal because it's cheaper to keep a good employee than to hire and train a new one.

Working at home

Whether you call yourself an entrepreneur, telecommuter, or independent contract worker, millions of working parents, including homeschoolers, are basing their work at home.

There are numerous sources that can tell you how to find work-at-home employment, which is beyond the scope of this book. Basic steps include identifying the types of industries and positions that are suited to working at home: sales, publishing, real estate, childcare, travel, and record-keeping, to name a few. You must also decide what you really want to do and consider your existing qualifications, as well as any additional training or education you may need to achieve your work goals.

Can work and homeschooling coexist? "Yes," says Georgette Evans, who homeschools her six-year-old, and also has a four-and-a-half-year-old. "I run my own third-party billing business. This takes about

Watch Out!
Blending work
and home does
have its hazards.
When her printer
jammed, one
WAHM (work-at-
home mother)
discovered a
Pokemon card
stuck in the
paper tray!

three to four hours a day, but on the last five days of the month and the first five days of the new month I work about 10 to 12 hours a day." It can be done, says Evans. "However, we do have a few more pet 'dust bunnies' than we used to have."

A great deal also depends on the age of your children and their level of independence.

There's more to a home office than deciding whether or not to get out of your pajamas. Consider your personal situation, while weighing the potential advantages and drawbacks of working at home.

The advantages include:

- Being there for your kids when they're sick or otherwise need you

- Enriching family relationships

- Independence and pride in running your own show

- Your family seeing you in another capacity

- Your children being exposed to adult responsibilities, including money and financial matters, which may inspire their own career development

- Having no boss or little interaction with one

- Reduced childcare and work-related expenses, such as lunches out and dry cleaning

The drawbacks include:

- Inevitable disruptions that may test your patience and force you into alien working habits

- Inconsistent income and the risk of business failure

- Resentment from family members who feel they have to compete with work for your attention, which may cause some children to act out

- Missing recognition from peers and others at the workplace

- Resentment from your spouse, who may be stuck in the 9-to-5 conventional job that pays most of the bills

- Clients and associates making demands at all hours

- The potential for work and family schedules to be easily thrown off by a sudden deadline or by a babysitter who cancels at the last minute

- Isolation from peers

Involve the family in your decision

You may have your alternative work scheme all figured out; now it needs to be discussed with your family. Introduce your plan to them and explain every aspect, from why this is important to you and how you are going to balance the needs of your family, homeschooling, and spouse, to how much space you require. Encourage their opinions and remain open to their ideas. After all, a home enterprise will impact everyone's life.

"Close that door" and other home office guidelines

You may choose to leave the door wide open, of course, or maybe you're set up on the kitchen table, and there is no door! Since work/family/homeschooling situations vary so widely, the following guidelines may or may not apply to your situation:

- **Set up your work space.** A separate area is ideal for avoiding distractions and establishing the home/office boundary. Install all

I am a single mom of two children, ages 8 and 4. I just started homeschooling. I'm also a registered home daycare provider, so I have the luxury of staying home with my children. I provide childcare for six others, two of those six are being homeschooled by me. It's working for all of us.
—Lisa M. Henderson

99

Bright Idea
A decision as important as a change in work must be reviewed with your spouse. Discuss how it will affect your family budget and lifestyle, as well as the long-term personal and professional goals for both of you.

necessary hardware, extra phone lines, modem, and other equipment. Provide "office equipment" for younger children, who might be underfoot while you're on an important phone call. Include a pretend desk, toy phone, and their own pad of stickies.

▪ **Devise a work/family schedule.** Define when your workday begins and ends. Be clear with everyone—clients and relatives alike—about your situation, and let them know the hours you are available. Incorporate family/homeschooling/household duties into your formal schedule, but be realistic about what you can accomplish in a day.

▪ **Be realistic about your childcare needs and plan ahead.** Consider every alternative, from available relatives and students to exchanging babysitting among your homeschooling support group. In any case, have a backup. Prepare your children, and establish how you will work when a babysitter is in the house.

▪ **Put your house in order.** Involve the family in chores and cooking, and hire some help, if you can afford it. With so much going on, it's inevitable that dust will build and laundry will grow into a mountainous pile. Embrace chaos, or just maybe lower your standards a bit.

▪ **Just as you do with homeschooling, take time for you and your family to stand back and draw a long breath.** Understand that there will be a transition period for everyone and, inevitably, rough spots along the way. Children, especially, are sensitive to stresses in the home environment; they may exhibit changes in behavior and learning.

Starting a home-based business

Many homeschoolers take the entrepreneurial plunge and start their own business. Such a venture may grow out of a common family interest, which can involve the children. Sharing a home business also enables both parents to participate in home-schooling. All the elements of working at home, described previously, apply to a home business.

How-to guidance is beyond the scope of this book, but resources in this area are widely available. There are books, Web sites, periodicals, and associations, all offering tips on how to start and run a successful home enterprise.

Beware: Home business scams

Many people who want to work at home begin by looking for a home-based job. Tempting opportunities abound in popular magazines, telephone solicitations, Internet offers, and cable-television infomercials. Aimed particularly at stay-at-home moms, these ads promise flexible work and large profits for little effort.

These work-at-home schemes claim many victims, who are losing more money than ever. Losses can range from $10 to $70,000 or more.

In truth, successful work-at-home situations are rarely found through a typical ad in the classified section. A more likely start is to build on your current experience or skills.

Typical scams include assembly work at home, multi-level marketing distributorships, unsolicited e-mail come-ons, and chain letters. One of the worst scams is envelope stuffing, which, because of the sophisticated technology that can do this work quickly and efficiently, does not produce the income as alleged.

Timesaver
Keeping a work-at-home journal will help you evaluate how you spend your time. Review it at the end of each week. You may find that you got too caught up with busywork, or your projected daily goals are not realistic.

Unofficially...
According to the Federal Trade Commission, Americans lose $100 million each year to bogus business opportunity schemes.

Ten tips for avoiding scams

Here are a few things to keep in mind to avoid being taken:

- Do your research. Check out the company through your local Better Business Bureau (BBB), the Federal Trade Commission (FTC), or other appropriate agency.

- Be skeptical of promotions that state "Earn hundreds in your spare time!" or make other exaggerated claims.

- Question offers of insider information or a "privileged" opportunity.

- Watch out for direct marketing schemes that push you to recruit others into the program, rather than sell the product.

- Follow the golden rule of scams: If it sounds too good to be true, it probably is.

- Before you sign a contract or send in money, get everything in writing, including written substantiation of the potential earnings the company has advertised, and background on the owners.

- Request a list of people who have participated in the business opportunity, whom you can contact as references.

- If you fall victim to a scheme, ask them to refund your money. Keep careful records of all communication with the company.

- Report the scam to the advertising manager of the publication that ran the ad, the state attorney general's office, the BBB, and the FTC. If mail was involved, contact the U.S. Postal Service Criminal Investigations Office.

■ Follow your instincts, and pursue opportunities that truly interest you.

Should both spouses work?

The expense of raising a family today would seem to demand two incomes. But have you considered that it may actually *cost* you money to have a spouse work outside the home? For example, it's conceivable that someone making $25,000 a year may only be taking home a grand total of $1,500 a year. How so? The second income may push your family into a higher tax bracket, cutting your take-home pay by up to 40 percent. You also have to pay for child-care and daily work-related expenses, such as dry-cleaning, that further reduce your net contribution to the family.

You may have already decided that one of you will remain at home or cut back from a full-time job, but you might like to see that there are financial reasons to support that decision. Complete the following form and calculate the net benefit of a second income:

---

1) The second gross income: _____

2) Federal tax: _____

3) State tax: _____

4) Social Security: _____

5) Medicare: _____

6) **Total amount withheld:** _____

7) Childcare: _____

8) Commuting (tolls, gas, maintenance of second car):_____

9) Car insurance: _____

---

10) Clothes and grooming
(work-related attire, dry
cleaning, hairdresser,
cosmetics, etc.): _____

11) Restaurant meals
(i.e., lunch): _____

12) Convenience foods
(i.e., take-out dinners): _____

13) Housekeeping: _____

14) Children's entertainment: _____

15) Other expenses
(i.e., unreimbursed
business supplies,
convenience services): _____

16) **Total expenses:** _____

17) Add lines 6 and 16: _____

18) Subtract line 17 from
line 1: _____

19) Add to line 18 any tax
benefits (i.e., child care
credit): _____

Before making any employment decision, review your own family situation with your spouse. In any case, you will need to map out your family budget and consider all your options, taking into account all issues, such as savings and other assets, debts, and any other expenses, such as child support. You may also want to factor in the long-term losses associated with giving up one income, such as decreased health and retirement benefits and lower earning potential when you return to the job market without work experience.

At-home spouses can still choose to work, such as on a part-time or free-lance basis. In fact, you may find that you can bring in less, and keep more, because you won't be subtracting all the expenses of going to work. And of course, the intangible value of being home with your kids is obvious.

Just the facts

- The cost of homeschooling varies widely among families. The growing population has spawned a burgeoning marketplace in which you can buy lots of things, so be a wise consumer and thoroughly research your purchases.

- Homeschooling will undoubtedly impact all aspects of family life, including work. In many cases, one parent stays at home. Part-time work and telecommuting are among your options; however, the feasibility of such alternative arrangements depends on the type of work you do.

- Many homeschoolers try working from home, but juggling home/work/learning under one roof can be a challenge.

- Home business scams—many targeted at stay-at-home parents—claim many victims each year. Be cautious when you encounter an opportunity that promises easy money.

- Concerned about losing a second income? Factor in childcare, taxes, clothing and food; you may find that the second paycheck isn't worth the net gain.

66
The trouble with the rat race is that even if you win, you're still a rat.
—Lily Tomlin
99

GET THE SCOOP ON...
Homeschooling under the law ▪ Finding the right
form of homeschooling for you ▪ The lowdown
on homeschool evaluation ▪ Handling problems
with officials

State and Local Homeschooling Requirements

Chapter 5

I n December 1996, a town constable, truant notice in hand, knocked on the door of Cindy Wade, a homeschooling mother of two in East Wallingford, Vermont. Wade had been "reported" for failing to have her home program formally approved by the state. Although she refused to sign the document, Wade invited the officer in, and introduced her two children. Over coffee, the constable proceeded to tell her how poor the local school was, because his own son was a student there, and, in fact, would be in the same class as Wade's daughter. Wade then contacted the school's principal to explain her perspective, that parents, not the school district, were responsible for a child's education. She also pointed out the expense of taking them to court. The school district decided to leave them alone.

While such experiences are rare, it is important that you are aware of your legal rights and responsibilities when it comes to homeschooling.

In this chapter I'll describe issues commonly faced by homeschoolers concerning state education law, which may or may not include statutes that specifically govern homeschooling. Regulations vary widely across the country, from the fairly permissive (such as Wisconsin and Montana) to the more bureaucratic (Pennsylvania and New York). Advocates continue to lobby on the legislative front, successfully repealing teacher certification and other requirements, as well as fighting new efforts at restricting homeschooling.

Know the laws in your state

Of course, you should familiarize yourself with your own state and local laws, which you can do by:

- Contacting your local support group or state homeschooling network. Knowing the ins and outs of compliance, your fellow homeschoolers can help you negotiate the system and provide other assistance.

- Obtaining a copy of your state's compulsory education law and related education statutes. Your local librarian can help you look them up yourself, but make sure the laws are current. You can also contact your state department of education (listed in Appendix B) to request a copy of the applicable laws, or, in some cases, you can download them from the state Web site.

Depending on your area, local officials may have little experience with homeschooling, and it's not uncommon for them to make requests that exceed the law. You could also be visited by unfriendly officials, as a few homeschool families are every year.

Understand your legal requirements, but know your rights as well. I will cover the nuts and bolts of compliance later in this chapter.

Homeschooling under the law

Each state defines different forms of homeschooling under the law, and each state has its own requirements for satisfying the law. Some regions allow more than one option for homeschooling. If such is the case, how do you choose? Consider the following:

- How much independence do you want in determining your home instruction plan?

- Would you be more comfortable associating with a "cover" institution or program?

- What is the local climate for homeschooling? Perhaps one form or another might lead to harassment from school officials.

Review all available options and speak with other homeschoolers, who can give you some insight about their experience regarding compliance.

In the following sections, I discuss the general provisions for homeschooling. Again, make sure you know the laws that would apply to your situation.

"Equivalent instruction"

Under this option, parents can teach children at home provided the children receive instruction "equivalent" to that offered in the public schools. The vagueness of these laws generally frees homeschoolers from stringent regulations. Teacher requirements, if required, may include a high school diploma, college degree, or state teacher's certificate.

Timesaver
Some state and local support groups offer a beginner's packet on homeschooling in their region. Providing a summary of the law, sample forms, and other information, it's usually available for free or a nominal printing cost.

Watch Out!
Make sure your cover program fulfills your state requirements. Iowa, for example, requires the school to be a member of a recognized national or regional accrediting association.

Establishing and operating a private school

In this option, homeschoolers register as a private or religious school. Choosing this option will allow you a great degree of independence and freedom in directing your child's education. While largely free of government restrictions, you must follow the same rules that apply to private schools, which vary according to state.

In New Jersey, for example, academic subjects covered are comparable to public school subjects; no method for reporting subject coverage, however, is prescribed. Private school teachers in California are not required to have teacher certification, and private school students are not required to submit to annual achievement testing. Michigan homeschoolers, however, must comply with teacher certification (unless they claim religious exemption). In Nebraska, private schools must provide evidence of compliance with safety regulations.

You will be responsible for answering any inquiries regarding your school, so know your law. Many regions, for instance, mandate the teaching of certain subjects such as reading, social studies, math, and science. But, in most cases, you decide what specific topics (such as American history, geometry, or biology) are covered and how they are to be taught.

In order to register you as a private school, your state may require specific notification. California, for example, requires those registering as a private school to file an R-4 affidavit. Those registering as a religious or private school in Alaska file a "Private School Enrollment Reporting Form" and a "Private and Denominational Schools Enrollment Report."

Be aware of filing deadlines. Nebraska families must file their notice of intent by August 1, or

30 days before the start of homeschooling. In Alaska, homeschoolers must file an enrollment report by the first day of public school and provide a school calendar to the state Department of Education by October 15.

"Umbrella" or "cover" programs

In some areas, homeschooling is allowed under the cover of a state-approved home study program. Virginia homeschoolers, for instance, may choose to enroll in a state-approved correspondence course or participate in a program approved by their local superintendent.

Cover schools offer reassurance that you are in full compliance with the law. Public or private, these programs offer homeschoolers a range of choices, from a full curriculum and teacher guidance to complete independence. The cost of these programs cover a range: for a private independent study program, you may spend $400 to $1,000 per year. The yearly tuition for a distance learning program can cost $700 to $2,000. You may also choose a publicly-financed program option. The ins and outs of these programs, along with other education alternatives, such as correspondence and distance-learning programs, are fully described in Chapter 6.

Independent study programs (ISPs)

Independent study programs (ISPs) are formal programs in which homeschoolers function as satellites to existing institutions. The structure and philosophy of ISPs will vary by institution, with some offering complete curricula and assignments, and others functioning primarily as a record-keeping service. ISPs can be offered through private or public schools, depending on your area.

Bright Idea
To preserve homeschooling rights in your area, support your state homeschool organization, which monitors the actions of government related to home education. Legislators may have their constituents' best interests at heart, but they may also be unaware of how legislation might affect homeschoolers.

Affiliation with a private institution holds many benefits for homeschoolers. Administrative matters will be handled by the private school, so that if a program comes under scrutiny, the school administrator may field questions from officials. A private school will also provide teaching materials and facilities.

On the other hand, such an affiliation may be expensive. Some homeschoolers also find curriculum guidelines provided by private institutions to be restrictive and resent interference in their homes by program staff or administration.

Of course, teaching and program assistance depends on the individual school. Some private ISPs offer curriculum packages and guidance, while others leave you largely on your own.

You must comply with the rules and regulations of the particular school, which may include campus visits, and submit attendance records and a course of study.

The cost generally involves a yearly fee. You can find private satellite programs listed in homeschool magazines, on the Web, or through your local support group or state network.

Public schools also offer ISPs, which are sometimes called home study programs. Because public ISPs require enrollment in the school, your child will be a public school student and must comply with all applicable rules. The traditional structure may be reassuring to some, particularly those families planning to homeschool temporarily or those giving it a trial run.

Depending on the particular school, public school ISPs offer access to materials and facilities, including computer and science labs and support services. Affiliation with such a program generally guarantees compliance with the law. Unfortunately, such an affiliation will also subject you to the dictates of state and local authorities, and the terms of agreement may be onerous. The quality of both program and teaching staff varies greatly from school to school.

You will have to sign an agreement, which may call for regular attendance and testing, among other requirements. The amount of control you have over your child's education depends on school policy and the assigned teacher who oversees your program. As with private institutions, the offerings of the program depend on the particular school and district.

To learn more about how an ISP works, see Chapter 6.

Charter schools

A relatively recent option in some areas, charter schools are public schools organized by an independent group of teachers, parents, community members, or others, and sponsored by the local school board or county board of education. While their goals and procedures are dictated by an agreement with the board, charter schools are largely free of state regulations.

Some charter schools have home study programs (HSPs), and homeschool organizations are forming charter schools of their own. At present, only charters in Alaska and California have provisions for home-based programs. In 26 other states, charters specifically prohibit home-based programs.

If you don't live within the district, you may be able to request an interdistrict transfer. (Recent legislation in California imposes certain residency requirements that limit enrollment in home-based

Unofficially...
The Family Partnership Charter School in Anchorage, Alaska, offers a unique program in which homeschooling parents forge partnerships with certified teachers. Parents and teachers devise a contract and, together, design an education plan according to the individual needs of the child.

Unofficially...
Curious about charter schools? At the U.S. Charter Schools Web site (www.uscharterschools.org) you'll learn about starting and running a charter school, from developing a mission statement to finance issues; charter school profiles, by state; and more.

charter programs.). The charter school may assign a teacher or facilitator who will help you establish a course of study for your child. Throughout the year, the teacher may meet regularly with you, make home visits, help secure tutoring, and provide other needed assistance.

Charter school home programs can be full- or part-time, partly classroom or home-based. An annual stipend, as much as $1,000 per student, can be used for educational expenditures, from science kits to music lessons, depending on the school. Report cards, end-of-year transcripts, and state-certified diplomas may also be offered.

Teressa Morris of Napa, California, has a son enrolled in a charter school program. "This has been our first year in the program. We are given 100 units (dollars) in curriculum choices every month for our son. We can only choose from "approved" catalogs (no religious agendas), but we have got some great stuff from DK, Math-U-See, etc., and it was all my choice!

"This school is very hands-off. We meet with a facilitator (certified teacher) once a month to hand in our learning records, sign attendance sheets, and order curriculum. We can e-mail or mail in our records if we want. So all in all, it's worked out great!"

Research your particular charter school and talk to families enrolled there. For more information on charter schools, see Chapter 6.

Government homeschool programs: A hot topic

Charter schools, public ISPs, and other government programs are controversial. With public schools now reaching out to homeschoolers, many warn that the potentially adverse effects on homeschooling outweigh the short-term benefits to individual families, who are opting for these arrangements in increasing numbers.

Some view public programs as luring homeschoolers back into the public system with cash stipends and other "free" goodies, which compromise their independence and undermine homeschooling.

While ISPs are considered by some as just another homeschooling option, critics claim they establish a framework for overriding government control. The community is divided over this issue, with some rejecting those families who participate in government programs as not being homeschoolers.

The potential drawbacks of public programs are summarized in Chapter 6.

Tutoring

Tutoring is another option in some states. In California, for example, a parent with a current state teacher's credential may teach his or her child under the private tutorial exemption. The state does not require filing or attendance records. The minimum hours of instruction and required subject list vary by state.

The parent/tutor can use this option only for the grades and subjects their credential covers. In other words, your elementary credential would not meet the requirements when your child reaches the high school stage. Keep in mind that acquiring a credential involves at least a year of graduate study in addition to student teaching.

Parents may also hire a credentialed tutor, although this option may be expensive.

Watch Out!
In California, a public school ISP asked participating homeschool parents to sign a statement stipulating certain rules and procedures, according to The Link, a homeschooling newspaper. The same requirements did not apply to conventional public school students.

Homeschooling outside the law

Most homeschoolers comply with the law; in fact, requirements in most states are relatively simple. But others, based on religious or other philosophical convictions, choose to "go underground."

Depending on where you live, defiance of the law may put you at risk for:

- Unnecessary investigations
- A visit by the truancy officer
- The disruption of your child's education
- Monetary fines
- Incarceration

Other homeschooling legislation

Other state laws affect homeschoolers, and I summarize these in the following sections.

Access to extracurricular activities and sports

Several states have enacted laws that entitle homeschoolers to participate in extracurricular and interscholastic activities at their local schools. However, there may be caveats. In Colorado, for instance, homeschoolers must first meet certain district requirements and are subject to a participation fee. Still other areas have no such legislation, and the decision of homeschooler access is left up to the local school district.

A separate issue is school sports, which is not governed by the school district, but by an independent sports association. In most cases, homeschoolers wishing to participate in sports have met with resistance. However, homeschoolers have been successful in pushing through legislation in 10 states, which now mandate that homeschoolers be allowed to play on public school teams.

Other sports opportunities, including home-school leagues, are discussed in Chapter 6.

Driver's license law

Recent legislation tying driver's license eligibility to a student's academic status has implications for homeschoolers.

An Oklahoma law stipulates that children (age 16–18) who wish to apply for a driver's license must provide proof of school enrollment and pass an eighth-grade-level reading test. An alternative proof of enrollment form must be completed by homeschoolers.

In Kentucky, high school dropouts can lose their driver's license. Homeschooling parents must provide a statement that their child is being schooled at home and is not academically deficient.

Contact your local Department of Motor Vehicles or state transportation department for information. They can also provide the requirements for driver's education courses, which, in some areas, can be taught at home. Some states allow nonpublic school students to enroll in the local district driver's ed course.

Curfew laws

In an effort to discourage juvenile crime, cities across America are enacting daytime curfews, in which police may stop and question young people who are not in school during conventional school hours. Those without sufficient reason for not being in school can be fined or taken into custody.

Curfews are widely opposed as a violation of civil liberties. For homeschoolers they are particularly restrictive to learning and working out in the community. Consequently, some existing laws have been

Watch Out!
Homeschooled teens may have trouble getting a "good student" discount from car insurance companies, which may question homeschool documentation of academic achievement.

modified to exempt homeschoolers, who are given special identification.

Despite such accommodations, homeschoolers remain vigilant against further curfew legislation.

The nuts and bolts of compliance

Your experience with the district and other officials will depend on the community in which you homeschool. While homeschooling is legal in all 50 states, laws and their effects vary widely—from the onerous statutes with detailed requirements, to the very lax statutes, which allow families to educate their children relatively hassle-free. The laws can be quite vague in still other areas, where homeschoolers may be subject to the interpretation of individual officials and their personal views on homeschooling.

In the following section, I'll cover the practical aspects of compliance and what you might expect regarding assessment and testing. Your homeschooling group can provide details on how to comply locally.

First step: Notifying your school district

If your state requires it, the first step you will need to take is to formally notify the public school superintendent or local school district of your intention to homeschool your child.

If you are required to submit a notice or statement of intent, learn answers to the following (again, your local support group is your best source of information):

- Who needs to notify? (parents or legal guardians of students of compulsory school age outlined in the state code)
- To whom should I send notification and when? (usually the local school superintendent

and a specified period from the start of homeschooling)

■ What is the required minimum number of hours or instructional days? (relates to the number of instructional days/hours stipulated for the district school year)

■ Are there required teacher qualifications?

■ Is immunization required?

■ What are the curriculum requirements?

■ Are there requirements for testing or other assessments?

■ What if my child withdraws from public school during the school year?

■ Is there an official form? (In some instances, you can create your own)

■ How often do I need to file? (generally, you must file for each year of homeschooling)

■ What happens if my form is rejected?

Within a specified time period you should receive a formal response either accepting your record or notifying you that the form is unacceptable, at which point, you can seek guidance from your support group. In most cases, forms are rejected for being incomplete.

The homeschool facilitator

Homeschooling has grown so popular that almost every state maintains personnel to assist these families. Well-versed in homeschool law, a homeschool facilitator can answer your questions and otherwise assist you with compliance. Facilitators generally have close relations with area support groups, who may also designate a contact member to assist new homeschoolers.

Watch Out!
Supplying extra information on your notice of intent may do a disservice to your fellow homeschoolers, as those who follow you could be asked to supply information beyond that required by law.

Your notice or statement of intent

Beyond such basic information as your name and address, birthdate of children, immunization record, and similar items, notification under a more restrictive law may involve additional material related to the following key requirements:

Education requirements for parents

Virginia, for example, requires parent/instructors to hold a baccalaureate degree or teaching license. Documentation must accompany the notice of intent. (Currently, eight states require a high school diploma or GED.) New York stipulates that the home teacher be "competent."

Curriculum

Find out what your state requires regarding curriculum. Pennsylvania requires a curriculum outline that is subject to approval. It must contain an outline of all subjects and activities prescribed by the state, instructional objectives, suggested activities, and methods of evaluation. New Hampshire residents have greater latitude in defining their "educational plan." "Planned educational activities" are required, but parents are free to choose their educational methods, curricula, or other materials.

Other states require a listing of texts, commercial curricula, and other materials, which you must attach to your notice of intent.

Your local support group can advise you on how to complete this part of the form. A list of core subjects is available from the local school district.

Testing and assessment

On many state forms you must stipulate how you will assess your child's progress. Options may include standardized testing, portfolio review, evaluation by

Bright Idea
If you have a choice in assessment, choose a method appropriate for your curriculum. If you use traditional texts, your child may be comfortable with test-taking strategies, so a standardized test might work. If your program is more flexible, consider alternatives like portfolios, interviews, or a third-party review.

a third party, or another alternative agreed upon by the superintendent. Pennsylvania requires testing at grades 3, 5, and 8, plus an annual portfolio evaluation by a certified teacher.

Parents may have to attach year-end test results or assessment materials to the notice of intent for the subsequent year.

Withdrawing from school

To proceed with homeschooling, you will have to withdraw your child from public school, if he or she is enrolled. Check with your homeschool organization about the recommended procedures for your region, which may involve sending a letter. In many cases, this is merely a courtesy and not a formal requirement.

You are not obligated to provide explanations or rationale for your choice. Arrange for school property (textbooks) to be returned and the student's personal belongings to be claimed.

As the administrator/teacher, you are now responsible for maintaining the required records. You may want to submit a written request for a certified copy of your child's school records.

Certain requirements may apply to those students who withdraw after the school year has started. If this will be the case with your homeschool, find out the procedure for withdrawal.

For information on preparing your child for homeschooling, see Chapter 2.

Working with a supervisory teacher

Some states, including Washington and New Hampshire, allow a home program under the supervision of a certified or licensed teacher. The supervisory teacher can be the parent, in some cases, if he

Bright Idea
Organize a separate file for your statement of intent and other homeschooling documents. Include copies of all correspondence and certified mail receipts, and keep the file with your other important documents.

66
My grandmother wanted me to have an education, so she kept me out of school.
—Margaret Mead
99

Watch Out!
Officials may ask to discuss your motivations for homeschooling, in person or by phone. Know your rights—you are not obligated to provide this information.

or she holds a teaching certificate or license appropriate to the grade level of the student, or a third party.

Iowa homeschoolers who choose to work throughout the year with an approved teacher are exempt from additional assessment, including testing and portfolio approval. In this case, the supervisory teacher must meet with the family at least twice per 45 instruction days.

A supervisory teacher may provide assistance with:

- Setting educational goals
- Lesson plans
- Textbooks and other materials
- Teaching techniques
- Evaluation and assessment
- Interpretation of test results
- Record-keeping
- Referral to special education services

Moneysaver
When a licensed teacher is engaged to supervise a homeschool program, fees are worked out between the teacher and the family. Some arrange a barter, such as exchanging services.

A potential source of support, a supervisory teacher can be an asset to homeschooling. A homeschooling mother in Cedar Rapids, Iowa says of her supervising teacher: "She trusts my judgment and knows that I work very hard with my children to teach them what they need to know. She and I have a great rapport and our trust is mutual."

Assessment

Procedures for evaluation and assessment differ according to your state. Here's an overview of the typical options.

Portfolio review

Many states provide for a portfolio review in which a homeschooler is assessed through a representative collection of their work, which may include completed workbooks, a journal, writing samples, completed science or other projects. In Connecticut, the portfolio review fulfills the assessment requirements, while Pennsylvania requires testing in addition to a portfolio.

What must a portfolio contain? New Hampshire law only specifies a log of reading materials, in addition to other materials that will demonstrate sufficient progress. New Hampshire homeschoolers recommend supplying one or two pages within each subject area that your child has studied. Other states specify an itemized list for homeschool portfolios, as well as the format (typically a three-ring binder).

Formal assessment procedures will also depend on where you live. In Connecticut, portfolio reviews are intended only to demonstrate that you have been fulfilling the schooling promised in your notice of intent. A reviewer is not entitled to evaluate your work. In other areas, a reviewer may score each item in the portfolio and rank the child's overall performance. Some portfolios are graded; others are followed up with a progress report.

Other reporting methods

Other areas require additional filing. Paperwork can be time-consuming, and experienced homeschoolers often find themselves providing less and less information beyond the minimum required for compliance.

"I used to believe that I would enjoy filing the quarterly reports to the school department (which are required in New York state)," says Jamie Shafer. "I thought it would give me a chance to see what we've covered and reflect on where we should go. But it's mostly been a pain. If I actually wrote all that

Timesaver
Take time at the end of the year to evaluate for your own purposes, beyond the required assessment. Let your past work determine your future homeschooling. Also, schedule fun things you can look forward to, such as trips you'd like to take in the coming year.

we covered each quarter, the report would be extremely long. I end up writing a brief list for each subject. I avoid sentences."

The homeschool evaluator

Evaluation by a trained third party is an assessment option for many homeschoolers. Such is the case in Louisiana, where evaluation may be conducted by a certified teacher, a local education agency panel, or a panel of homeschoolers that includes a certified teacher. Evaluation in Ohio is made by a certified teacher or a mutually agreed-upon person.

Support groups frequently provide a list of independent evaluators and the areas that they serve. In choosing an evaluator, make sure the person holds the required credentials. Certain areas require teaching certification according to grade level, others do not. Ideally, the evaluator is familiar with homeschooling, and perhaps homeschools his or her own children.

Set up your appointment with an evaluator well ahead of the deadline and find out exactly what the procedure will involve. In Florida, evaluation usually takes place in the home and includes an oral screening, in addition to any written requirements, such as a portfolio. The discussion with the child will vary according to the particular evaluator; some may simply discuss the portfolio with the child, while others may screen for basic skills.

Some states require evaluations be submitted in written form. The evaluator may be responsible for submitting the report, or sometimes it is the parent's job.

The law usually specifies to whom you should submit the results of the evaluation. An evaluation, in most cases, requires the parent's signature. If you believe the report is not accurate, you may not wish to sign it. You may be able to seek a second opinion. In any case, try to secure a copy for review.

Testing

Many homeschoolers are required to have their children tested periodically. Currently, 29 states require standardized testing or evaluation, while 16 require standardized testing. Thirteen states provide for alternative methods of assessment.

See Chapter 8 and Appendix E for more information on testing and state requirements.

Evaluation results

After your results are submitted for evaluation and accepted as satisfactory, you may have no further contact with the district.

Unsatisfactory results bring about various procedures, depending on the state, which may affect your eligibility to continue homeschooling. Most states will only be concerned if your child scores in the lowest 30th percentile.

Some states allow an opportunity for reassessment, while others do not. For example, if a superintendent deems a child's progress as unsatisfactory in Oregon, that child may be sent to school for the remainder of the school year. See Appendix E for more information.

Handling problems with officials

While legal entanglements involving homeschooling are rare, some families do experience run-ins with school officials. In a great majority of these situations, these officials are simply not familiar with the law.

Again, your local or state networks may have suggestions about how to handle situations particular

Moneysaver
Testing in your region may be offered through the public school free of charge. Consider whether a public, group setting is an optimal test-taking environment for your child before choosing this option.

to your area. Other members, in fact, may have encountered the same difficulties.

When contacted by an official, these are basic guidelines:

- Remain calm and polite.
- Request the caller's name and title.
- Request the legal citation to support her/his action.
- If necessary, consider contacting their supervisor, or the school board.
- Keep records of all interactions, and put things in writing whenever possible to establish a paper trail.

If you can't resolve the problem on your own, consider speaking to your family lawyer, or one recommended by your homeschool group, who may be familiar with the laws involved in homeschooling.

National legal organizations may be another option. They include the Home School Legal Defense Association and the Rutherford Institute, both Christian organizations; the American Civil Liberties Union; and the National Association for the Legal Support of Alternative Schools.

Before hiring any legal counsel, consider the following:

- Is counsel licensed to practice in your state?
- Under what conditions will they consider accepting your case?
- What legal expenses are you expected to cover?
- How much control will you have in running your case?
- Will your case possibly become a tool for a larger platform?

- Is the group involved in other causes that you
support?

If you have concerns about the law, speak to your
fellow homeschoolers. Local veterans, in particular,
will know the history of homeschooling in the area
and will be glad to share their experience.

Just the facts

- Compliance today is pretty straightforward;
however, make sure you learn your requirements as part of your preparation for homeschooling. A local support group is a good
place to start for up-to-date information.

- Legal options available to home educators vary
state by state, and in some cases, there may
be more than one way to go in your area.
Consider the degree of independence you
desire, as well as other factors, such as mandatory testing and record-keeping requirements,
before you decide which is right for you.

- If you must file formal notification for your
intent to homeschool, know exactly what information is required. If you provide anything
additional, you may be setting an unfair precedent for other homeschoolers.

- Families rarely encounter legal problems
involving homeschooling. If you are concerned, consult fellow homeschoolers or your
local group, who may refer you to legal counsel or national organizations, such as the
Home School Legal Defense Association.

Preparing to Teach

GET THE SCOOP ON...
The pros and cons of public school programs
■ What alternative learning centers can provide
■ Questions to ask about correspondence
programs ■ Accessing extracurricular activities
and other school services

PART III

Other Education Options

Chapter 6

Traditional homeschooling conjures up an image of children being instructed by mom around the dining room table. But in practice, homeschooling can involve many forms of alternative education, from part-time attendance at a traditional school or alternative center to correspondence and distance learning programs.

Debate abounds over whether these alternatives are consistent with homeschooling. Public programs are particularly controversial. However, increasing numbers of homeschooling families partake in some form of assisted homeschooling. In fact, researchers Brian Ray, Maralee Mayberry, and Gary Knowles found that 75 percent of home school families said they need or would like to enroll their children part-time in private or public school courses.

Participating parents say that having such a program gave them the confidence to begin homeschooling, or that they provide invaluable support with certain subject areas or special services.

Increasingly many school districts sponsor cooperative arrangements with homeschoolers, as do many private schools.

Homeschooling support groups have organized their own free-standing centers and schools, and entrepreneurial distance learning programs are popping up all over the Web. This chapter describes the ins and outs of these alternative programs, to help you decide if they're right for your family. Your options will depend on your state regulations and what's available in your area.

Private homeschooling programs

Many families choose "assisted" homeschooling by enrolling in a formal program. These options include:

- Correspondence schools
- Independent study programs
- Distance learning programs
- Other private options

Some are highly structured, offering complete curricula, while others flexibly adapt a program to your individual design. Some cover schools—those institutions that oversee the program of homeschool enrollees, and insure their compliance with education laws—simply provide a record-keeping service. A number of institutions are Christian, while others have no religious affiliation.

With so much available, more families are finding programs that fit their needs, and the choices in programs are increasing as homeschooling grows in popularity. Some of the benefits for homeschooling families include:

- Reassurance that everything is being covered, particularly advanced or specialized subjects.

Unofficially...
In 1996, 16 students enrolled in the (grade 5–12) online learning program of Laurel Springs School, a private school in Ojai, California. Just three years later, enrollment jumped to 840 students, all of whom are homeschooled.

This is very important to many parents of older students.

■ Compliance with state requirements.

■ An end to the hassle of record-keeping and dealing with school officials, because these are taken over by the school.

■ Online courses, which can be an ideal format for self-motivated learners.

Of course, there's a downside to involvement with these kinds of programs:

■ Accreditation varies among these institutions. Secondary-level students looking ahead to college, in particular, will need to check a prospective school's accreditation status.

■ Once committed to a program, you may be reluctant to try out your own teaching ideas or investigate other resources.

■ The cost of such a program may be expensive, including additional fees or required program supplementation.

■ Many curricula are textbook-based or otherwise very traditional in format.

When considering such a program, ask the school the following:

■ Is the program flexible? (Do participants have a certain choice in courses to fulfill the program?)

■ Can you incorporate other learning experiences and materials?

■ What are the state requirements for enrollment? (In California, for instance, families enrolled in out-of-state programs are required by state law to be enrolled in a California

> 66
> Rather than being threatened by home-schoolers and unschoolers, educators would do well to see us as colleagues and sources of information on the nature of learning and motivation. After all, we spend nearly all of our waking hours observing, studying and participating in this fascinating endeavor.
> —Jan Hunt, director, The Natural Child Project
> 99

private school, with a California address. This means following the procedures for registering your home as a private school.)

- Will program administrators mediate with officials?

- How are records kept?

- What services does the company provide? (Look for such services as record-keeping, an advisory teaching service, and an 800 number.)

- How are online classes structured? (Do you communicate only through e-mail with the instructor, or are students attending "class" at the same time?)

- Is the program easy to follow? Lessons should provide clear guidance for home instructors.

- What are the methods of assessment?

- How much does it cost? Are there extra lab or materials fees?

- What is the enrollment period? Can a student enroll in the middle of the term?

- How long does a course take to complete?

- Can you enroll in just one subject? Perhaps you want to pick and choose to supplement your own program.

- Can you view a sample? Homeschool curriculum fairs are a good opportunity to look over different programs. You may also be able to view a sample on their Web site.

- What is the refund policy?

After accessing this information, you'll need to consider how the program fits in with your personal learning goals.

You can access a list of independent study and correspondence programs through some of the Web sites listed in Appendix B.

How do you choose among these options? Make sure to research your prospects thoroughly. Talk to other homeschoolers about what they use. Find out what aspects they find especially effective as well as any potential drawbacks.

While individuals may be gung ho about their program, don't make choices based on personal opinion alone, no matter how enthusiastic. A method of homeschooling that's right for one family may not necessarily fit another.

Distance learning

Computer technology is an incredible educational tool, and homeschoolers are taking full advantage. According to the National Home Education Research Institute, 85.6 percent of homeschool families report owning a computer, and 73.7 percent say their children use it in their education. Compared to the national norms for all U.S. families (34 and 26 percent, respectively), homeschoolers are way ahead in this regard.

While public school districts remain saddled with obsolete hardware and outdated networked programs, homeschoolers are able to keep up with rapid advances and put to use the best, most up-to-date programs for learning.

Because of their computer skills, homeschoolers are able to take advantage of distance learning programs. Briefly defined, "distance learning" refers to an alternative mode of education in which teacher and student(s) in different locations communicate using technology such as

Bright Idea
A homeschool "computer" course may mean different things. Find out what's involved. Do teacher and student communicate through e-mail? Does the program use Web resources? Does it teach skills, such as how to create a Web page?

videotape, cable/satellite communication, CD-ROM, and the Internet. Distance learning can also be described as correspondence study, independent study, distributed education, or Web-based instruction. Homeschoolers are logging onto these programs in increasing numbers. One of the largest online programs sponsored by a public school system is the Internet Academy in Washington. About 60 percent of Internet Academy students are homeschooled, according to Linda McInturff, the program's administrator. Other private online programs also report burgeoning enrollments.

Distance learning appeals to homeschoolers because it does the following:

- Encourages self-directed learning.

- Allows interaction among a wide, potentially global audience.

- Provides good (virtual) classroom experience for homeschoolers, allowing them to engage in group activities and encounter a variety of opinions.

- Promotes equity among participants. Computer communication helps give voice to otherwise shy students and allows learner contributions to be judged on their own merit.

- Allows course content to be easily updated.

The drawbacks include:

- Hampered delivery of sound video and graphics due to limited bandwidth and slow modems.

- Heavy reliance on initiative on the part of the learner, which can be hard for those lacking motivation.

Timesaver
Distance education is a terrific opportunity to enhance home learning. But before you begin researching specific programs, make sure this is right for your child. No matter the program, the level of success depends primarily on their motivation and ability to work independently.

- Heavy dependency on students' technical abilities and Internet navigation.

- A lack of nonverbal cues, which may hinder communication.

- A potential for isolation.

- A potential for breeding passivity, as television can.

While many homeschoolers use such courses to supplement their children's learning, some depend on them for a full curriculum. Some are critical of the emphasis on online courses, warning that families can become overly dependent on them. Even Tom Layton, founder of Cyberschool, an online program run by the school district of Eugene, Oregon, warns against taking too many of these classes.

Here are some tips for successful distance learning:

- Before signing up, evaluate the course and the background of the teachers. Consider whether the course has been suitably adapted for distance learning.

- Make sure you have the required hardware—a compatible computer with adequate hard disk space, and a modem—along with other tools, such as access to a fax machine.

- Locate your workstation in the optimal environment for work and study.

- Establish a schedule, including a regular time for study.

- Recognize that ideal courses are interactive and encourage outside work.

Unofficially...
One Utah school district plans to build a "school of the future," in which a third of the student body would telecommute at least part of the day from home, local libraries, or community centers.

- Teachers should assist students with information management, selection, and critical assessment of Internet resources.

- Look for programs that enhance interaction by introducing participants, assigning partners and group projects.

- The program should provide support for technical issues.

- Without the benefit of visual clues as to how a student is doing, teachers should actively communicate with students and make note of those who don't participate in online discussions.

While online courses are great for self-motivated learners, you need to remain involved. Even those in the business admit that online learning is no substitute for face-to-face interaction. Some parents may already have concerns about the amount of time their child spends in front of the computer.

Public schools open their doors to homeschoolers

Increasingly, public institutions are taking a more cooperative attitude toward homeschooling. In addition to helping parents comply with home-education requirements, many districts welcome homeschoolers on campus, offering part-time enrollment, access to the computer lab and other resources, and opportunities to participate in school life. Some districts feature established centers, where homeschool families can take classes or obtain materials and instructional support.

Such cooperative arrangements can benefit both the school system and home students. The district can still collect state money for the child, and the family can enrich their home program with a range of valuable services.

Why homeschoolers are wary of public school extension programs

In general, the homeschooling community has serious reservations about public extension programs. Consider the potential drawbacks:

■ **The seduction of homeschoolers into or back into the public system.** Many fear that once homeschoolers re-enter the institution, the administration may try to mainstream children back into full-time public school enrollment.

■ **The surrender of parental control.** You don't get something for nothing, as the saying goes, and this apparently holds true for publicly funded education. In exchange for school resources and other goodies, homeschoolers may be subject to the same bureaucratic rules and a one-size-fits-all curriculum that motivated them to homeschool in the first place. Your control over your child's curriculum and course of study, to some degree or another, may be compromised by the fine print of your cooperative agreement.

■ **Increased state regulation of all homeschoolers.** As more and more families cross into the public system, it's only a short step for legislators to mandate this type of arrangement for homeschoolers across the board, or enact even more restrictive laws.

■ **The misrepresentation of homeschooling.** Public school users are more visible, and thus "represent" homeschooling to the general

Bright Idea
Homeschooling organizations strongly urge prospective homeschoolers to come to them first to learn about all their available education options. Too often parents go directly to the district, which might push its program as the only way to go.

public and educators, who may decide this is the way homeschooling should work. In addition, the source of funding for these programs is often associated with "at risk" students, which may lead observers to lump all homeschoolers into this category.

- **Money, money, money.** The temptation of cash grants may blind families to the other issues. Money also places an emphasis on consumerism and fosters a sense of dependence on the school. One mother found that the required purchase of materials at the beginning of the year interfered with her ability to respond to and support the individual interests of her child as they developed through the school year. In addition, certain areas stipulate that government funds cannot be used for materials having religious content.

- **Conflict within the homeschooling community.** Public programs are already a divisive issue. Many groups reject extension programs, along with individual participants, who, in their view, are not "real" homeschoolers.

Even more moderate experts insist that public school alternative programs not be mislabeled "homeschooling programs." They feel a distinct terminology is necessary to clearly separate publicly funded offerings from genuine homeschooling.

Public independent study programs (ISPs)

For some, an independent study program is the basis of their homeschooling arrangement. In California, for example, children can enroll in an ISP through a public school, then base their studies in the home. Others employ an ISP to pursue an in-depth program in a particular area of study.

Unofficially...
While cost must be considered, private ISPs and other programs often feature more flexible arrangements, such as allowing parents greater input on the course of study.

Here's how it works: Once an ISP student is enrolled, the school will draw up an agreement outlining the key concepts of study. The student will also be required to meet with a teacher a specified number of times per week, and complete a certain number of home assignments. Students must demonstrate mastery at appropriate checkpoints to continue this arrangement for the rest of the unit. They may be required to participate in selected group activities, complete an independent project, or take a final exam.

By and large, children enrolled in public school ISPs become public school students, subject to the rules and regulations of both the district and state. For this reason, ISPs are very controversial among homeschoolers. Before enrolling in a program, be sure to ask the following:

- Can parents/home students help design their program?
- What are the terms of the agreement?
- Are there unusual clauses, such as those regarding behavior?
- Is the student required to participate in class or group activities?
- Can you refuse testing?
- Do parents share responsibility with the school for evaluation of the student's work?

Charter schools

Charter schools are public schools run by an independent board of trustees. The board—usually comprised of concerned parents (in some cases, homeschoolers), teachers, and community representatives—determines the school's curriculum,

Moneysaver
Many homeschool groups have devised cost-efficient, effective approaches to teaching academic subjects, such as cooperative teaching, or pooling funds to hire specialists in math, science, and other subjects.

scheduling, and methods of instruction, independent of most state regulation.

Charter schools must be open to all students living within the district, charge no tuition, and have no religious affiliation.

This promising alternative could potentially help poor and middle-income parents find better schools for their children and break up the monopoly of the one-size-fits-all philosophy of education. Currently, only California and Alaska have laws that allow for charter schools that are mainly home-based.

Charter home-based programs may be full or part-time and usually involve a yearly stipend (up to $1,000) that can be used to pay for educational expenses, such as supplemental tutoring or books.

One such program is the Santa Barbara HomeBased Partnership, which serves over 40 homeschooled children, ages five to 12, and their families. The homeschoolers are on campus two days a week, during which time they have the option of attending classes taught by specialists in various subjects, working independently, or working with others using available facilities. The homeschool portion of the week is completely directed by the parents. A teacher/facilitator meets with them to provide feedback and offer support.

Lorie Bacon, whose daughter is in the program, appreciates the new perspectives and teaching styles that tutor/specialists provide both children and their parents. Through the program, Bacon has a math tutor come to their home twice a week, and last year had a drama coach work with her home-school group. "I can't imagine working completely alone," says Bacon, "but I don't see 'teachers,' per se, as being particularly necessary. I see experts and specialists being a very important element of the process, however."

Here's a sampling of what a charter might offer:

- A teacher/facilitator for home-based learning
- Part-time classes that feature multi-age groupings
- Separate offerings for older students
- Outreach programs with local museums and other institutions
- Language courses
- Performing arts classes, such as theater arts and storytelling
- Math and science courses
- A lending library
- Group activities, such as sports
- Enrichment activities

A listing of individual schools, along with more information on charter schools, can be accessed through the U.S. Charter Schools Web site (www. uscharterschools.org/).

Dual enrollment

Dual enrollment occurs when a child enrolls in public school on a part-time basis. This arrangement may suit a homeschooled student who needs a specialized or upper-level course, such as biology, advanced math, language, shop, or lab classes. Teens who are ready for more advanced coursework may want to pursue joint enrollment at a community college. See Chapter 15 for information on teens.

Regulations vary by state and among districts. Washington and Iowa state law require public

Watch Out!
Part-time attendance may affect your homeschool status. If your children receive more than half their schoolwork outside the home, you may not be in compliance with the conditions you've established for homeschooling.

schools to enroll children on a part-time basis if they apply. Other areas have no specific laws regarding dual enrollment, in which case applicants can approach their district or local school on an individual basis.

Also find out what credit they will grant your home study, and whether you can earn a high school diploma by attending on a part-time basis.

To enter a public school, home students are generally required to complete a district application, get approval from the district administrator, and secure an interdistrict transfer. In some districts, a homeschool coordinator may assist in this process. Testing may also be involved, as well as other requirements. If you are planning part-time enrollment or reentry into public school, it's a good idea to plan ahead—(prepare for any academic adjustment, coordinate with the administration) perhaps as much as a year or two.

Check with your local homeschooling support group for more information on dual enrollment. Most likely they can put you in touch with other homeschoolers who have dealt with your school, or perhaps they've tried such an arrangement themselves. Their experience can help you determine if the school plan can enhance your child's education.

The advantages of dual enrollment include:

- Access to particular academic courses
- Access to support resources and facilities
- Social interaction with peers who attend school
- An opportunity to "get in the groove" of traditional school, particularly for those planning on full-time reentry

- Homeschoolers often enhance a classroom, contributing new ideas, which stimulate the other students

    Potential drawbacks include:

- Difficult academic adjustment

- Conflict with the school environment: conformity, uninspired teaching, mandatory testing

- Social issues, difficulty fitting in with peers

- Beyond a natural curiosity about homeschooling, some peers or teachers may disapprove of your choice, and any bias may adversely affect your child

- Some believe part-time compromises a family's commitment to home education

Afterschooling

Another education alternative is afterschooling, which involves additional instruction by parents whose child is enrolled in school full-time. Some parents afterschool as a way to "test the waters" before fully committing to homeschooling.

Other reasons for afterschooling include:

- A desire to provide supplemental help to your children

- A way to adapt home instruction when there are two full-time working parents

- A change in circumstances for a full-time homeschooling family, such as illness

- Living abroad, traveling, or taking on a work assignment in another location temporarily

    Part-timers should keep in mind the following:

- A limited course of study should be based on your child's need or special interest.

Watch Out!
Part-time home-schoolers may feel out of place in certain support groups, some of which take a hard line against any variant outside of traditional, full-time home-schooling. Pursue an inclusive group, and get the support that you need.

- If you're homeschooling part-time, tailor your program accordingly, and don't attempt a comprehensive curriculum.

- Schedule homeschooling at the optimal time for your child, not a four-hour stretch immediately following the school day.

- Summer is a great time to give homeschooling a try.

Extracurricular activities and other school services

In addition to classes, homeschoolers may be able to access other programs and services of their local school system. These may include:

- Textbooks

- The computer lab or other facilities

- The library

- Special education classes

- Gifted programs

- Ancillary services—health and nursing, vision and dental screening, speech and language therapy, counseling, reading enrichment (in some cases, applicants must be found to have a qualifying impairment before accessing certain services)

- Extracurricular activities—on-campus clubs, sports, school dances, and other social events

Access varies widely by state and even among districts within a state. Alaska, California, Idaho, and Iowa are among the states allowing access to classrooms. Colorado, Illinois, Oregon, and Washington grant access to after-school activities.

Some laws allow homeschoolers to partake in specific offerings. Others have no such laws, but generally accept homeschoolers on a case-by-case basis. Still others admit homeschoolers with certain caveats, such as requiring the student to be dually enrolled in the school.

Overall, public schools are reluctant to allow homeschooled children to participate in sports. This is primarily due to the eligibility requirements of school athletes regarding attendance and academic achievement; the governing sports organizations claim these are impossible to enforce in homeschoolers.

How to approach your school

"If you are going the school route," advises one mother, "you need to work the system." First, check with local homeschoolers or your regional support group to see if there is any precedent at your school. And, if you're not already familiar with the home-school contact at the district level, ask for the name of this person.

When directly approaching the administration, be specific about your plan and stress the positive aspects of the school as well as the school's potential as a community resource. Pushiness, of course, can backfire. And as determined as you may be to get in, don't set a negative precedent for other homeschoolers by accepting tighter control of your home program in exchange for admission to programs.

If the school resists your proposal, you can approach the school board for a formal policy decision.

Sports

School sports can present even greater bureaucratic hurdles for homeschoolers. Beyond simply entering

Watch Out!
Know your law regarding homeschoolers' rights to extracurricular activities, which can be arbitrarily overruled by local school officials. One school superintendent, for example, denied a homeschooler's entry to a social event when he decided that a school dance qualified as a classroom activity!

the campus, there are rules regarding admission to teams and rules for league competition.

The Interscholastic Athletic Association, the governing body of high school competition, once stated that any school that used homeschoolers to compete on a team would be disqualified. A recent letter campaign has effectively brought them around. The National Collegiate Athletic Association (NCAA), also under pressure to change its policy, now accommodates homeschooled athletes who can submit homeschool records in applying for eligibility waivers..

But despite their growing acceptance on the playing fields, homeschoolers still run up against team requirements regarding grade point average, attendance, and behavior. Some also consider it unfair for a nonstudent to displace a full-time student from a spot on the team.

Homeschoolers argue that academic standards could easily be assessed based on the individual course of study, and that homeschoolers do not contribute to disorderly conduct in school. Moreover, their tax dollars entitle them to such programs.

Even so, some home students, having outgrown parks and recreational programs, are forced to consider full-time enrollment to participate in sports.

Another option is to join independent sports groups, including Pop Warner football and Little League. The homeschooler-friendly Amateur Athletic Union (AAU) offers competitive leagues in a variety of sports. With its stated purpose, "Sports for All, Forever," the AAU is the largest nonprofit multi-sport organization, boasting 58 charters nationwide. Children of all age groups are welcome.

Unofficially...
Jason Taylor, defensive end for the Miami Dolphins, was a 1992 homeschool graduate. Taylor won a $100,000 football scholarship to Akron University, which was denied by the NCAA. After intervention by the Home School Legal Defense Association, and a sympathetic article in *Sports Illustrated,* the scholarship was reinstated.

Magic Johnson, Wilma Rudolph, Mark Spitz, and Greg Louganis, among other sports stars, once participated in AAU programs.

Growing numbers of homeschoolers are creating their own sports opportunities. In basketball alone, homeschool coaches estimate 500–1,000 such teams now compete nationwide. Another homegrown program is the Homeschool Symphony Orchestra. Ask your support group if there are such opportunities in your region.

Driver's education

In many states, parents have the option of teaching driver's ed at home, or homeschoolers may be allowed to enter district driver's ed classes.

Contact the Department of Motor Vehicles or your state transportation department for information and a description of requirements for driver's ed courses.

Just the facts

- Correspondence schools, ISPs, and other programs are available to provide as much support of your homeschooling as you wish. Homeschoolers voice strong opinions about these things, so make sure you keep your own needs and goals foremost in mind when you research these programs.

- While many homeschoolers take advantage of publicly funded programs—which are becoming more prevalent—make sure you understand the requirements involved in entering the public system, as well as the potential larger implications for homeschooling.

- Depending on your region, you may also have the choice of an alternative learning center, which provides viable options for many families.

- Afterschooling is a good way for any parent to supplement their child's traditional education and incorporate alternative learning methods. It's also a good way to "test the waters" before deciding to homeschool.

- Homeschoolers have been increasing their demands for access to public programs and activities, with sports causing the most difficulties. But other options are available for off-campus leagues.

GET THE SCOOP ON...
The ins and outs of homeschool philosophies
■ How to prepare for a unit study ■ Developing
an eclectic approach ■ How to find a learning
method that's right for your child

Homeschooling Methods

Chapter 7

As a group, homeschoolers uniformly believe that they can do a better job of educating their children. But in most other respects, say researchers Susan Groover and Richard Endsley, "homeschoolers are as different among themselves as they are different from non-homeschoolers."

This is especially evident in the diversity of their methods of teaching—which may center around a particular philosophy, as in unschooling or Montessori; involve specific plans for teaching, such as unit studies; or combine a number of these elements.

In this chapter, I'll summarize some of the more common approaches, from the structured method and classical education to unit studies and eclectic homeschooling.

Over the course of homeschooling, you may find that a certain method just doesn't work for you or that your needs have changed. You are free to simply drop the approach and try another, which is one of the advantages of homeschooling.

135

Bright Idea
When using packaged curriculum, particularly computer software, stay actively involved as the teacher. Discuss the material with your child, or ask your child to write about it. By doing this, you'll be making sure your child isn't simply memorizing facts.

Interest-initiated learning

Also known as child-directed learning, interest-initiated learning is more than just another teaching method: It is a basic tenet of homeschooling, overlapping many philosophies and constituting the heart of unschooling. Homeschoolers believe that children are self-directed learners by nature, and child-directed learning allows the child's interests to dictate his or her educational direction.

So what is the parents' role? To best facilitate child-directed learning, you should do the following:

- Respect and trust them

- Engage them in discussion and encourage their questions

- Provide opportunities for varied activities and experiences

- Avoid the habit of doing things for them, rather than letting them try on their own

- Encourage them to risk taking on challenges and view mistakes as part of the learning process

- Encourage strategies for them to take the initiative when learning bogs down

- Facilitate a stimulating environment, providing a range of learning materials

- Demonstrate, by your example, that learning is a lifelong process.

- Savor accomplishments

Wendy Priesnitz, Canadian education activist and author of *School Free: The Home Schooling Handbook* (see Appendix C), recommends "providing the time for children to investigate their own ideas, and being a flexible and patient observer of a process that is not particularly sequential or organized, in spite of what some educational theorists would have us believe."

Unschooling

Unschooling has come to mean many different things since John Holt coined the term that describes learning without going to school. During the 1960s and 1970s, Holt, a school teacher, advocated progressive alternative schools. At first, he believed educators would transform schools, from overly structured institutions that smothered a child's natural curiosity, to places that would allow learning to be directed by a child's interests. Ultimately, however, Holt surmised that even alternative schools did not go far enough, and he began to champion learning at home. The work and writings of John Holt helped popularize the modern homeschooling movement.

Holt said, "Birds fly, fish swim; man thinks and learns. Therefore, we do not need to 'motivate' children into learning by wheedling, bribing, or bullying. What we need to do, and all we need to do, is to…give children as much help and guidance as they ask for; listen respectfully when they feel like talking; and then get out of the way. We can trust them to do the rest."

The philosophy of child-directed learning forms the basis of unschooling. Unschooling implies a trust in the natural curiosity of a child, that, if provided with a rich and stimulating environment, will lead to learning. Unlike the traditional education model—generally a top-down approach that dictates what children will learn, when, and how—the child takes the lead in unschooling. As a result, a child learns what he or she needs to know; in this

"
My husband doesn't help with the day-to-day teaching of academics, but he is very involved by being supportive and encouraging. He turns a blind eye to a frequently messy house. He eats "creative" dinners without complaint. This year he will teach our oldest about computers…
—April Morris, homeschooling mother
"

way, content becomes more meaningful because it relates to what is important to that child.

By and large, unschooling rejects the precepts of traditional school: its hierarchy and structure, school years and schedules, dividing learning and playtime, group rewards and punishments, assembly-line curriculum in which subject matter is divorced from context, segregation by chronological age, separation from family and the "real world," and all the trappings—from standing in lines to jumping at the sound of a bell.

Unschoolers even have a name for this process in which a child overcomes many of the negative aspects of traditional school as he makes the transition to homeschool; it is called deschooling.

Deschooling is usually associated with the unschooling approach. But other homeschoolers, as well, undergo a similar adjustment in which the entire family must break free from old habits, and prepare to learn in a different way.

"Radical" unschoolers impose little or no structure. Others allow children to choose what they learn, but provide guidance and some degree of organization to help the students reach their goals. Unschoolers use a variety of resources, including curricula and textbooks for core subjects, but are freer with others. Most try to integrate learning with the activities of everyday life.

Unschooling parents surround the child with learning opportunities, ask and respond to questions, and generally provide a model of lifetime learning.

If you decide to unschool your children, you will spend much of your time doing the following:

- Responding to and encouraging your child's curiosity

- Finding learning value in elements and experiences that occur outside a "classroom."

- Fostering creative and cooperative problem-solving, and, as much as possible, allowing children to devise their own solutions.

- Accessing a variety of resources and information to support your child's interests. Hands-on activities and real-life experiences are particularly valuable.

- Considering different styles and modes of learning. How do we learn best? How have others that you know—family members, friends, figures in history—followed their own interests?

- Modeling lifetime learning, by exploring your own interests, and engaging in the process of discovery alongside your child.

Watch Out!
A potential challenge within the unschooling approach is record-keeping. Make sure you understand your state requirements for compliance.

Multiple intelligences and learning styles

Utilizing this theory, families approach education and materials based on how their children learn best.

This approach is based on the findings of Harvard psychologist Dr. Howard Gardner, who theorized that all people possess seven distinct intelligences, or capabilities. Every individual possesses varying degrees of these intelligences, according to Dr. Gardner, "but the way in which intelligences combine and blend are as varied as the faces and the personalities of individuals." The multiple intelligences that Dr. Gardner identified are listed and briefly defined below:

- *Linguistic:* A linguistic learner uses words effectively, either verbally or in writing, and enjoys reading. Optimal techniques include keeping a journal and providing written directions.

- *Logical-Mathematical:* The ability to reason well and use numbers effectively. Those exercising these skills include accountants, computer programmers, and statisticians.

- *Spatial:* Exercised by architects and artists, spatial intelligence is used to perceive and interpret what we may or may not physically see.

- *Musical:* The capacity to perceive, discriminate, and express musical forms. Prior to Dr. Gardner's theory, innate musical ability was not perceived as a distinct intelligence.

- *Kinesthetic:* Most school-age children are kinesthetic/tactual learners, who excel through total engagement with the material. They learn best through hands-on activity.

- *Interpersonal:* Why do some people make excellent leaders? Interpersonal intelligence involves the ability to affect others by perceiving their moods, intentions, motivations and feelings. Without interpersonal acuity, we would be unable to exist socially.

- *Intrapersonal:* The capacity for self-knowledge, and the ability to adapt according to that knowledge. Intrapersonal intelligence relates to self-esteem.

- *Naturalist:* Following his initial study, Dr. Gardner named an eighth intelligence, which involves the ability to classify patterns in nature, a particular awareness of one's own environment.

Determining learning styles aids parents in choosing curriculum, teaching methods, and activities. For example, unit studies are ideal for kinesthetic learners, with facts and concepts taught through activities.

Learning styles can be assessed through tests based on the Learning Style Inventory, or more informal measurements. The Web site Index of Learning Styles (www.crc4mse.org/ILS/Index. htm/), sponsored by The Materials Science and Engineering Career Resource Center, includes a self-test, which you can take online and submit for scoring.

Structured or traditional method

This technique, sometimes described as "bringing school home," involves developing a very organized home program. In practice, it may involve having separate class times for each subject, and using textbooks, workbooks, tests, and other elements of a structured curriculum. This is how most adults were schooled, and because of this, many homeschoolers are most comfortable starting with this approach. As they become more confident with homeschooling, some gradually change to another approach, or adapt others.

Annette, a home educator, describes her program as eclectic, but she does incorporate structure within her home program. "It seems that the older my children get, the more I lean toward more forms of structure because I want to make sure everything is covered. Probably math and language are the most structured for us," she says.

Critics caution that adhering too closely to "regular school" leads to burnout of both parent/ teachers and children, who can become enslaved by an overly rigid schedule. Traditional methods can also bore kids, leading to attention and motivation

Unofficially...
Approximately 20 to 30 percent of the school-age population remembers what is heard; 40 percent recalls well visually the things that are seen or read; other people cannot internalize information or skills unless they use them in real-life activities.
—*Teaching Students to Read Through Their Individual Learning Styles* by Marie Carbo, Rita Stafford Dunn, and Kenneth J. Dunn

problems and other related issues. Traditional assessment, grades and standardized tests, in particular, may be inappropriate. Make sure you remain responsive to your child's needs and interests.

Still, many families successfully apply a structured approach to some aspect of their child's education. Proponents claim that traditional methods can work more effectively in the home than in public schools, because the one-on-one tutorial is an advantage.

Unit studies

This popular approach integrates multiple subjects (language arts, science, etc.) and skill areas while focusing on a central theme. A unit study on space, for example, might include the study of the aerodynamics of flight (science and math), reading about famous astronomers (language), building a rocket (hands-on activity), and visiting the NASA Web site. Additional language skills could be practiced through writing papers and keeping a journal.

The key features of unit studies include:

- Complete immersion into the topic so the subject is seen as a whole instead of a bunch of isolated facts, resulting in greater comprehension of the material.

- A higher interest level than a standard curriculum, from combining a variety of resources and learning tools, including hands-on activities.

- The ability to teach all ages simultaneously, with each child working around the same theme, but with assignments suited to their abilities.

- Significant savings—with unit studies, parents don't have to buy, assign, and teach separate materials for each child, therefore saving time and money.

Commercial unit studies are readily available; however, going this route can get expensive. You can easily custom-design your own.

Here are a few tips on how to plan and get the most from a unit study:

- Select your general topic. Consider the source of your ideas: are you working from curricular guidelines, or is this a subject of personal interest? Also, depending on your available resources, certain subjects may be more conducive to a unit study than others.

- Write down your objectives, what you hope to accomplish from the study. If you start with a very broad topic, let's say American History, you'll need to focus your objectives (a particular period or event, or a political or social theme, for example)

- Do your research. Adequate planning is key to a successful unit study. In your research, consider how the unit relates to other studies, and take care not to repeat what you've already covered. From here you can begin to form an outline; streamline your record-keeping by creating your own unit study template.

- List the subject or skills you hope to cover (such as reading, basic arithmetic concepts). Experienced homeschoolers caution against trying to work too many subjects into an activity. Also, unit studies may not completely

Moneysaver
Looking for unit study curricula? Check out the numerous unit studies sites on the Web, where you can find free, printable units on a variety of subjects, from space exploration to family travel. To view a general list of links, begin by searching "unit studies" and "homeschooling."

substitute for more systematic methods of teaching math and language skills.

- List activities, field trips, materials, religious references, and any other related items that you hope to involve in your study. Consider your child's suggestions for activities. To prevent burnout, be careful to balance out trips and hands-on activities with other modes of study, such as reading.

Timesaver
If you're looking for general guidelines for a course of study, ask your local school district for a copy of their scope & sequence (curricular guidelines).

- Maintain a reading list of books and other literature, including bibliographic data (publisher, date, volume number, and pages) and where you expect to obtain these materials.

- Don't forget online sources. You'll need to be a discriminating consumer here, particularly if you are logging on for research purposes. Make sure to check the authorship of all Web sites. Multimedia resources—videos and CD ROMs—should also be listed.

- Estimate the duration of the unit and relate it to your overall schedule. Depending on the age and interest level of your child, enthusiasm may wane if units start to drag beyond four to six weeks.

Charlotte Mason method

Also called the Living Books approach, this method is based upon the work of Charlotte Mason, an early 19th-century British educator. Advocating the education of children across all classes of British society, Mason lectured widely and published her views in her 1886 book, *Home Education*. She disparaged modern education for breaking down knowledge into isolated bits of information to be fed into "container" children. Mason respected the abilities of children, and advocated their involvement in real-life situations and in allowing them to read really good "whole" books instead of what she called "twaddle"—inferior, superficial material, such as textbooks. Much of Mason's original approach involved instruction from the Bible.

In academics, Mason advocated a firm rooting in the core subjects of reading, writing, and math skills, with exposure to the best sources for all other subjects, including the arts. This involves providing experiences such as nature walks, observing wildlife, visiting art galleries, and reading "living books" as opposed to textbooks, which she believed stifle creative thinking. Particularly recommended are autobiographies and diaries, which offer firsthand accounts of events.

The Mason method also involves the practice of narration, in which children recite what they've learned. Mason believed the natural desire for children to share in this regard has great educational value, reinforcing and helping them organize their knowledge. Teachers are encouraged to read aloud to children, who recite back the material. In this way, comprehension and vocabulary skills are encouraged. A child can also absorb material within his own interpretive framework. Charlotte Mason students also read independently and discuss the material with the teacher/parent. The Mason method also prescribes the formation of good habits, including attention, imagining, and remembering.

Charlotte Mason students keep Nature Notebooks or Diaries, in which they record their impressions of the natural world. These may include drawings, poetry, and species identification. The

> **"**
> Who remembers the scraps of knowledge he labored over as a child? And would not the application of a few hours in later life effect more than a year's drudgery at any one subject in childhood?
> —Charlotte Mason
> **"**

Notebooks help children develop powers of observation and an appreciation for nature, and they inspire families to share in outdoor activities.

Karen Andreola, author of *A Charlotte Mason Companion* (Charlotte Mason Research & Supply Co., 1998)), defines the objective behind the Notebooks: "We are trying to help our children develop a spirit of joy and praise, admiring God's work in creation. Let us avoid criticism unless it is to give helpful suggestions. These Notebooks, in the words of 19th-century naturalist Anna Botsford Comstock, 'of whatever quality, are precious beyond price to their owners. And why not? For they represent what cannot be bought or sold—personal experience in the happy world of out-of-doors.'"

Those not partial to a child-centered approach may not adapt well to Charlotte Mason. Also, it may be less applicable for very young children, and older students may require supplementation in advanced level subjects.

Moore formula

Raymond and Dorothy Moore are both educators and early pioneers of the modern homeschool movement. Through their early research and in several books, including *The Successful Homeschooling Family Handbook* (Thomas Nelson, 1994), the Moores advocate the delay of formal education until a child is developmentally prepared to learn.

Their simple guidelines for homeschooling, referred to as the Moore Formula, follow two basic tenets:

- Study, balanced by work and service, both at home and in the community.

- A child's relative maturity should determine when formal study is introduced, usually not before age eight to 10, or even 12 years old.

The Moores promote informal learning in the early ages through games, life experiences, and the reading of books. In accommodating a child's interests and abilities, they recommend, among other resources, unit studies. In addition to academic work, the Moores value the benefits of keeping a personal schedule, with regular times for rising, eating, and going to bed.

While many successful homeschoolers incorporate the Moore Formula, some consider the prescribed schedule to be somewhat rigid.

Classical education

A classical, Christian education concentrates on teaching children critical thinking skills, classic languages such as Latin and Greek, with a curriculum based on the "great books" of Western civilization.

To foster the development of independent thought, Dorothy Sayers, a British writer and medieval expert, became a modern proponent of classical education.

The classical approach is based on the trivium, a teaching model that attempts to correspond the curriculum with a child's cognitive development. In the grammar stage, when children readily absorb factual information (up to age 12), they are taught reading and writing. Listening and observation skills are also emphasized. Next is the logic stage (middle grades), when children begin to acquire independent or abstract thought.

Through discussion and reading criticism, the child develops analytic thinking and a greater understanding of the subject matter. In the final

Bright Idea
The mere mention of the word "textbook" will raise eyebrows among some homeschoolers. Yet texts are used to some extent by many, including one homeschooling mom who disassembles textbooks, filing pages by subject for future use.

phase of the trivium, the rhetoric or wisdom stage, the student (in the later teens) expresses all she has learned in language, both written and spoken, that is eloquent and pursuasive.

This approach fosters independent thinking skills, as well as the development of verbal and written language; however, critics believe the concentration on classics may be limiting.

Montessori

Based on the studies of Dr. Maria Montessori, Montessori education promotes a multi-sensory environment in which children learn at their own individual pace, according to a wide choice of activities. In a formal Montessori classroom, the elementary program is characterized by:

Watch Out!
The name "Montessori" is used freely by institutions and programs, who may have little relation to the authentic Montessori technique. Look for affiliation and teacher accreditation, which is offered by the Association Montessori Internationale or the American Montessori Society.

- Individual and small group work of the student's choice.

- An attitude of cooperation rather than competition, including a reduced emphasis on conventional tests.

- The development of individual responsibility. Students maintain the classroom and help develop class rules.

Many homeschoolers subscribe to Montessori methods, or incorporate certain aspects, such as following the child's interest, and encouraging his or her participation in home activities, such as cooking meals. The Montessori de-emphasis on competition, so much a part of the traditional school environment, is also easily promoted in the home. While it is more closely associated with preschool-age children, Montessori methods can be applied to older students as well. These methods may not specifically relate, however, to learning upper-level subjects.

Waldorf school

The first Waldorf school opened in a German ciga-
rette factory in 1918, under the direction of
philosopher Rudolf Steiner. Steiner viewed the
interconnected development of spirit, intellect, and
body as unfolding in three distinct stages: early
childhood, middle childhood, and adolescence.
This dynamic informs the Waldorf philosophy,
which emphasizes experiential learning.

Steiner's revolutionary school sought independence from governmental control and allowed
teachers a great degree of freedom to teach within
the goals of the program. Steiner designed the curriculum to "nurture the intuition, imagination, and
spiritual capacities of the child." Today there are
98 Waldorf schools in North America alone, with
Waldorf methods incorporated in many public
schools and home programs.

In the early years, a Waldorf program encourages a rich environment that affords the young
child opportunities for meaningful imitation and
creative play. Songs, poems, and storytelling foster
the enjoyment of language; puppet shows, pretend
play, house building, and gardening are a few forms
of creative play.

The elementary and middle ages introduce subject matter, enlisting the child's natural imaginative
powers. For example, the number system and the
four mathematical processes (addition, subtraction,
multiplication, and division) are introduced as characters in a drama that can be acted out by first-
graders.

In a traditional Waldorf curriculum, an uninter-
rupted main lesson provides the day's focus, in
addition to concentrated blocks of study, which are

66

True education is
not the inculca-
tion of facts and
skills into a pas-
sive student but
is [instead] an
Art—the Art of
awakening what
is actually there
within the
human being.
—Rudolf Steiner

pursued over time. To promote concentration and self-discipline, handwork is encouraged through knitting, weaving, toymaking, and woodworking, among other activities. Waldorf training in later years prepares the adolescent to take on self-education.

"I love having the Waldorf curriculum outline as a guide, and I find many of their ways of teaching certain subjects excellent and fun (skipping and clapping games for times tables, gnome stories to learn the four math processes)," says Lyn Turner. "I have let my children do a lot of exploring on their own, but they also really enjoy their 'Waldorf school' time!"

The Eclectic Approach

While many homeschoolers may incorporate certain aspects of other methods, eclectics truly expound the smorgasbord approach to homeschooling.

They pick and choose from the array of philosophies, teaching methods, and curricula, employing whatever happens to work in their home at a particular time. This doesn't imply a haphazard attitude; eclectics make deliberate choices according to their child's nature and abilities.

For example, an eclectic homeschooler may adapt the unschooling concept of child-directed education. He may draw on the traditional approach, employing textbooks to teach core subjects, such as math. He may devote a period of time to a certain topic, integrating primary resources and hands-on activities, as in unit studies.

"Eclectic homeschooling seems to fit many, many different kinds of homeschoolers," says Beverly Krueger, editor of *Eclectic Homeschooling* magazine. "You'll find sit-down-at-the-table, pull-out-the-workbooks homeschoolers calling themselves eclectic, as well as those who might unschool, but use a math text for math." According to Krueger, eclectic homeschooling fits the core reasons most homeschoolers choose to educate their children at home. "It is choosing from a variety of methods, curriculum, resources, and ideas to meet the homeschool needs of your family."

Keeping up with so many choices may become a job in itself, potentially frustrating both parent and child. Also, dropping curricula and other materials that don't work can be costly. But if you can remain focused on your child's needs, the eclectic approach can be an effective form of homeschooling.

Other homeschooling methods and philosophies

There are other philosophies within homeschooling. One is the principle approach, which emphasizes developing moral character through a Christian outlook or Biblical worldview. Students learn how to reason with Biblical principles, as applied to every aspect of life.

Centered on child-directed learning, relaxed homeschooling encourages children, particularly in the early years, toward learning as a process of self-discovery, with gentle guidance from parents. Relaxed homeschooling incorporates greater structure for teaching basic skills (math and language).

Devising your own homeschool philosophy

This chapter provides an overview of the approaches currently popular among homeschoolers. It is not intended to direct you toward

Timesaver
Students with ability might consider taking CLEP or AP examinations, and begin earning college credit early.

one or the other, as a framework within which you should fit your own program. A great many people homeschool successfully by adapting only the aspects of a particular philosophy that suit them, and omitting the rest.

Whatever elements you choose to employ, homeschooling is a process that provides parents an opportunity to develop their own personal philosophy of learning.

Just the facts

- Some families choose to follow a particular philosophy or approach to homeschooling. If you're interested in learning more, there are resources—books, catalogs, and Web sites—devoted to each practice.

- The various approaches to homeschooling incorporate diverse elements. For example, unschooling is largely free of any advance planning, whereas the Moore Formula stresses the value of a regular schedule.

- Everyone processes information differently—some respond well to written instructions, while others learn best by getting their hands dirty. In discovering your child's learning style, you can tailor your methods accordingly.

- By engaging in a variety of activities and materials that center around a single subject, information becomes more meaningful to a student. Unit studies are popular across the broad spectrum of homeschoolers.

- In practice, probably more homeschoolers are eclectic, choosing what works best for their child at a given stage. Over time, many homeschoolers come to develop their own philosophy of learning.

GET THE SCOOP ON...
The pros and cons of packaged curricula ▪
Where to find a curriculum guide ▪ What to
include in a portfolio ▪ The ins and outs of
testing and record-keeping

Your Homeschool Plan

Chapter 8

With the growing market in homeschool curricula, it might appear that home-school planning is simply a matter of choosing and purchasing a curriculum.

For the majority of homeschoolers, this is simply not the case.

According to a National Home Education Research Institute study of 1,657 families, 71.1 percent said they custom-design their curriculum to suit their child's needs. So how do they do it?

This chapter covers the issues you need to consider before forming your own plan, including first and foremost, defining your personal requirements. I'll give you the lowdown on curriculum guides, which can help you create your own curriculum. If you decide to go with a commercial package, I'll offer some tips to consider before making that purchase. Schedules and record-keeping, in their various forms, are also described, as well as testing.

Devising your own plan

Once you've considered the different teaching approaches, it's time to start working on a practical plan. Ask yourself the following questions:

- What are your legal requirements and options for homeschooling? Some states specify the subjects to be covered at each grade (see Chapter 5).

- What educational goals do you have for your child(ren)? Sketch them out for the coming year, as well as your long-term objectives.

- What interests do your children have? Remain responsive to their questions over the course of the coming year. Older kids may take a leading role in determining their program.

- How does your child learn best? Find your child's optimal learning style (see Chapter 7).

- What is your own personal teaching style? Consider the relative amount of structure that you'll need in the first year.

- What are your or your spouse's special inter-ests, skills, and delights that you would like to pass on to your children?

- What is your child's educational level? For example, preschool curriculum packages are expensive, and many parents recommend against formal methods at this age. For young ones, veterans rely on available materials at the library and lots of reading. Does your child have difficulties with math? Remediation strategies and materials are available that involve alternative approaches to teaching math concepts, as well as language skills.

- How much can you afford to spend? Curricular purchases quickly add up.

- Are you aware of all your available resources? Evaluate your personal resources (hobbies, professional background, and skills). Does your community offer a nature center, cultural activities, a museum, vocational workshops, or other learning opportunities?

- Will you be participating in a public or private program, or operating independently? (For more on assisted homeschooling, see Chapter 6.)

- Are you leaning toward a packaged curriculum? Have you considered creating your own?

Bright Idea
At first glance your state subject requirements may seem overwhelming. Keep in mind these are guidelines for what you should cover over time—you don't have to cover each subject every day.

Ready-made curricula

If homeschooling with more structure appeals to you, you can find a wide variety of ready-made curricula to suit your situation. A comprehensive package generally includes everything you need: grade-appropriate workbooks, texts, and lesson plans. You can also find curricula designed for teaching a specific subject.

Because of the security offered by an established course, beginning homeschoolers often choose a packaged curriculum. If you are unsure of covering all the bases, a packaged curriculum can help build your confidence, encouraging you to branch out and try other resources. Additionally, a thorough curriculum can provide useful ideas that you can use for years to come.

Packaged curricula: Be an educated consumer

Before you buy any curriculum package, be aware that a formal curriculum may not always fulfill the best interests of your child. Consider the following:

- Formal curricula are largely based on the average child's interest, abilities, and learning style—one-size-fits-all again.

- Even if a curriculum is a good fit, most homeschoolers find it to be lacking in some aspects, making it less than "comprehensive."

- A package may hinder the development of your own instincts, or your overall goals, affecting your independence as well as your child's.

- The potential for burnout is higher with a formal curriculum. Along with other elements of the school-at-home style, packages may put a damper on spontaneity and your child's curiosity.

- Some packages require an inordinate amount of time in teacher prep, with thick manuals to wade through before you begin teaching.

- With a package, families may find themselves chained to their desks, not taking advantage of outdoor activities, the community, and other outside opportunities for learning.

- A formal curriculum can be expensive, with a comprehensive package costing as much as $600.

- With an established program, you may feel the need to stick it out, even if it's not working.

Tips for choosing a curriculum

If you are shopping for curricula, ask the following: Does it appear to address the objectives we have for this child? Does it have a religious orientation, or is it secular? Is teacher support available? Is it comprehensive, or can you purchase according to subject? Consider whether the format is textbook, workbook, or unit-study based; some may have a little of everything. See if you can get a sample.

Once again, ask around. Network with other homeschoolers and find out what they use, or perhaps your local library may have some of these materials. Ask about the pluses and relative drawbacks of the program. At support group meetings, members often bring in their curricula to share with others.

Shop around and look at the catalogs. Consider attending a homeschool conference or curriculum fair to examine the choices available, and only purchase according to your present needs.

Curriculum guides

Whether you follow them to a tee or use them as a reference for informing your original course of study, curriculum guides are useful tools.

Curriculum guides, detailed lists of the concepts students are expected to cover in grades K-12, are widely available from a host of sources, including your state or local district scope and sequence (the formal education term for guidelines on what to study when). Others include:

- *Typical Course of Study: Kindergarten through Grade 12,* available free of charge from World Book Educational Products, P.O. Box 980, Orland Park, IL 60462; 708/ 873-1533; www.worldbook.com/ptre/html/ curr.htm

- The Web page "National Standards" (www.ash. udel.edu/ash/teacher/standards.html), which links to sites concerning national and state standards

Moneysaver
Delay your first curriculum purchase for at least a few months. Give everyone time to decompress from school, then begin to assess your child's interests and needs.

❝

The notion of a
curriculum, an
essential body of
knowledge,
would be absurd
even if children
remembered
everything we
'taught' them.
We don't and
can't agree on
what knowledge
is essential.
—John Holt,
How Children Fail

❞

A curricular guide for social studies, for example, might outline the following topics and concepts: Suggestions for kindergartners might include the exploration of holidays and traditions, and the meanings behind them. A related topic would be the appreciation of other cultures. Social studies goals for grade 3 might list history of the local community, or local or U.S. geography, and for grade 7, specific periods such as the Middle Ages or the Renaissance. Goals for Language Arts may range from experiencing stories and phonics for Kindergartners, to analysis of plays and advanced research skills for 12th graders.

Again how you relate such an outline to your own program is entirely up to you. As with packaged curricula, some of the same reservations apply to curricular guides. When considering such guidance, remember to prioritize your personal goals, and be aware that any suggestions for study may reflect a particular perspective or philosophy.

Creating your own

There are no set rules for building a plan of study from scratch. Asking yourself questions such as the following may help spark some ideas:

- What are your child's interests?
- What are your family's favorite activities and places to visit?
- What personal interests of yours would you like to explore with your child?
- What do you enjoy talking about together?
- What sorts of questions does your child ask?
- What kinds of books does your child like to read?

- What daily activities around your home offer opportunities for your child's involvement?

- What other resources offer educational opportunities?

Homeschoolers have many creative options. Georgia Ana Larson, an unschooler, told me, "Our educational goals are personal, set at irregular intervals as necessary, and receive the unqualified support of other family members. For instance, after several passionate years spent learning theater and teaching theater to younger learners, my daughter decided to spend this year studying science (especially paleontology and archaeology), ballet, and Celtic harp. So, we have begun a 'Florida Explore' club with similar-minded unschoolers and have planned real-life digs, are conducting interviews with scientists and amateur paleontologists, will be dissecting owl pellets next week, collecting fossil shark teeth the next, etc. We learn as we go, passion sparking passion, building deep relationships with fellow learners (kids and adults alike). I have a calendar which keeps our record of the journeys and our best questions, and I post related reading, pertinent video and tape entries, and miscellaneous resources there as well. We take lots of photographs... We also videotape-interview Juliana and her friends, and she makes videos of her own."

Lesson plans

In preparation for specific lessons some homeschoolers may find it helpful to create some sort of written plan. Lesson plans can help insure coverage of important details and concerns, and may also help to clarify your objectives. Generally, a plan incorporates a concise statement of the goals at

Timesaver
Don't be intimidated by a prescribed scope and sequence. As they work through the curriculum, many homeschoolers find themselves completing the course of study well ahead of schedule. Others discover that their own goals actually exceed those of a standard curriculum.

hand, followed by the actual lesson. Here are other elements you may wish to include:

- The relationship of the lesson to curricular, or overall goals

- Rationale: Why are we learning this?

- Resources: Related activities, reading, Web sites, and the like.

Adhering too rigidly to a plan may prevent you from following spontaneous opportunities for learning. Even if you're a super-organized, Day-Runner-type, home education demands that you remain flexible and open to your child's questions as they arise.

Schedules

A schedule, especially to unschoolers, may seem anathema to home education. But in practice, a schedule can bring order to the day, helping focus efforts for both you and your children. The beauty of a schedule is that it can be tailored according to your life, accommodating work, the individual needs of several children, daily home activities, and spontaneous plans such as an impromptu field trip.

Don't allow a schedule to enslave you, or become so much work that it becomes a job in itself. Use it as a tool to help you organize, fend off boredom, and motivate your kids.

The school year

Many homeschoolers stick to the traditional September–June school calendar. It certainly can be the most convenient, particularly in accommodating state-required hours of home instruction and filing forms, which are generally submitted just prior to the fall.

"
I have felt that educating my kids is simply an extension of parenting... But it does take a determined commitment... and an understanding that having my kids at home all the time means I have to say "no" to other opportunities, such as Bible studies and other ministries.
—Pam Sautbine, homeschooling mother
"

Still others are having so much fun they find themselves extending "school" into the summer months. Family vacations and warm-weather activities present additional opportunities for learning.

The school day

"So, what do you do all day?" is the second most frequently asked question of homeschoolers (after socialization). It draws a variety of responses as broadly diverse as homeschoolers, ranging from a structured day complete with lunch and recess "periods," to a loose, no-schedule approach that allows the family to take advantage of educational opportunities as they arise throughout the day.

The amount of time spent homeschooling also varies, according to the ages and temperaments of the children, among other factors. On the whole, though, it's much shorter than the average school day. Contrary to the institutional setting, where time is consumed in changing classes, taking roll call, dealing with disruptive behavior, repeating explanations, and other interruptions, homeschooling has the edge in time efficiency.

On average, homeschoolers spend from two to four hours in formal "class time." This can be one solid stretch, or spread out over the course of the day, particularly if you desire one-on-one time with multiple children. One mother, for example, had older ones doing school between 9 and 11am, while she cared for four- and two-year-olds, shuttling back and forth as her children needed her. After 11am, the learning continued for the entire family, when they read stories, took nature walks, or explored museums.

"School" may officially begin at 9am but may also flow into the rest of the day. "Some of the best

education comes from 'free time,' says Giovanna
Gomez. "Even though it is free time [my child] is
still learning and doing interesting things. He has a
big interest in the solar system and during our free
time we will sometimes read a good book about
outer space or do something related to that. He
doesn't see this as 'school' even though there is
learning taking place. I love that!"

Some families complete formal instruction
before 3pm, the traditional end of the school day,
when their children's friends start returning home
from school.

No matter your schedule, you'll want some
way to organize or track what you're doing. Homeschoolers keep logbooks, note their activities on
calendars, or employ homeschool organizational
software. In her weekly records for her two
children, Andreas and Danike, homeschooler Sonja
Becker-Boelter has devised her own shorthand
to streamline her notes. Under "English," a seven
inside a square indicates they have covered page 7
in the review section. Under "Reading/Workbook,"
Becker-Boelter jots down page numbers; numbers
preceded by a "w" are pages completed in the
workbook.

Your homeschool records and evaluation

The record-keeping and evaluation methods you
choose depend on the purposes for which they will
be used. What are your state's requirements for
records and assessment? What are your personal
goals for tracking your child's progress? Could your
child return to school sometime in the future? Are
you looking ahead to what your child will need for
employment or college admissions? The major

types of record-keeping are discussed in the following sections.

Portfolios

The portfolio is favored by artists, photographers, and many other professionals as the format in which they present their work. Homeschoolers, too, assemble student work and other elements within a portfolio, which, taken together, can provide a clear picture of the student's progress and accomplishments.

Portfolios can include a variety of items, among them:

- Essays, short stories, poetry, and other writing assignments
- Artwork
- Reading lists
- Photographs of projects, videos, audio tapes, and other technological samplings
- Attendance records (a requirement in some areas)
- Daily or weekly logs
- Exhibition or performance programs; ticket stubs
- Test results
- School district records (if applicable)

Representing the progression of individual achievement, portfolios are an effective means of evaluation without grade-labeling. In addition, the process of building and reviewing a portfolio allows parents to connect the disparate physical elements—a drawing here, a poem there—into a true understanding of their child's learning process.

Watch Out!
Some states specify the items to be included in your portfolio. Make sure you are prepared for your evaluation.

Homeschool portfolios may be quite informal, or they may involve inventories or scoring methods that lend a "professional" appearance for the benefit of district evaluators. (For information on portfolio evaluations, see Chapter 5.) Portfolios can also offer:

- Flexibility in their organization. For example, you can subdivide them according to subject or incorporate other assessment tools, such as teacher inventories.

- Structure to interest-led curriculums, particularly unschooling.

- Guidance in determining your direction for the coming year.

- Evidence of the relative effectiveness of your teaching tools and methods.

- An opportunity for children to evaluate their own learning.

Journals

In addition to other written forms such as lists and daily logs, journals provide an effective way of record-keeping. With the continuity of a written narrative, journals can offer a unique perspective of your homeschool experience. Unlike other recording methods, good journals communicate not only the subjects covered and the accomplishments, but also the full spectrum of homeschooling days, from the doubtful moments to the major breakthroughs. There are pros and cons to journal keeping, including the following:

- Journals can be time-consuming. Set aside time for entry writing, taking care not to let it intrude on learning time. Also, consider having the kids help contribute.

- Journals encourage the good habit of regular writing.

- The narrative form may not translate easily into a transcript.

- As with portfolios, journals are effective tools for interpreting the learning process.

- Journals become treasured personal records that your family will revisit and enjoy for years to come.

Transcripts and grades

Another record keeping/assessment option is the more traditional method: grades. Grades are simple to understand and familiar to most of us. However, most homeschoolers object to letter grades, saying they're an ineffective way to gauge a student's achievement. Even so, a traditional transcript may appear more acceptable to school officials and concerned relatives.

Homeschooler Debra Marcotte manages her records using several different methods, described in her words as follows:

1. **A daily log**—"Because so much of our day is composed of activities and not just written work, I log our activities each day and assign a subject to them. This is for me mostly, so I can see that we are doing something even on days I don't feel we accomplish a lot. I also use it to write a summary at the end of the year of what we have done, for evaluation purposes."

2. **A photo album**—"I have a camera that I use strictly for homeschool. I take pictures of large projects we do, activities and field trips, Cam working on a project, anything to document work being done. My son often will read about

Unofficially...
The Garden Book, Thomas Jefferson's 60-year gardening journal, contains detailed notes and observations on everything from building plans to a description of the first spring blooming of the purple hyacinth. Jefferson learned from his notes, using them to save time and labor and improve the next growing season.

Watch Out!
If your state
mandates testing
for home-
schoolers, find
out the specific
standardized test
that is required.
Some districts
require adminis-
tration by a cer-
tified teacher,
not the parent.

something and then create a model of what he
has read about, or create a costume and spend
hours play-acting. This is the way he learns
best, but it's hard to show it without pictures!"

3. **A main lesson book**—"This is what the Oak
Meadow curriculum uses. It is a large sketchbook, either one for all work or a separate one
for each subject. Work is done directly on the
sketchbook paper, or I rubber-cement things to
pages."

The controversy over testing

Testing may become an issue, particularly if it's
required of homeschoolers in your state, in which
case you have little choice. Even when it isn't
mandatory, many homeschoolers seeking reassurance from an "outside" assessment consider testing
their child.

The controversy over testing's capacity to accurately measure a child's intelligence, achievement,
and competence continues to be debated among
homeschoolers and educators at large. Test scores
wield extraordinary power and have wrought serious consequences not only for the school system,
but also for the educational possibilities for many
children.

When considering testing, ask yourself the
following:

- Why would you test your children? Because
  it is required in your state, to satisfy worried
  relatives, or for your own peace of mind?

- What are your state's specific legal requirements? Some states require testing annually,
  and others only at specific grade levels.

- Which tests are used? Some regulations offer parents a choice of tests.

- Does the law allow alternative assessments? Some stipulate options such as portfolio review or another assessment, pending approval by the superintendent.

- Who needs to see the results? In some areas, scores may have to be submitted to your local district; others don't require that scores be reported at all.

- How are test results used? Some states require a minimum score in order to maintain your eligibility to homeschool.

- What are the conditions of the test? Can you administer a test at home? Is there a flexible time limit, and can portions be administered orally?

- How does testing affect the learner and the parent? The fallout from testing can include anxiety, self-esteem issues, or a reconsideration of your teaching methods.

Moneysaver
Group discounts are offered by some testing services.

What are standardized tests?

Any test that is administered to students, scored, and interpreted in a uniform manner can be called a standardized test. Most often, though, the national tests—like those mentioned in the following list—are the first that come to mind, and they are created and distributed by commercial test publishers. Standardized tests can take many forms, from multiple choice to essays to oral examinations. Every student supposedly takes the test under the same conditions, and each student's performance on a standardized test is compared to a "norm group" of students of the same age or grade who took the same test.

The three basic test types are:

- **Achievement tests,** which measure a student's knowledge and skills within a specific subject area, such as mathematics, language arts, or social studies. These include the CAT (California Achievement Test); the California Test of Basic Skills; the Comprehensive Test of Basic Skills; the Metropolitan Achievement Test; the Iowa Test of Basic Skills; the Stanford Achievement Test; and the PIAT-R (Peabody Individual Achievement Test).

- **Aptitude tests,** which measure a student's ability to learn, and how well they are likely to perform in future schoolwork. These include the Wechsler Intelligence Scales for Children (WISC-R); the Differential Aptitude Test (DAT); and the Stanford-Binet Intelligence Scale.

- **Scholastic aptitude tests,** which are widely used to determine college admissions. These include the ACT (American College Testing Program) and the SAT (Scholastic Assessment Test). These tests and the college admissions process are described in detail in Chapter 16.

Fulfilling state requirements

If you will be testing in compliance with the law, find out what to expect well in advance of the testing date. In addition to the type and grade-level of the test, learn how it will be given, and whether you have a choice in selecting an administrator. Seek advice from your support group, which may also be able to direct you to test administrators and/or home-school evaluators. Some homeschool parents who are also certified teachers serve in this capacity. In some areas you can administer the test yourself, under certain conditions. The Iowa test, for example, requires the administrator to be a college graduate or a certified teacher.

Consider how you will prepare your child. A practice test is often helpful, though having it in hand too early in the year may tempt you to "teach to the test"—that is, you may restrict yourself to teaching the information or concepts that will appear on the exam. Understanding the limitations of testing will enable you to keep the whole process in perspective.

When homeschoolers choose to test

If testing is optional in your area, you may still wish to test for your own purposes. It may be an appropriate assessment, particularly for those using a curriculum or structured methods.

Do your homework—evaluate the available tests, and have an idea about what you want the test to measure. Alternatives to standardized tests include PASS (Personalized Achievement Summary System), which is designed specifically for homeschoolers. PASS is offered by Hewitt Homeschooling Resources for assessing grades 3 through 8 only, and measures achievement in language arts and math. The appropriate testing level of a student is identified by an initial placement test. PASS is untimed and can be administered at home.

Learn how to evaluate a test so you can derive the greatest possible value from the results. Find out for whom the test is designed, and consider content validity: Do the test questions represent the skills in the specified subject area? Make sure you understand the error of measurement, which is inherent in all test scores.

Bright Idea
Some testing companies offer test samples online, writing evaluations, and other services.

Unofficially...
Part of a growing trend, applicants to public universities in Texas do not have to submit SAT or ACT scores if they finish in the top 10 percent of their high school classes. State research concluded that "except at the extremes, SAT/ACT scores do not adequately predict grades in core freshman courses or the probability of college graduation."
—FairTest: the national center for fair and open testing

Make sure to discuss testing with your children, gauging their perspective. Some may view tests as interesting challenges, while others may be completely overwhelmed.

Finally, keep test results in perspective. Both educators and parents tend to give far too much weight to test scores. No educational situation should rely exclusively on tests. Make sure to incorporate other forms of assessment, such as personal observation and analysis of writing skills and problem-solving abilities.

Just the facts

- Before purchasing a curriculum, define your personal goals, your child's interests, your learning objectives, and your personal style.

- Readily available from several sources, curricular guides are a helpful reference. However, avoid becoming so concerned about covering everything on the list that you are less willing to allow your child to pursue his or her particular interests.

- There is no prescribed schedule for homeschooling. Your day-to-day routine will evolve, based on your academic goals, the size of your family, and your other commitments.

- True representations of learning, portfolios and journals also promote self-evaluation. Even if they aren't required by local regulations, consider maintaining these records.

- Testing is a controversial measure of learning. Standardized testing may or may not be required in your state. If you choose to test, make sure you understand the options available and how to derive meaning from the results.

Living and Learning

PART IV

GET THE SCOOP ON...
Joining a support group or starting your own
▪ The benefits of co-ops and resource centers
▪ The politics of homeschooling ▪ The lowdown
on shopping for used curricula

Joining the Homeschool Community

Chapter 9

Homeschoolers tend to be independent types—the very nature of the endeavor implies self-sufficiency. But rather than sequester themselves in complete isolation, the vast majority of homeschoolers come together in groups that provide support and encouragement, an exchange of information, and a sense of belonging.

"I have found two support groups in my area...I would feel very alone without them!" says one homeschooling mother, Deb Marcotte. "I have learned so much from the other 'seasoned' parents...And I have felt supported when I was having doubts. I always come away from the parent meetings recommitted to homeschooling."

In this chapter, I'll describe all you need to know about support groups, from how to find the right group to the various benefits of homeschool resource centers. Included, too, is information on connecting to the online homeschool community—with a sample list of e-groups you might like to join.

I'll also cover homeschooling conferences and curriculum fairs and show you how to get the most from these events.

Finding a support group

The first piece of advice most new homeschoolers get is to join a support group—it's advice I've given throughout this book. Whether you are looking for encouragement, assistance in complying with state law, or just an opportunity for you and your children to socialize, a supportive group of homeschoolers probably meets right in your area.

With a little help from my friends

In addition to general encouragement and the fellowship of other homeschoolers, local support groups offer a range of services, including:

- Information and personal advice on homeschooling, including recommendations on specific curricula

- Assistance to newcomers, including materials and a designated contact to answer questions

- A member directory

- Teaching seminars

- Educational and social events, from field trips to Mom's Night Out

- Special programs for your children, including mentoring, 4-H, Presidential Physical Fitness testing, spelling bees, and a teen ministry

- Sports instruction, teams, and league competition

- Scholarships

- Discounts, curriculum exchange, and other savings

- A newsletter and other publications
- A lending library
- Community outreach

Support groups may also provide accountability organizations, which assist in complying with the law, providing record-keeping, evaluation, and other services.

State networks

You should also contact your state homeschooling organization, which may also be called a network, if they sponsor a membership of local chapters. Here's what state networks do:

- Monitor state and local laws, pending legislation, and court cases related to home education
- Organize political action
- Provide a communication network for homeschoolers
- Sponsor state-wide activities, such as conventions
- Produce a handbook or guide to home-schooling in your region
- Refer homeschoolers to local groups, education consultants, and other services
- Sponsor and assist local groups (for example, helping them set up their own Web pages, or allowing them to post notices on the state Web site)

How to find a local support group

Start by asking other homeschoolers you know or consult your local librarian, who may be acquainted with homeschoolers who patronize the library. You

Bright Idea
Parents interested in preserving home-schooling rights in their state can participate in these efforts through their state home-schooling organization.

Moneysaver
Some home-
schooling groups
provide a
membership card
that entitles
you to discounts
at local book-
stores and other
educational
suppliers.

can check the state-by-state list at the back of this book, where you'll also find national homeschool organizations that can connect you with a local group.

Many homeschooling Web sites have links to support groups. Once you link to a support group's Web site you can review their mission statement or philosophy, member policy, a sample newsletter, a list of upcoming events, a summary of your state's homeschool law, and homeschooling FAQs (Frequently Asked Questions).

But is it the right group for me?

So you've found a group. Before signing up, consider the following and how these issues relate to your needs:

- Is the group secular, or does it have a religious affiliation? Most groups with a religious affiliation state this upfront as part of their mission statement. They may also state whether the group is "inclusive," meaning they welcome all homeschoolers.

- Do they have a specific philosophy or emphasis? For example, are the members proponents of unschooling, or do the group activities focus on the interests of teens?

- What is involved in membership? In addition to any fees (which range from $12 to $35 for membership in a national organization), families may be asked to commit a minimum number of hours or to assist with a program or activity. Some religious groups require members to sign a statement of faith.

- Is there a contact person you can call with questions? If you are new to homeschooling, you'll need help to get started.

- When and how often are meetings held? Meetings are generally scheduled on a regular basis. Make sure the time and location are convenient for you.

- How is the group governed? What is the leadership? Are decisions made by consensus, or by a central board of officers? Clear bylaws ensure smooth operation of the group and are essential for resolving any conflicts.

- How does the group communicate? A good organization has a clearly established line of communication. The group may have a phone-tree system for relaying messages, in which a designated coordinator contacts phone-tree group leaders, who then call members on their list.

- Is member information kept confidential? Many groups clearly state their policy regarding distribution of the membership list, which may include information about children. Make sure the list will not be sold or posted without your consent.

Call the newcomer contact or other representative who can tell you how the group works.

If everyone does their share

Support group veterans advise newcomers to become active members. "The advantages of a group can't be realized by sending in a form and money," said one homeschooler. "Getting involved and developing relationships with other homeschoolers is the main benefit."

Group leaders often lament the fact that the bulk of organizing always falls to the same individuals, with many members apathetic about participation. Any group, homeschooling or otherwise, is

Timesaver
Before you join a support group, attend one of their meetings, which are usually open to nonmembers. Then you can decide if it's right for you.

only as good as its members. Find a way to contribute—offer your special talents to lead a workshop for kids, write for the newsletter, or volunteer to host a social event.

Take your turn in a leadership position. Most groups depend on a rotating system, in which every member serves a position, from treasurer to new homeschooler contact. Many homeschoolers also become ambassadors for their education choice, spreading the word and sharing their experience both within and outside the homeschooling community.

Homeschool co-ops and resource centers

Support groups—or as few as two or three like-minded homeschooling families—may sponsor offshoots, organizing classes and team-teaching through homeschool co-ops, or providing materials, mentoring, and other services through a central resource center.

Homeschooling is quite an undertaking for a single family. Co-ops and centers are a way to share the experience, with members pooling their funds, efforts, and individual contributions to everyone's benefit.

Resource libraries provide parents, particularly new homeschoolers, with access to a variety of materials. Typical offerings include homeschooling books, back issues of magazines, convention tapes, sample curricula, reference books, manipulatives and other teaching tools, a copy machine, and other items the group desires.

Members of the community may also wish to contribute to a resource library. A local business, for example, may be supporting your local public school through apprentice programs, materials and

Bright Idea
"Remember that [homeschool support] groups are often run by individuals volunteering their time and money to provide a service to homeschooling families. If requesting that information be sent to you, please include a self-addressed, stamped envelope (and perhaps a couple of dollars)."
—*Home Education Magazine*

equipment (such as used software or computers), scholarships, donating or loaning corporate space, or technical support. Perhaps they could contribute to your homeschool group or resource center or offer a meeting space. The publicity would benefit both the contributing business and homeschooling.

As with support groups, a co-op or center needs to determine its organizational style. On the one hand, too rigid a structure may turn membership into an onerous chore. But a lack of order may result in chaos. Does each family pitch in, or do families pay for services as they use them? (Some resource centers may receive additional funding from a church, which may also provide the space.) Who determines purchases or the classes to be offered? Issues such as these can be addressed in some form of organizational bylaws.

National organizations

As with any member organization, you need to consider carefully before joining. Examine their mission statement and what's involved in membership. Are there religious or political agendas that you may find objectionable or that you might consider as being outside the realm of homeschooling? Is the leadership member-based? Do their activities and services relate to your family's needs? Consider the opinions of homeschooling friends, then judge for yourself whether to sign up.

That said, many homeschoolers assert that their local and state groups adequately meet their needs in terms of services and networking. Moreover, many busy parents simply don't have enough time and energy to devote to yet another group.

If you seek a larger role in advocating for homeschooling, some advise that the most effective way to serve the homeschooling community is at the state level (since legislation affecting homeschooling occurs at the state level).

It's okay not to join

Perhaps you're not a joiner, or large gatherings aren't your style. Or maybe the local group isn't quite the right "fit." A formal group isn't mandatory to becoming a successful homeschooler.

Many homeschoolers choose to get together with just one other family, around shared interests, and at times convenient to both. You might get together once a month for a regular field trip, double up on a science project, or take turns watching the kids so you can run errands.

Some of those who've been homeschooling for a few years may feel that their initial needs have been served by their support group, or their kids have grown older, and moved on. Still others seek fellowship in church and other organizations, such as Scouts.

When a support group doesn't work out

While all groups begin with the best intentions of providing families with support and fellowship, it doesn't always work that way in practice. Members may experience differences of philosophy or personalities may conflict. Group dynamics may shift with a change in leadership.

One mother found her group simply became too cliquish. Squabbling ensued over petty differences, until she decided enough was enough and struck out on her own. Many families become uncomfortable over the particular focus of a group. "I consider myself a very religious person," says Kathleen Roberts, a homeschooling mother. "I feel very strongly about my beliefs, but I'm uncomfortable with people who assume we have the same beliefs and interrogate me when they find out differently. I love honest questions, but I'm not into heated debates. A group that focuses on fun and learning for the kids instead of 'doctrine' is best for me…"

Starting your own group

If no existing group fits your needs, perhaps you could start your own. Here are a few tips:

- **Consider the orientation of your group.** Will it be geared toward a particular teaching method? Will it have any particular philosophical or worldview emphasis?

- **Determine its structure.** Will it be loosely organized or formal? Will you allow an unlimited number of members, or do you favor the intimacy of a small group?

- **Decide on your objectives.** Find out the needs of local homeschoolers. Most groups can't possibly provide all the services and activities listed earlier. Focus on some service that another local group doesn't provide, such as organizing activities for a specific age.

- **Secure a meeting place.** You might be able to arrange to use space at the library or your church.

- **Get the word out.** Post notices in the library, market, and anywhere else parents might see them. A press release might get you publicity in your community newspaper, library newsletter, or on a local radio station, especially if you can tie it into a current event or noteworthy issue.

A support group is not all taking—it is giving also. I have helped link people across the country to used curriculum and interesting Web sites, and given them a shoulder to cry on. We cheer ourselves on and praise our children's victories, even when they are small.
—a homeschooling mom in Iowa
99

Detailed instructions for starting a support group are available from state networks, including the California Homeschool Network, which sells a *Support Group Guide.*

Networking online

Homeschoolers also connect electronically. Literally hundreds of such opportunities exist, from the Homeschooling on a Shoestring mailing list to a used book–swapping e-group.

Many homeschooling Web sites provide links to these online opportunities for networking. They include Finding Homeschool Support (www. geocities.com/Athens/8259/), and Jon's Homeschool Resource Page (www.midnightbeach.com/ hs/Talk.f.htm/). In addition to listing the major homeschooling bulletin boards, e-mail groups, chat rooms, etc., both of these sites provide brief summaries describing how each mode works..

Here are the ins and outs of electronic homeschool networking:

- **Check it out.** First see if it's your cup of tea before investing your time in signing up and participating. Most groups clearly state any religious orientation or emphasis on a particular form of homeschooling (such as unit studies). Some are quite specialized and restrict their discussion to related subjects.

- **Read the archives.** If the group has a viewable archive, review the postings to see if the discussion is of interest to you. Is the information relevant to your needs, or is it just a lot of gossip?

- **Is the list moderated or unmoderated?** With a moderated list, an administrator or a list owner

Unofficially...
Some sample postings from Homeschool bulletin boards: Hello, from a newcomer; Tadpole Trouble; What exactly is Unit Studies?; Geography Bee in Dallas; Managing Mom Time???; My wife likes public school; Need advice on Saxon Math; Home Sunday school; Help! My daughter can't spell!; Where do you get owl pellets?

reviews postings and otherwise manages content. In case of any problems, you can e-mail the moderator.

- **Discern relative activity.** Does the bulletin board appear to have many visitors? Some groups post the number of members and current postings.

- **You've got mail.** With e-mail groups, be prepared for a lot of it! You might choose to receive messages in "digest form" as opposed to single or individual messages. Digest means that all the mail for the day will be combined and delivered as one e-mail message. Some lists let you turn off the mailbox if you will be away, so your mailbox isn't crammed with messages upon your return. Don't sign up for too many groups at one time—you may have trouble keeping up with the mail.

- **Follow the rules.** Many homeschoolers online—especially experienced ones—wish to avoid certain topics, including basic questions of newbies and debates on socialization. (There are sites and groups specific to new homeschoolers and other general homeschooling issues.) Most discussion groups do not allow selling or commercial messages, although there may be a separate area for posting member services.

- **Flaming, spamming, and other spurious comments are not allowed.** Given the vast choice of e-groups within homeschooling, there's probably a venue specifically for such venting. (Learn more about the rules of online etiquette in the next section.)

> **❝**
> Focus on homeschooling. No one should have to walk on eggshells, nor should anyone need to feel ashamed for why or how they choose to homeschool...maybe we can all work harder at working together, and encourage some crossover and discussion.
> —Shari Henry, "When Diversity Isn't," *Home Education Magazine,* 1995
> **❞**

- **Optimize your experience.** Follow any suggestions of the group, such as encouragement to share bookmarks. There's often space to post a member profile; take the time to introduce yourself.

- **Be specific with your questions.** "What's involved in homeschooling?" may bring few responses or information that you don't need. An example would be "Is there a support group near Atascadero, California?"

How do I join?

Registration is usually a simple process, which includes completing an online form with basic information, establishing a user name (you can choose an alias), and choosing a password. In some cases, membership must be approved by the list owner. Be aware of what exactly will appear on-screen, and whether your message or post can be viewed by anyone or only group members.

Now that you're ready to begin submitting messages, keep in mind the following points of online etiquette:

- Keep your message length short—long lines are difficult to follow.

- Watch typos, spelling, and grammar.

- When you reply to a post, trim that message to the minimum needed to set the context for your reply.

- Don't make criticism personal.

- Take private disagreements or discussion to e-mail.

- Don't use the lists for chain letters or off-topic posts.

Watch Out!
Online sources may have inaccurate or dated information regarding home-school laws and should never be relied on for legal advice. Get a copy of the current law, and talk to your area homeschool organization for information on compliance.

Kids online

Many youngsters use the computer to connect with other homeschoolers. Especially popular among kids are chat rooms, where you can talk to other homeschoolers in real-time; and electronic pen pals, listings through which you can exchange mail.

You will need to register (there is a maximum capacity for the room), as well as obtain any required plug-ins for your Web browser. Here, too, there are rules to observe, including polite conversation only, no advertising, no solicitation of names and addresses of others in the room, and the moderator has absolute discretion. There will be a schedule of chats, with some general in nature and others restricted to a topic.

Chat rules for kids

The Internet is a relatively safe place for kids to meet and talk with others all over the world. But as you would in any public place, you need to supervise your child.

First, make sure the chat is appropriate for kids. Don't allow your child to give out personal information—you don't really know who's in the room—and they should never share their ID or messenger ID (used with a pager or instant messaging system). Review the rules together to make sure your child acts appropriately, and consider setting up your own family guidelines. (See Chapter 10 for more about online safety for kids.)

If the room is unmoderated, you might opt to find a moderated one. This will not prevent inappropriate messages, but if there are problems you can e-mail the moderator, who usually takes care of the offender immediately. Depending on chat room policy, offenders may be kicked out of

Watch Out!
When creating a family Web page, don't include your child's name, photo, school, or other information that might allow anyone to identify your child and possibly locate them.

the room and blocked from access to the site. If the abuse warrants it, the moderator will file a report with the ISP of the offending party, who may also be subject to criminal charges.

A filtering mechanism can guard against offensive language, or can be designed to ignore specific chatters. You can also block messages coming from a certain address or ID. A variety of software filtering programs can be purchased and downloaded via the Internet, with some versions designed for use on specific online servers.

If you are victimized by spamming—receiving unsolicited messages—do not respond. And never blame your child for problems that arise: You don't want them to be afraid to alert you in the future.

Here are just a few sites among the hundreds that are just for homeschooled kids:

Free_Teens: www.onelist.com/ubscribe.cgi/Free teens
This [mailing] list is for unschooled, and homeschooled, teens and those looking to explore alternative education.

Homeschooled Kidz: www.homeschoolcenter.com/kidz.html
This site includes an e-mail list, chats, pen pals, and a message board just for kids.

Home Learning Teens: www.onelist.com/subscribe/homelearningteens
A mailing list for homeschoolers ages 11 and up. "Everyone here is friendly, and all are welcome." For safety reasons, lurkers (people who watch but don't participate) will be unsubscribed after three weeks.

Homeschooling conferences and curriculum fairs

These events are worthwhile to attend, particularly for new homeschoolers. Variously sponsored by state networks, homeschool publications, and others, conferences are events for homeschoolers to come together, meet with their peers, and explore new ideas and teaching techniques. A major conference or curriculum fair will enable you to see a range of materials, in addition to product demos, teaching workshops, and informative speakers—all of which can get you geared up for homeschooling.

With so much to take in, such events can also bewilder and exhaust the uninitiated. Before attending, it's helpful to do some research. Talk to other homeschoolers about the materials they're using. Ask questions about what worked for them and what didn't. Check online message boards and groups for discussion about specific curricula, and peruse the catalogs. (For more on choosing a curriculum, see Chapter 8.)

How to get the most from a homeschooling event

Here are a few more tips for getting the most out of a conference or curriculum fair:

- Try to get a schedule in advance of the event. Then you can map out your plan, prioritizing the "must-see" speakers or demonstrations.

- Although children may be welcome, these events can be tiring for young ones, who might be better off staying at home (although in some cases, childcare may be provided on-site). Older kids might like to come along; many events feature teen or youth workshops.

Moneysaver
If you've decided on a curriculum, vendors frequently offer a discount on purchases made at the fair.

- It's impossible to attend every workshop. Choose only those that really interest you, and be prepared to take notes. Perhaps your spouse can attend certain events.

- You won't be able to hear every speaker. Tapes are often available for purchase, which you can then share with your support group.

- While vendors can offer helpful advice, keep in mind that all are trying to sell a product—something, perhaps, that you don't really need.

- To avoid impulse buying and overspending, set a budget. Or take a certain amount of cash, leaving your credit cards at home.

- If you're not prepared to purchase a curriculum, pick up catalogs to study at home.

Event calendars

Your local or state group maintains a schedule of upcoming events in your area, many of which are sponsored by the groups themselves. You can also find homeschool calendars online at the following sites:

- Kaleidoscape's The Home Educators' Calendar of Events: www.kaleidoscapes.com/cgi-bin/Calendar_3.0/calendar.cgi

- Christian Home Educators Electronic Convention: www.cheec.com/lobby.asp

- Homeschooling conferences by state: www.sound.net/~ejcol/confer.html

- Homeschooling Today, master list of homeschool fairs and conventions: www.homeschooltoday.com/hfc.htm

Timesaver
Local support groups frequently host their own "curriculum nights," when members can bring in and discuss what they've used in an informal setting. These are good opportunities for parents to learn from seasoned homeschoolers before making the larger investment of attending a convention.

Keeping costs down

Homeschooling expenditures can quickly add up, especially for first-timers. In addition to establishing a homeschool budget, you can hold down costs in other ways.

Homeschoolers shop creatively. Used texts and other materials are available from a variety of sources, including college and university bookstores or religious and private schools. Some school districts make extra or used books available on a first-come, first-served basis. Inquire at your local education agency. The sale shelf at the public library can also yield great finds, at only 25 or 50 cents a pop.

Used curricula and other homeschooling materials are another option. The ins and outs of resale outlets and swapping are discussed next.

Shopping for a used curriculum

Listing for several hundred dollars and up, curricula, for many families, is the single largest homeschooling purchase. No wonder used curricula has become such a popular option.

In addition to all kinds of curricula, used outlets offer:

- Books
- Tapes
- Software
- Holiday supplies
- Science kits
- Used microscopes and other equipment
- Math manipulatives
- Costumes
- Games
- Manufacturer overstocks or discontinued items

Bright Idea
Local businesses frequently make donations to their public schools in the form of used equipment and other supplies. Ask them to consider doing the same for your homeschooling group or co-op.

Commercial outlets abound in both catalog form and online. Some are more organized than others, with offerings subdivided into categories. Some Web sites, such as the Homeschooler's Bookmobile Online (http://bookmobileonline. com/bookmobile/index.mv?HANEleftcoIBKMBL), are searchable by keyword. A few also take consignments.

Also popular are electronic message and swap boards, with several devoted exclusively to the exchange of used material. With some sites experiencing hundreds of visitors each day, this can be an efficient way to buy and sell material.

Although each site may have specific rules, the following guidelines will help you negotiate these boards:

- Listings may be free or involve a monthly fee.

- These forums are usually reserved for individuals and don't allow dealers or commercial advertisements.

- Exchanges can list items for sale, and those wanted to buy.

- Before selling an item, first check the wanted board to buy posts, and vice versa.

- There may be restrictions on certain items (such as no toys).

- Postings are variously organized, such as by subject or grade level.

- Listings are usually limited to a specified time period, such as six months, after which they may be automatically deleted. Sold items may also be held for a limited time.

- Responsibility for listings remains with the originating party and not the sponsoring site.

- Be sure to follow any requirements for posting an ad. With books, for example, you may be asked to include the date of publication and the edition number. Be sure to include your e-mail address, so you can correspond throughout a transaction. Always indicate when an item has been sold.

- Some sites offer pricing guidelines (one recommends half of retail, depending on the condition and popularity of the item) which may require that you include shipping in your price.

- Generally, the method of payment is negotiated between buyer and seller (COD is usually recommended).

- You buy and sell at your own risk.

When there's a problem

Most transactions are trouble-free; both buyers and sellers want to maintain a good reputation. But if there's an issue which cannot be resolved directly with the offending party, there is usually a board for posting problems. Beyond that, fraudulent parties may be subject to prosecution, regardless of the value in question.

Just the facts

- Support groups offer a range of activities and support services that are especially valuable to new homeschoolers, but make sure the group is right for you. Be aware that these groups tend to organize around a common philosophy. There may be a secular or religious distinction.

- Once you decide to join, becoming an active member will benefit everyone. Look for ways

Watch Out!
Shipping costs may be expensive relative to the value of the item ordered from a used outlet.

to contribute—help support existing programs or instigate a new one, such as team-teaching, or other cooperative activities.

- Homeschoolers are independent types, and many hold strong views on homeschooling and other issues. Decide your own level of involvement, and be prepared for conflicting views.

- Joining a support group is not a requirement to being a homeschooler. Just getting together with one or two good friends could be all the support you need.

- The homeschool community is on the Net. Check out the electronic board, or join a mailing list or newsgroup. You might want to observe a bit to get a feel for the discussion before posting a message.

GET THE SCOOP ON...
Great Web sites for learning ▪ Keeping your
kids safe online ▪ Learning resources in
your community

Tools of the Trade

Books and more books. Across the board, homeschoolers are unanimous in their enthusiasm for books. "The absolute staple of any homeschool!" says Melissa, a homeschooling mother. "And of course I'm referring to 'living' books. In my opinion, textbooks are good for math, high school science, and college. If you don't have room for books, you've got too much furniture."

In a recent survey conducted by Brian Ray of the National Home Education Research Institute, 53 percent of homeschoolers reported visiting a library at least once or twice a month. Nearly half, 47 percent, reported that they go even more often. In the same survey, 83.7 percent of homeschoolers said that their children use a computer in their home.

In this chapter, I'll show you how to get the most from these and other tools of the trade.

For the love of books

Use books to build a foundation for learning, beginning in your home. Surround your family with books. Even infants can enjoy the physical pleasure

Chapter 10

of books: Let them grab, fondle, and even taste the chunky variety. Your own daily use of books, magazines, and newspapers will instill in your children a love of reading, opening the door to independent learning.

Read aloud to your children—the earlier the better—and continue to read to them even after they have gained the skill for themselves. Encourage their skills by having them read to you, and discuss what you've read. If interest wanes, choose another title. Recommendations of books for children are available from the American Library Association, the Library of Congress, and your local library, which may publish recommended lists of their own.

Build a home library

It will take time to create your home library because most of your purchases will be chosen according to your evolving needs. When looking for educational titles, don't restrict your child by buying a certain grade level. Instead, shop according to subject categories, while remaining in touch with your child's abilities. Also allow them the freedom to explore adult volumes, if they choose.

Most homeschool libraries have good references on hand, such as encyclopedias and dictionaries (hard copy or electronic versions). Many references are also available in current Internet editions (see recommended Web sites later in this chapter).

Animated by sound and video, CDROM encyclopedias are dynamic tools that are particularly appealing to kids. A far cry from bulky, multi-volume sets, this format can store the same amount of information, including sound and video clips, on one or two CDs, and many update themselves automatically via the Internet. Searching is easy, with many editions featuring automatic cross-referencing hyperlinks, and bookmarking. CDROM encyclopedias also represent a tremendous savings over hard copy editions. Popular hard-bound encyclopedias are priced from about $50 to $400—CD versions, around $20 to $50.

Finding great books

Each year, the American Library Association awards the Newbery Medal to the best in children's literature. The Caldecott Medal, which honors the best picture books for children, is also presented annually by the ALA.

Named for the 18th-century English bookseller, John Newbery, the Newbery Medal has been awarded since 1922. Following are the award winning titles for the last 20 years.

Newbery Medal Winners, 1960–2000

- 2000: *Bud, Not Buddy* by Christopher Paul Curtis (Delacorte)
- 1999: *Holes* by Louis Sachar (Frances Foster)
- 1998: *Out of the Dust* by Karen Hesse (Scholastic)
- 1997: *The View from Saturday* by E.L. Konigsburg (Jean Karl/Atheneum)
- 1996: *The Midwife's Apprentice* by Karen Cushman (Clarion)
- 1995: *Walk Two Moons* by Sharon Creech (HarperCollins)
- 1994: *The Giver* by Lois Lowry (Houghton)
- 1993: *Missing May* by Cynthia Rylant (Jackson/Orchard)
- 1992: *Shiloh* by Phyllis Reynolds Naylor (Atheneum)

Watch Out!
Though they might represent a bargain, keep in mind the relative usefulness of reference books purchased from thrift shops or garage sales, most of which will be outdated.

- 1991: *Maniac Magee* by Jerry Spinelli (Little, Brown)

- 1990: *Number the Stars* by Lois Lowry (Houghton)

- 1989: *Joyful Noise: Poems for Two Voices* by Paul Fleischman (Harper)

- 1988: *Lincoln: A Photobiography* by Russell Freedman (Clarion)

- 1987: *The Whipping Boy* by Sid Fleischman (Greenwillow)

- 1986: *Sarah, Plain and Tall* by Patricia MacLachlan (Harper)

- 1985: *The Hero and the Crown* by Robin McKinley (Greenwillow)

- 1984: *Dear Mr. Henshaw* by Beverly Cleary (Morrow)

- 1983: *Dicey's Song* by Cynthia Voight (Atheneum)

- 1982: *A Visit to William Blake's Inn: Poems for Innocent and Experienced Travelers* by Nancy Willard (Harcourt)

- 1981: *Jacob Have I Loved* by Katherine Paterson (Crowell)

Courtesy of American Library Association

Other recommendations for children's reading appear in The Horn Book, a bi-monthly publication that reviews new children's books, available at libraries, or their Web site (www.hbook.com). Also on the Web is AtoZebra (www.atozebra.com), a searchable database of children's book reviews. Older students may wish to review college preparatory reading lists.

Visit your public library

Make a regular trip to the library part of your routine. Almost everyone has a public library nearby, and depending on your area, you may also have access to school and college libraries, or specialty collections such as historical societies or business and law libraries.

Resources commonly offered at a public library include:

- A children's librarian specially trained to help you find the right materials

- Reference services

- Interlibrary loan (ILL) opportunities

- A library Web site offering 24-hour access to the library catalog, library services, and events

- Web pages especially geared toward kids

- A variety of non-book offerings—videos, books on tape, book/cassette kits, and CDs

- Computer workstations and computer courses

- Special needs services, and connection to a nationwide network of Braille and talking book services

- Foreign language materials

- Parenting information, workshops, and parent/child activities

- Preschool programs to stimulate the development of infants and toddlers

- Young people's programming: story hours and summer reading programs

- A homework hotline

- Contests

Bright Idea
When reading a book to your child, include the author's dedication. This is a fun and simple way for kids to connect with the book as someone's personal creation.

- Offerings for older kids, such as writing workshops, career resources, and information on college and financial aid

- Volunteer opportunities and tutoring

- Adult events: reading groups, poetry readings, community bulletin board, and other events

- Mobile services

Libraries in general have become increasingly aware of their homeschooling clientele. To better serve their needs, many librarians maintain home-school files, containing a copy of the local education laws and a directory of support groups in the area. They may also offer special workshops geared toward homeschoolers as well as other services.

Tips for helping your children use the library

In traditional school, library skills are often taught as part of the curriculum. Do the same for your child, and learn how to use the library alongside them.

First, orient yourselves to the library's organization. A public library is generally divided in the following manner: a children's section (up to 6th grade), a section for young adults (ages 12–18), and an adult section (ages 18 and up). Each is in turn divided into circulating and non-circulating collections, including a reference section with periodicals. New books may be featured in special displays.

You'll need to know how to navigate your way around. You can simply browse (a good time to learn or refresh your memory of the Dewey Decimal numbering system), or familiarize yourself with the library's public access catalog. To help get you started, ask a librarian, who can also show you how to access other collections and bibliographies.

Periodical searches can start with bound copies, the *Reader's Guide,* or online magazine and newspaper indexes. Ask the reference librarian about other abstracting or indexing services. Many libraries also maintain print files of clippings, photos, and other materials that may not be in the main electronic catalog.

Most libraries will issue a library card to children who can print their names. Parents will have to co-sign for them. Make sure everyone knows the rules for checking out books and understands that the books belong to everyone and should be handled accordingly. Teach your children how to use a table of contents and index, and advise them to consult more than one source when researching a topic.

Building a relationship with a librarian is especially important for homeschoolers. Whenever possible, you should encourage your children to ask on their own for help in finding books and materials. Prepare specific questions (see the following section), since a librarian can only direct you to different choices—he or she is not responsible for helping you find a topic of study. Remind your children, including those who will be spending time in the library on their own, that the library is a public place and they should respect other patrons.

A research checklist

To maximize your time at the library, it's best to take a systematic approach. To prepare for a visit, ask yourself the following:

- How much information do I need—a few good articles or in-depth coverage of the topic?
- Do I want current or historical information?

Unofficially...
Depending on the particular day, a librarian may be trying to answer as many as 30 questions per hour.
—*How to Use the Library* by Frank Ferrow and Nolan Lushington

Timesaver
Approach your librarian about scheduling a brief orientation to the library for your homeschool group.

- Am I looking for books or periodicals? Journal articles will usually provide the most up-to-date information in science, for example.

- Am I looking for information geared toward the non-specialist, as in an encyclopedia entry, or more scholarly material?

It might also help to begin thinking of the keywords you will use in your research. Other research tools, such as comprehensive bibliographies and database searching, are part of advanced research techniques.

Volunteering at the library

You can help support your local library and gain valuable experience by offering your services as a volunteer. For many homeschoolers, this is a great way to learn even more about the library, while you help others access library services. Opportunities range from storytelling to book repair; contact your local library for available volunteer positions.

Librarians and the needs of homeschoolers

As mentioned previously, librarians are beginning to serve the specific needs of their homeschool patrons. However, this may not be the case in every community.

To help your library better serve homeschoolers:

- Make your needs known. Give your librarian an idea of where to start—do they need to refer homeschoolers to appropriate state laws? Perhaps they could stock curriculum catalogs or textbook samples. Libraries can respond more quickly to direct requests.

- Present your recommendations/requests in writing. A library might be overwhelmed by a deluge of individual requests. Get together with other homeschoolers, and make a formal list of the most important items.

- Volunteer to speak at a library staff or board meeting. In addition to raising awareness of homeschoolers, you can begin to establish relationships with library personnel.

- Invite your librarian and other staff members to attend a meeting of your support group, where everyone can meet and exchange ideas.

Audiotapes/CDs

A remarkable wealth of offerings for children is available on tape. Beyond the obvious choices within music, you can find books on tape and original storytelling, poetry, foreign language instruction, folklore, dramatizations, and more. You can find reviews of audio recordings in professional journals, such as *Booklist,* and the American Library Association (ALA) issues their notable recordings list each year.

Quality children's music and audiotapes are not widely available through retail shops. The library is a good source; you can also order from commercial suppliers (see Appendix B).

The Internet

In a nutshell, computer technology can:

- Encourage children to be self-motivated in researching topics and developing concepts

- Allow you to get a lot closer to your subject

- Make lessons more meaningful

- Allow you and your child to work together as a problem-solving team

Moneysaver
If your community doesn't already have one, create a toy library, where young children can engage in play as a learning experience. Toy libraries may also provide disabled children with quality specially-adapted toys, as well as other resources. For more information, contact the USA Toy Library Association, 1213 Wilmette Ave., Suite 201, Wilmette, IL 60091 or view their Web site: usatla. deltacollege.org/ index.html.

Whether you wish to travel back in time to an ancient Native American village, peer inside the cavity of a frog, or participate in a rainforest survey on the other side of the world, the Internet can take you there.

How to evaluate a Web site

The number of Web sites is multiplying at an incredible rate. Anyone can publish on the Internet, but what are their qualifications? Is the information accurate and or up to date? Unedited and unreviewed, much of the material on the Web may not, in fact, be accurate or appropriate at all. Therefore, it's important for both you and your kids to view sites with a critical eye. (Online safety issues are described later.)

When you evaluate a Web site, use the following basic criteria to guide you:

- Who is the site's author, and what is his or her expertise? Is the Web site affiliated with a major organization or institution?

- Does the site have a stated purpose? Is it trying to entertain, sell, educate, or persuade?

- Is the information useful? Original? When was the site last updated? Does it cite primary research sources?

- Does the site provide information unavailable elsewhere, such as the library?

- Is the site well-designed and easy to navigate, with active links and clear directions for accessing information?

- How does the site relate to your area of study?

- Does the site support opportunities for interaction?

- Has the site received any awards or been favorably reviewed by reputable professionals?

As you and your children search the Web, be wary of those who are highly interested in acquiring information about your children—marketers. Children of middle- and upper-middle income families are considered the most lucrative target market. Strategists employ appealing cartoon characters, contests, and other seductive means to elicit marketing information direct from your home keyboard.

Objectionable sites

Most everyone is aware that pornography (and other objectionable material) is rampant on the Internet. Even if your child isn't likely to be searching for inappropriate sites, the frequency of unintentional exposure demands that you confront this issue.

Banning Internet use would be a shameful waste of a great educational tool. Instead, the American Library Association strongly urges parents to supervise their children's Internet time. Let your child know your views regarding inappropriate material, and help them make informed choices. You may also wish to consider installing a software filtering program that will screen certain Web sites.

Before employing such a program, examine the relative pros and cons. Here is what a software filtering program might offer:

- A custom-editing feature, allowing parents to determine objectionable sites. You may also be able to customize levels of access for multiple users.

I never write for children. It's just that what I have to say is often too difficult for adults to understand.
—Madeleine L'Engle, author of *A Wrinkle in Time*

Timesaver
Very often you can tell a lot about a Web site's content by looking at its address. Commercial sites usually end in .com, sites sponsored by the federal government end in .gov, and college and university Web addresses generally end in .edu. A tilde (~) usually indicates that a page is maintained by an individual.

Unofficially...
An analysis of a major search engine revealed the following subjects had the following number of online pages: sex, 14,896,710; politics, 2,996,060; wine, 2,324,620; dogs, 1,893,440.
—SuperKids, www.superkids. com

- E-mail filtering, which may monitor chatrooms, bounce offensive messages, or prevent personal disclosures.

- Monitoring of Web site activity, including logging reports. Parents may also be able to limit Web access to certain hours of the day.

However, these programs often:

- Aren't compatible with certain Internet service providers

- Don't enable parents to edit a predetermined list of banned sites

- Are ineffective, since new Web pages are added every day

- Reflect the subjective rating criteria of the software publishers

Kids' rules for online safety

Talk to your children about online safety. Post the following rules near the computer:

1. I will not give out personal information such as my address, telephone number, parents' work address/telephone number, or the name and location of my school without my parents' permission.

2. I will tell my parents right away if I come across any information that makes me feel uncomfortable.

3. I will never agree to get together with someone I "meet" online without first checking with my parents. If my parents agree to the meeting, I will be sure that it is in a public place and I will bring my mother or father along.

4. I will never send a person my picture or anything else without first checking with my parents.

5. I will not respond to any messages that are mean or in any way make me feel uncomfortable. It's not my fault if I get a message like that. If I do, I will tell my parents right away so that they can contact the service provider.

6. I will talk with my parents so that we can set up rules for going online. We will decide on the time of day that I can be online, the length of time I can be online, and appropriate areas for me to visit. I will not access other areas or break these rules without their permission.

7. I will not give out my Internet password to anyone (even my best friends) other than my parents.

8. I will be a good online citizen and not do anything that hurts other people or is against the law.

These rules are posted at www.safekids.com. Rules one through six are adapted from the brochure "Child Safety on the Information Highway" by Lawrence J. Magid. Printed copies are available free by calling 800/843-5678.

Tips on choosing children's software

Nothing takes the place of books and hands-on activities. But when the right program is used appropriately, software can help children visualize concepts or reinforce skills that they've learned. For instance, a creative writing program may spark a child's enthusiasm more effectively than a blank

Bright Idea
Locate your computer in a common area in the house. This allows you to periodically check on internet use. A child's bedroom is not the place for a computer.

journal page. Other effective applications are available to teach foreign language, math, and geography, among other subjects.

When choosing software, keep the following points in mind:

- *Compatibility with your computer model and operating system.* Also, find out how much RAM (random access memory) is needed to run the program, as well as how much storage (hard disk space) is required, and any additional features such as sound cards.

- *Your child's particular skills and interests.* The age range printed on the box may be misleading. Many educational programs, for example, have a game element, which may frustrate a child who doesn't have those particular skills.

- *Your purpose.* Are you looking for coverage of a specific subject, drills, or a thinking game?

- *An innovative and engaging presentation.* A good program will present familiar subject matter in a new way.

- *Ease and flexibility of use.* Content should be presented in a variety of activities which are easy to navigate. A child should never feel locked into an activity.

- *Positive feedback.* Feedback should be positive or neutral, nothing that would discourage a child, such as a sad face.

Watch Out!
Manufacturers of educational software may license their titles to video games, which do not offer the same learning value as the original programs.

The market is flooded with "educational" software; before making a purchase, you'll need to do some research. Read several reviews on a specific title and familiarize yourself with the retailer's return policy. You might also consult other homeschoolers about the software they have used. For basic drill and practice lessons, certain shareware programs are less expensive alternatives. (These software programs are available free of charge through e-mail or other electronic media. In exchange for some payment, shareware users may purchase support, documentation, or additional functions.)

Learning activities, creativity, and games

When a child actively searches for answers or engages in a discovery process, learning happens. While computers are useful tools, active learning adds another dimension by engaging all the senses, promoting problem-solving skills and emotional as well as intellectual growth.

Readily available sources contain ideas for hundreds of projects, activities, and games that cover main skills and concepts in all subject areas across all ages. (For a list of resources, see Appendix B.)

Not be confused with the mass-market variety, learning toys are designed to inspire creative play. Your retail outlet may not have a wide selection; some of the best products are only available through specialty stores, catalogs, independent toy shops, museum stores, and children's bookstores. Of course, some of the best toys and activities are those that you create yourself.

These questions may help you choose appropriate learning activities:

- Is it age-appropriate?
- How does the activity relate to your child's specific interest or area of study?

Timesaver
Sometimes a planned learning activity falls short of expectations— experiments fail, children lose interest, or learning concepts are too abstract. Be prepared to scrap what you're doing and move on to something else.

- Is there a purpose? For example, will it help with visual perception, math readiness, or language development?

- What is the relative activity level? Is too much sit-down work required?

- What skills are required? An inappropriate level may leave your child frustrated or bored.

- For the make-your-own variety, are the ideas practical, using readily available materials?

- Can games or projects be done independently? Some may be designed for group or classroom use.

- Are children actively involved, or are you doing all the creating/playing?

Television as a learning tool

Visual media are powerful tools that exert a magnetic attraction over children and adults alike. But when viewing is selective, TV can be an effective educational tool that inspires your child and promotes creativity.

Unofficially...
Children who watched *Sesame Street* and other educational programs have been found to have a higher degree of reading ability.
—University of Kansas, Center for Research on the Influences of Television on Children, 1995

Take the time to gauge your present viewing habits. Keep a chart, listing all TV shows watched in a week. Where is your set located? Research shows that people watch less TV if it's not in the most prominent location in the room. Monitoring your child's viewing may be more difficult if there is a TV in his or her bedroom. According to the American Academy of Pediatrics, parents should limit their children's TV viewing to one to two hours of quality programming a day.

Don't simply allow your kids to watch television. Decide on a specific program, and when it's over, turn off the TV and move on to another activity. Let them help establish the rules, such as times when viewing is allowed, and make the rules as clear as possible. Consider issuing points for chores, which they can cash in for viewing time.

Select programs that encourage reading, further conversation, and activities. Avoid those that promote problem solving through violence and negative behavior. If in doubt, get more information from independent sources, such as KidScore (a system for rating media content sponsored by the National Institute on Media and the Family), or discuss programming with other parents. If you view something that you particularly like or don't like, express your opinions to TV and radio stations. They do listen. Look at Peggy Charon, one woman who founded Action for Children's Television, whose lobbying efforts spurred regulation of children's programming.

Getting the most out of videos

As with television, the judicious use of videos can help support your child's learning. Follow these tips for video-watching:

- Consider the content of all videos you plan to show your children.

- Schedule time for viewing videos together.

- As with television, remain an active viewer; relate what you've seen to hands-on activities or reading a related book.

- Make use of the VCR capabilities of pausing, stopping, and rewinding to reinforce important points or review something the child doesn't understand.

- Build upon your children's interests. Let their enthusiasms dictate your next viewing selection.

Bright Idea
"I use it [the Internet] for myself—a good resource for information. But even high schoolers find the library less time-consuming and easier to use than the Internet."
—Lin McBee, homeschooling mother

Purchasing videos can be expensive. Check the video collection at your library, including the adult section for documentaries and foreign language tapes. Teaching titles, including those specifically intended for homeschooling, are also available. If your homeschool support group hasn't already organized a resource or lending library, consider starting one.

Resources for videos and other homeschool supplies appear in Appendix B.

Exploring community resources

Community resources are important to all homeschoolers. Unschoolers and those following unit studies, particularly, depend on creative use of these opportunities.

Following are just a few options that may be available in your community. Some may be obvious, while others you may not have viewed previously for their educational value:

- Youth organizations (4-H, Girl Scouts, Boy Scouts, YWCA)
- Your church (youth group, choir)
- Book discussion or reading groups
- Volunteer or service opportunities
- Museums
- Historical sites
- Natural areas (bird sanctuaries, state parks, nature centers)
- Specialty shops (demonstrations, workshops)
- Libraries
- Government facilities (local or state agencies, legislative offices, courthouses, police or fire stations)

- Local experts (apprenticeships, private lessons, lectures)
- Bookstores (free events, readings, book signings, workshops)
- Local industry (tours, internships)
- Athletic organizations (competitive leagues, coaching)
- Public and private schools (classes, facilities, special services)
- Local colleges or universities (advanced courses, special programs, libraries, tutors)
- Special-interest organizations (such as chess, bird-watching, stamp collecting, quilt making, and others)
- Nonprofit organizations (mentors)

With increasing numbers of homeschool visitors, several institutions have begun to install special services. In Virginia, for example, Colonial Williamsburg offers Home Educator Weeks, with themed programs designed especially for homeschoolers, including Creating Colonial Citizens, Tools, Trade and Technology, and Choosing Revolution.

Old Sturbridge Village in Sturbridge, Massachusetts, hosts four Homeschool Days, which feature pre-visit materials, hands-on activities, and self-guided tours of Village exhibits. In this outdoor museum that re-creates everyday life in an early 19th-century New England town, homeschoolers participate in special activities, such as decorative arts, apple harvesting, candle making, and reverse glass painting. Even if you don't go to these places, you can still access their Web sites, which frequently offer educational materials.

> **66**
> Last year, a Brazilian student stayed with a homeschooling family. The family put together an incredible Brazilian open house, with maps, Brazilian products, a question and answer session, and food! The children loved it and the student felt very welcome and cherished as they shared their culture.
> —A homeschooling mom in Cedar Rapids
> **99**

Special-interest organizations often present good opportunities for the entire family to participate together. When considering getting involved, ask:

- Is membership open to children?

- Can you get involved as a volunteer? This is a good way to get started before committing to membership. Volunteering also demonstrates your genuine interest.

- Are activities appropriate for families? Or do group meetings consist of adult cocktail parties?

- Does it complement your learning? If your youngster is looking for performing experience, your local theater group may not be appropriate if their activities are centered around classroom lectures on theory.

- Visit a meeting. Check it out with your child to decide if the group is right for you.

Homeschoolers denied access

Homeschoolers may encounter difficulties accessing certain resources, particularly at large institutions, where they may not have an official policy in place to deal with homeschoolers. You may have more luck approaching them formally as a group. If you appear well-organized, they may establish provisions to the benefit of all homeschoolers.

Your options will depend on local resources and their receptivity toward homeschoolers. One family, for example, had difficulty participating in a local parks and recreation program, primarily due to personal biases against homeschooling among the program's leadership.

Still, there are many resources that specifically welcome homeschoolers, such as 4-H. As homeschooling becomes more widely accepted, the diversity of opportunities is sure to increase as well.

Just the facts

- While the Internet can enhance your program, books remain the primary learning resource for homeschoolers. Provide your child a variety of titles and become familiar with your local library. A librarian can assist you with appropriate choices; however, having your child search out his own reading encourages independent learning.

- Educational games, CDs, and tapes are widely available through commercial outlets. With so much out there, you have to be a wise consumer; research what's available and talk to other parents about products they have used.

- There are even more choices on the Internet, and not everything is educational or appropriate for a child. Supervise their time online and have a frank discussion about objectionable sites.

- The outside world offers rich resources for homeschoolers. Explore what's available in your community. Some institutions and organizations may have never dealt with homeschoolers before; consider ways you can bridge that gap.

GET THE SCOOP ON...
The value of play ▪ Fun writing activities
for the whole family ▪ A cool experiment
that's edible too! ▪ How to get the most
from a field trip

More Ideas for Resources and Materials

Some of the best learning resources are those that homeschoolers create themselves. Whether it's soliciting a local craftsperson for a demonstration, tracing historical events through a family genealogy project, or conducting a science experiment in the kitchen, homeschooling can involve creative yet inexpensive ways in which the whole family can learn together.

The community also offers rich learning resources. I'll show you how to take advantage of what's available where you live. Then there are virtual tours that will take you anywhere in the world and even into the solar system. I'll also show you how to find fun, educational freebies that will enhance your children's learning experiences.

Creative learning opportunities at home

While the market is flooded with educational products, a wide choice of curricula, and texts, successful

Chapter 11

Bright Idea
Get together
with your
youngsters in
the kitchen and
test your sense
of smell or taste.
Select various
items and have
the subject wear
a blindfold.

homeschoolers rely on a very important resource: their own ingenuity in creating learning tools and experiences for their children.

Homeschoolers are extraordinarily resourceful in this area, with their children's interests or enthusiasms most commonly leading the way. You can create your own games from scratch and use them to teach math concepts or link simple art activities to reading development. No wonder, then, that many veterans name their favorite homeschooling tools as paper—reams of it—index cards, a dry-erase board, and the like.

Homeschool magazines are also full of good ideas. Talk to other homeschoolers, and peruse the electronic bulletin boards and mailing lists or post a question. You'll find other parents are a great source for trading information and innovative ideas.

Not just playin' around

The educational value of play continues beyond preschool into a child's school-age years. Active, hands-on learning harnesses children's natural energy levels and improves powers of concentration, builds self-esteem and skills, and reinforces the study of related subjects.

Parents should always be careful to choose projects and activities appropriate to the child's level. Five- to seven-year-olds are usually not ready for competitive games—rules are difficult to follow, and losing is too hard. If you find your children in a competitive situation, be your children's ally, giving them insights that will help them improve their play. Children at this age are also particularly sensitive to criticism. They need lots of praise and success.

Play is equally important for children in the middle years, though it becomes much more serious as they test and stretch their growing skills. Games challenge their minds, encourage them to take chances, and increase their skills. They also begin to employ strategy at this age. Games with rules come into full play but allow them to make up their own rules if they choose, or modify existing ones.

Older teens, as well, can derive a great deal from games. A variety of offerings—from Scrabble to card and board games—challenge math, language, and problem-solving skills in entertaining ways.

Guidelines for games

To choose the games that will serve most effectively as tools for learning, consider the following:

- Capitalize on your children's interests. If they love dinosaurs, use pterodactyls and stegosaurs in matching and counting games.

- Don't force children to play. Even if you've taken some time to prepare a game, always allow them the option to change the rules, or participate at another time.

- Let their interest get you started. Stating, "Let's play a math game," may not always catch their attention. Instead, try leaving the cards or playing pieces on the table for them to discover, or ask a question that will intrigue them.

- Don't scold errors or attach moral significance to mistakes. Children will learn to prefer not to participate rather than take a risk of making a wrong move and becoming embarrassed.

- Keep things moving. Don't wait until a child becomes bored; if they begin to lose interest, change the game.

- Avoid a heavy competitive element that emphasizes winners and losers, particularly with young children.

The spirit behind such games should be a spirit of joy, foolishness, exuberance... [Games] give a child a stronger feeling of cause and effect, of one thing leading to another. Also, they help a child to feel that he makes a difference, that he can have some effect on the world around him.
—John Holt, *How Children Learn*

- Don't take it all so seriously that you kill enjoyment of the activity. It's just a game, after all.

Break out of the prepackaged-games mindset and create your own. Many don't require a lot of preparation, such as the classic 20 questions. Or you might try Tangrams, a game that originated in China two thousand years ago:

Tangrams
template

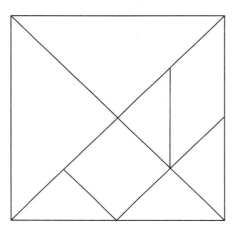

Tangrams help develop spatial visualization skills and problem solving. Appropriate for a range of ages, Tangrams can introduce geometric concepts, congruence, fractions, and the properties of polygons.

Tangram sets are available commercially, or you can easily make your own based on the above diagram. Trace or copy the pattern onto wood or stiff cardboard, and cut the pieces as precisely as possible for the best fit.

In one version of the game, the object is to use your imagination to create silhouettes of recognizable objects using all seven pieces. There are no fewer than 1,600 designs that can be created from a single Tangram set. Each figure you design must use no more and no fewer than the full set of seven pieces.

Portrait of the artist

Most parents and kids don't need much encouragement in this area. Art is fun, and it provides creative opportunities for learning, ties into academic studies, and allows children to try new skills.

Designate a space to encourage creativity, where kids can easily access materials and get a little messy. Older children will particularly appreciate their own space, where they can keep their projects separate from younger siblings and neat parents. A labeled pegboard for hanging their tools and other organizers will help facilitate cleanup and make sure they'll find things when they need them.

In addition to providing appropriate activities, parents can do much to allay frustrations and help their children get the most out of art experiences.

Children in the primary years are full of confidence in their artistic ability. Reinforce this with sincere praise. Teaching them "realistic" drawing is pointless—they're seldom ready and they don't need this type of instruction.

Children in upper elementary grades conclude that their earlier efforts, which once were so satisfying, don't look "real." They may ask, "How do you draw an airplane?" Rather than draw a picture for them, prompt them by discussion to draw the actions or images that they are trying to represent.

With older children, help expand their powers of observation by pointing out how light and distance change the size and color of things we see. Equally important in a child's art education is learning to view art. On trips to museums, discuss the

Unofficially...
The ancient game of Tangrams is believed to have started when a man named Tan accidentally dropped a beautiful ceramic tile on the floor; it shattered into seven pieces. Fiddling with the pieces, he found he could imitate all sorts of shapes: houses, boats, animals...and on it went.

Bright Idea
For a natural wind catcher, string a tree branch with grass and yarn to make a loom. Then weave found objects from nature—leaves, bark, seed pods, feathers, reeds—into the loom and hang it in a breezy place.

many ways artists from around the world and in different time periods have pictured reality.

For information on art as a subject, see Chapter 14.

Crafts

As current art educators recognize the genderizing of the terms art ("what men do") and crafts ("what women do"), distinctions between the two are blurring. Any activities that result in visual products are appropriately referred to as art. Under this more contemporary definition, many families discover artists among their members—Grandma with her afghans, Uncle Joe with his wooden duck decoys, and brother Bob with his customized hotrod. And in terms of homeschooling, so-called craft projects can teach the same things as so-called art projects. Knitting, for example, is very mathematical. Hobby store kits (whether labeled art or craft) that do the thinking for children may be effective time-fillers, but they teach little. You and your child can gather the materials needed for most projects, which will save you money and result in a more artistically successful product.

A visit to folk art and history museums or craft fairs may spark interests in projects the family can enjoy together. Some media include:

- **Art with fibers:** weaving, papier mâché, lanyards, beadwork, sewing, batiking, knitting, dyeing, costuming, and needlepoint

- **Art with paper:** printmaking, stenciling, papermaking, bookbinding, and creating albums

- **Art with other media:** tinwork, candle making, woodcarving, enameling, leather tooling, basket weaving, herb crafts, model making, jewelry, and flower pressing

Sample art project: Woodshop

Woodworking is a great hands-on activity. Promoting both confidence and competence in children, it's a valuable developmental activity and an integral aspect of the Waldorf philosophy of education. Girls and boys alike love to create their own toys and other practical things using real tools and materials.

As with any art activity, show them good examples first to provide them with ideas. Attempting to stimulate creativity by forcing children to generate their own entirely original ideas when they are beginning is poor teaching. Copying in the beginning stages is often a good idea. Children will voluntarily venture into their imaginations once they are familiar with a medium.

Soft woods of quarter- and half-inch widths are ideal, as are balsa wood and plywood. Mills or lumberyards will give away scrap lumber or sell it cheaply.

A low work table with a vise to hold wood in place is a must for sawing or drilling by hand. Young carpenters require more than toy tools, but lighter items than those found in the standard tool chest. A primary-age child can usually handle a lightweight hammer, and a short, but real, cross-cut saw (with proper supervision, always). A hand plane, pliers, screwdriver, screws, file, and hand drill may also be added to their equipment.

Beyond the initial exploring phase of working with tools and wood, young builders can make simple birdhouses, boats, airplanes, and doll's furniture. In the process, kids will develop math skills, learn about spatial relationships, and learn how to stick with a project until it's completed.

Moneysaver
Most knitting shops will provide free lessons if you buy your supplies there. Decorating stores often give away gorgeous wallpaper sample books they no longer need. Ask florists for their discarded flowers. Recycle found objects into interesting jewelry. Save your old magazines. Brown paper bags, flour, and water make great papier mâché.

Bright Idea
The old saying is true: "Measure twice, cut once." Show your children the importance of measuring carefully before they cut. Your finished project is only as good as the care you take with each part of it.

Write it

There are many creative activities that involve writing. The act of writing doesn't have to be solitary—many of the following ideas are great family entertainment. Young ones can get in on the act too: Allow them to dictate their contributions.

As with other activities, the level of success that you achieve derives largely from your approach. Avoid making assignments. Don't stress correctness—grammar and spelling—over substance. Your input should be helpful; discuss their writing, and help them discover what they want to say, while gently guiding them in the direction of proper grammar.

Moneysaver
Take advantage of resources in your community. Does your local home improvement center offer workshops for children?

Even the simplest activity can go a long way in encouraging your child's efforts. Make it fun, and these little exercises will set them on a path of creative adventure and help develop a lifelong skill that will touch their every endeavor.

The hardest part about writing is getting started. Only by doing it will you find what to write about. As Peter Stillman, author of *Families Writing* (second edition Calendar Islands, 1998), says, "Don't wait for the right word, there isn't any."

Here are some ideas to get you started:

- *Start a list.* Short on topics to write about? Brainstorm by creating lists—your favorite sayings, the most embarrassing moment in your life, and so on.

- *Keep a journal.* Journaling is a good habit that helps people visualize and recollect events and reason things out. Consider keeping a family journal; it's a good way for parents and children to communicate and share their feelings.

- *Write letters.* Become a regular correspondent, and ask your children to add their postscripts. Encourage them to write letters of their own, to relatives and others in their lives—even to imaginary ones, such as the Tooth Fairy.

- *Tell stories.* Build a story in round-robin fashion, going around the dinner table, with each member adding his or her contribution.

- *Publish your work.* Homeschooling journals and newsletters often provide opportunities for young contributors.

- *Rewrite a fable or popular story.* Try it from another point of view, such as the villain's. For Humpty Dumpty, tell it from the wall's perspective.

- *Compose group poetry.* One person starts with a line of verse, someone else creates the next line, starting with the last word from the preceding line, and so on.

- *Create an album.* For all those old snapshots lying around, compose silly captions and create an annotated album.

- *Create your own Web page.* This is a great project for the entire family. Begin by outlining your ideas on paper. A Web page can center on you, your family, or your hobbies. How about including information on homeschooling? You will need to know HTML, the computer language used to write a Web page, or use a Web page editing program. You'll need to design the visual presentation and incorporate graphics. Your finished page can

You always find things you didn't know you were going to say, and that is the adventure of writing.
—author John Updike

then be uploaded to the Internet. Space may be provided by your server or you can acquire space by signing up with an online community.

- ***Write your own greeting cards.*** Kids can compose an original message or a poem. Solicit their contributions for a holiday family newsletter.

- ***Find and post a quote of the week.*** You can suggest a theme, or ask them to extract an interesting quote or passage from their studies.

- ***Give your children a word, any word.*** Their challenge is to write it in a way that conveys its meaning.

Tying history to your family tree

Family history is an ideal subject for homeschooling that incorporates several valuable elements. Such study enables kids to learn research techniques (such as interviewing), helps them develop a personal relationship with historical events, strengthens family ties, and encourages writing skills.

Homeschooling mom Cheryl Hall utilizes family history in her program. Her children keep genealogy booklets, which they work on periodically. They also relate ancestors to a timeline, discussing where they fit in and the times and conditions in which they lived. "One of my ancestors," says Hall, "was a famous settler in our area." The family visits his restored home at least once a year.

"Also, one new thing we are planning on doing this year is to 'float pumpkins,'" Hall says. "One ancestor from around the early 1700s lived near a pond and grew pumpkins. When harvest time came they would wait for a blustery day and then put the pumpkins on the pond and float the pumpkins

Bright Idea
Traditions help define your family, provide stability, and keep generations in contact with one another. What are some traditions that your own family has started?

across the pond with the wind blowing them to get them to market. We plan on putting them in the wading pool in the backyard. Just a simple idea in memory of this ancestor."

How to discover your past

To begin a study of your family history, start by interviewing your family. Grandparents, in particular, will enjoy sharing their memories. You might ask:

- What are the origins of the family name? Have any names become traditional in the family as they have been passed down through generations?

- Where did our ancestors come from?

- What is our family's medical history? Discuss why this is important.

- How did your parents or grandparents come to meet and marry?

- How does our family celebrate holidays? Are there special traditions?

- What are the stories that everyone's heard dozens of times?

- Is there a notorious or infamous character in the family? Are the stories about him or her true?

- Are there any family heirlooms? What is their significance?

- Can you identify individuals in family photographs, and provide information about their significance?

- Are there any special family recipes? How were they passed down?

In addition to basic facts and figures, anecdotes will make your story more lively and interesting.

Watch Out!
If you are publishing a family history, take care not to harm anyone. Don't include stories or information that might shame or otherwise hurt a family member or their loved ones.

Traditionally, genealogies primarily focused on a family's highest achievements. Expand your coverage to provide a more comprehensive, personal portrait, and don't forget to include the antics of your more colorful relations.

With genealogy so popular these days, numerous resources can assist you in your search. Various guidebooks describe the different avenues of research, from church and military records to immigration papers and ship's passenger lists. Several software programs provide templates for family trees and other types of presentation.

The value of dramatic play

Appropriate for young and old alike, dramatic play allows participants to work out their feelings and emotions. Children can gain experience with social interactions, negotiate turns at playing roles, and learn to use language in meaningful and creative ways. Dramatic opportunities can also be used to further study of other subjects, particularly history.

Puppet shows are simple to set up and popular for a range of ages. The activity exercises the skills used in telling a story; the ability to recall the characters and the order of events support reading comprehension. Puppet shows can also encourage shy children, who may find it easier to talk through a puppet.

Props can enrich the make-believe play of young children, and they don't have to be expensive. Recycle a toy cash register, play money, old clothing, empty cans and bottles, tickets, a briefcase, old checkbooks, and so forth. Kids will use their imaginations to create their own props, which can be the most practical. As one teacher advises, "a cardboard box that's playable is preferable to a castle that must be cared for with fear."

Bright Idea
Parents can offer suggestions for dramatic activities, but should avoid playing director.

Older children and teens enjoy performing monologues, scenes, and short plays. They might also be interested in learning about the production aspect of theater or film, including script writing, set design and lighting, and other production techniques. Other opportunities in the performing arts may be available through your local community theater (many of which welcome volunteers). Many homeschooling groups have organized their own performances and drama clubs; ask your state network about what's available near you.

> Learn to teach yourself.
> —Anonymous graffiti

Kitchen science

Are you aware that you already possess a well-equipped science laboratory? Your kitchen has a supply of water for preparing solutions, studying reactions, and cultivating specimens; a source of heat, such as burners on the stove, for speeding up reactions; cold storage (a refrigerator), for slowing down reactions; and a supply of ingredients. Many experiments can be done at home, and some you can even eat, like this rock candy recipe. Note that this activity requires adult supervision. (For more on cooking with kids, see Chapter 12.)

Materials:

1 cup water	Food coloring (optional)
A small saucepan	
2 cups granulated sugar	A wooden spoon
	Flavoring extract (optional)
A heavy cord or some candy sticks	
	A glass jar
Additional sugar	

Directions:

1. Place the water in the saucepan and pour the sugar into the water. Heat the water and

sugar over medium heat, stirring with a wooden spoon until the sugar melts. Keep adding sugar until it will no longer dissolve in the water (some grains of sugar will remain on the bottom of the saucepan). This is a saturated solution.

2. Remove the pot from the stove and let it cool until it is just warm. (For the biggest crystals, heat the saturated solution a second time, then cool.)

3. Add food coloring or flavoring to the mixture as desired. Pour the liquid into the jar. Tie one end of a piece of heavy cord around the middle of a pencil. Place the pencil over the top of the glass jar, suspending the cord in the liquid. You can also suspend candy sticks.

4. Crystals will begin to form in a few hours. After a few days you may have to break and carefully remove the crust of crystals that form on the surface so that water can continue to evaporate. Leave undisturbed for up to a week.

After you have grown some sugar crystals, take a magnifying glass and compare them to the crystals of granulated sugar. Are they the same size and shape? How do sugar crystals compare to salt crystals?

Backyard science

Some of the best hands-on science activities take place in your own backyard. Homeschoolers raise animals, gauge weather, grow plants, and compost organic materials, among other projects that teach important concepts and spark a youngster's interest in the process of science.

Here's a backyard science experiment that's a lot of fun. Volcanoes are always fascinating to children, and building a working model is a great way to launch a study.

A volcano is produced over time as heat and pressure build up. While it would be impossible to recreate this process, a homemade version will help you visualize a volcano erupting with flowing lava.

You will need:

An adult helper

A shallow box or pan

For the volcano:

Clay, soil, or sand to create a small mountain

An empty soup or similar-size can

$^1/_4$ cup water

About a tablespoon of baking soda

A few drops of red food coloring

A few drops of liquid dishwashing detergent

$^1/_4$ cup vinegar

Directions:

1. Place the box or pan on the ground outside.

2. Build a mound around the can using clay, soil, or sand to build your version of a small mountain.

3. Pour the water into the can. Stir in the baking soda, food coloring, and detergent.

4. Pour in the vinegar and stand back for the eruption!

Here's how it works: The vinegar and baking soda combine to make carbon dioxide. This is a gas that is very light and causes the mixture to bubble and erupt.

Bright Idea
Take a blank calendar and create a weather journal. Use a simple gauge, such as a bucket, to measure rainfall. Chart the sunrise and sunset, changes in vegetation, and behavior of wildlife, and observe whether the days are getting shorter or longer.

You can also bake volcano cookies, using sugar cookie dough. Have your child make mounds with the dough, filling the top with strawberry jam. While the cookies bake, watch through the oven window as the jam bubbles over.

Compare these exercises to an actual volcanic eruption. Here are some related activities:

- Identify three kinds of volcanoes and the different mountains they form.

- Do some research on what causes an actual volcano to erupt.

- Write your account of a virtual trip to a volcanic area.

- Discover how volcanoes can be constructive as well as destructive forces. For example, the electrical energy generated from the Geysers geothermal field in northern California can meet the present power consumption of the city of San Francisco.

- Describe the changes caused by the 1980 eruption of Mount St. Helens.

- Research some other major volcanic eruptions in history.

- Find and mark active volcanoes on a world map.

- Learn about the Ring of Fire.

- Find out how the study of volcanic phenomena relates to our understanding of the earth.

Out and about: Field trips

Field trips are great opportunities to extend learning outside the home and break up the "school" routine. They're also a chance to get together with other homeschoolers and families with similar interests.

Such excursions needn't involve extensive travel; there are plenty of opportunities right in your neighborhood. See Chapter 10 for a list of community resources.

While traveling in a group can be fun, make sure the number of participants is manageable and appropriate to the setting. If you're not sure, inquire first, or make an initial visit with just your family.

To get the most out of a field trip, keep in mind the following:

- Preplan. Consider the purpose of the trip well beforehand; do any reading or other preparation that will enable your child to get the most out of the event. Consider questions you might want to ask.

- Make any necessary arrangements, such as group reservations, booking a docent (speaker), or purchasing advance tickets. If you're with others, be sure to let the site know the age range of your group, so they can tailor their presentation accordingly.

- Plan ahead for any meals, and carry a supply of snacks and water.

- Take any necessary equipment, including a camera and film (check to see whether photography is allowed), a notebook or sketchbook and a pencil or pen, a tape recorder, or binoculars.

- Plan an after-trip discussion.

- Write a note thanking anyone who hosted or assisted on the trip.

Moneysaver
Save by traveling with a group. Inquire in advance about family or group discounts on transportation and admission. Pot-luck picnics are also practical and a lot of fun.

Janet Griffin, who lives in Cimarron, New Mexico, is a homeschooling mother who knows how to use her local resources. "Our area is rich with history and geographical features," she says. "We have the only known Tyrannosaurus Rex footprints in the world here on Philmont. The National Zoo in D.C. has a cast of one of them, but we have the originals right here in Philmont. We have ancient cliff dwellings and petroglyphs within a couple of miles of our home. The Santa Fe trail runs through our neighbor's backyard, and Kit Carson's stage stop and home are a few miles down the road. This time of year, we go out at dusk and track elk herd. They are mating this time of year, and we sit and listen to them bugle, and watch the males fight for their mates. We have to take the public school children in town to see these wonders on Boy Scout or Youth Group outings, because they never see them as part of their school activities. My 14-year-old son is a docent at one of the Philmont museums, and he has gained so much knowledge and self-confidence."

Virtual Field Trips

Even if you don't live near a dinosaur site, you can still visit exciting places. Via a computer and a phone line, virtual field trips can whisk you off to explore distant locales, providing educational information, teaching ideas, and related activities. Following is just a sample of trips you can take with your family.

Americana

Williamsburg, Virginia: www.history.org

> Site includes tips on planning your visit, including educational information for home educators.

Welcome to the White House for Kids: www. whitehouse.gov

> A fun tour geared just for youngsters, with facts on White House kids and pets. Send an e-mail to the President.

Virtually Hawaii: www.satlab.hawaii.edu/space/hawaii/

> NASA images of Hawaii that teach about the islands, including image puzzles to unscramble, and the meanings of colors that appear in infra-red pictures.

Time travel

The Underground Railroad: www.national geographic.com/features/99/railroad/

> Take the journey of a Maryland slave of the 1850's to freedom in the North.

Machu Picchu, Home of the Ancients: www. shastahome.com/machu-picchu/guide/html

> Explore the ancient culture of the Inca.

The Catacombs of Paris: http://metalab.unc.edu/vm/paris/cata

> Detail images of the subterranean cemetery.

Seven Wonders of the Ancient World: http://ce.eng.usf.edu/pharos/wonders/

> An info-tour and related links, from the statue of Zeus at Olympia to the great pyramid of Giza.

Around the world

The Tower of London Virtual Tour: www. toweroflondontour.com/

> Features a specially-designed tour for kids, including a quiz and a fun maze.

Bolivia Virtual Field Trip: www.care.org/virtual_trip/bolivia/

A pictorial and cultural exploration, sponsored by the relief agency CARE.

Online Tour of Russia: www.cs.toronto.edu/~mes/russia

A photo collection arranged by region, including Moscow, Siberia and the Far East of Russia.

The Great Wall of China: www.chinavista.com/travel/greatwall/greatwall.htm

The history of the structure, and photos of representative sections.

Science and geography

Scientific American Frontiers—Destination: Galapagos Islands: www.pbs.org/saf/voyage.html

The island home of some of the world's most interesting and exotic wildlife, with video clips and expedition journals, all specifically designed for educators.

Volcano World Virtual Field Trips: http://volcano.und.nodak.edu/vwdocs/kids/vrtrips.html

Volcanoes around the world, including a 360-degree view of Mt. St. Helens.

Kelp Forest: www.nationalgeographic.com/monterey/ax/primary%5Ffs.htm

Climb inside a submersible for a virtual dive in California's Monterey Bay.

The Nine Planets—A Multimedia Tour of the Solar System: http://seds.lpl.arizona.edu/nineplanets/nineplanets

A trip into space, with pictures, sound, and movies.

Museums

Metropolitan Museum of Art: www.metmuseum.org/

> Searchable site with more than 3,500 works from the Met's collections. Of special interest are the "explore and learn" activities.

A-Bomb Museum: www.csi.ad.jp/ABOMB/index.htm/

> Facts about the A-Bomb, voices of survivors, reader contributions, and a tour of the Hiroshima Peace Park.

Freebies!

Some educational materials are available for free, or for a nominal cost, such as the cost of a self-addressed stamped envelope. Consider what you can actually use, and make sure to follow any instructions, such as submitting your request on a postcard or providing postage. The Internet offers plenty of goodies, too, including downloadable lesson plans, worksheets, and interactive games. Some offers may require you to fill out a survey or provide other information.

A good source is the clearinghouse for government publications, the Consumer Information Center: Dept. WWW, Pueblo, CO, 81009,1/888-878-3256, Web site: www.pueblo.gsa.gov/. The Web site Home Schooling Daily (www.infinet.com/~baugust/) features links to freebies sites, including one just for teachers, as well as several pages of freebies selected and screened for use by home-schoolers.

Just the facts

- Games can be fun, effective supplements to learning, but make sure you find the right match for your child's interests and abilities, and avoid those that overly emphasize competition.

- Journaling, simple crafts, and home experiments prove that learning materials don't have to be expensive or carry the label "educational."

- Incorporate writing into fun family activities, and you'll inspire your children to further explore and develop this lifelong skill.

- Family histories are ideal homeschooling projects, linking personal stories with events and strengthening family ties.

- Field trips, virtual and otherwise, prove that homeschool learning extends beyond the four walls.

GET THE SCOOP ON...
Getting your kids to help around the house
- Instilling values at home and beyond
  - Cultivating learning by gardening
    - Entrepreneurial kids

Learning Life Skills

Chapter 12

A dapting life skills in education is nothing new. Since Maria Montessori established the first Children's House in 1907, her widely respected teaching methods have recognized this important aspect of learning. In fact, the first of her five "subjects," Practical Life Activities, engages young children in everyday skills, from sweeping the floor to buttoning one's jacket.

If you're like most homeschooling parents, you want your children to learn more than just academic subjects: You want them to learn how to get things done, manage a home, make the right choices, take care of the community, nurture a business. Those are the things you need to do to be successful in your homeschooling efforts as well, and it requires an ongoing balancing act of all of the elements of your life. To achieve such a balance, you need a team effort.

With some organization, day-to-day activities provide a regular rhythm to life that provides a stable environment, optimal for learning. In this chapter, I'll show you how to get the whole team involved by delegating the household chores to each member of the family. Involving your children in these kinds of activities around the house—and in voluntary activities in the community—can teach them the importance of interdependency and responsibility, as well as promote new skills—all qualities that will serve them well beyond their "school" years.

66 Around the home

Since labor occupies most of us nearly one-third of our lives, a good work attitude contributes to our happiness. To instill the joy of working early in life is a very special accomplishment.
—Raymond Moore, *Home-Grown Kids: A Practical Handbook for Teaching Your Children at Home*

99

It stands to reason that housework and other chores will become a greater issue when everyone's living and working together "24/7." While everyone's standards of cleanliness may vary, applying some degree of organization will enable you to run your home more efficiently, which can positively influence your homeschooling.

Why can't I get my family to cooperate?

This is the 64-dollar question. Today, it's usually Mom who shoulders the greatest responsibility for managing the house, while many children are excused from even the most minor duties, such as picking up after themselves.

So how can parents arrange a workable solution? Families need to realize the importance of sharing the load, that a well-functioning home—achieved through teamwork—benefits all. When properly demonstrated to them, kids will understand that getting things done around the house leaves everyone happier and free to engage in other activities. They may resent busy work, but if given a chance, children like to know that they are needed and appreciated.

Moreover, a child acquires major life skills through involvement in the home. When established early, good work habits foster the qualities of responsibility and self-direction that cross over into their studies and all other aspects of life.

Call a family meeting

An effective tool to improve cooperation in a household is the family meeting. This presents a regular opportunity for the group to make plans, coordinate schedules, discuss any issue, and, oh yes, assign chores.

You might consider these ideas for your family meeting:

- Post an agenda on the fridge or another central location.

- Brainstorm ideas for how to make your home a better place. Encourage everyone's input on improvements or other suggestions.

- Report on the status of ongoing projects.

- Plan upcoming trips or activities.

- Distribute allowances.

- Work on resolving any issues that have arisen.

- Motivate attendance by serving food or a snack.

- Appoint someone to take notes.

- Take turns leading the meeting.

Try to hold meetings regularly. Before concluding a meeting, schedule the next one. Meetings don't have to be too formal—perhaps you're already having this sort of discussion over dinner. Whatever format you choose, any regular gathering is a worthwhile opportunity to promote communication and household organization.

Pitching in: How to get kids to do their chores

While "House Beautiful" standards may be unattainable, it's possible to improve on home management. The secret is to know how to motivate your children and your spouse.

Watch Out!
When a parent says, "I've told you a million times," a child might hear, "I'm a bad person." When a parent says, "Let's finish this together and go skating later," a child will hear, "We're a team at work and play."

Bright Idea
Are the kids arguing over whose turn it is to play a video game? Did a child promise to pick up her things in five minutes? Time to bring out your kitchen timer!

You've probably already realized that barking orders and telling them "Because Mom says so" doesn't really work. To maximize cooperation, involve your family in developing mutual standards. During the family meeting, discuss what needs to be done. Ask for their input and be prepared to compromise.

Here are some other tips for getting them to help:

■ **Be positive.** Such comments as "Your room looks like a pigpen" won't go far to inspire anyone.

■ **Take time to explain how taking care of the house will improve their lives.** "If the house is cleaner, you can have friends over." "The toys need to be put away or they might get lost, or start to clutter the house."

■ **Give them appropriate consequences.** For example, "We can't start dinner until all the toys are put away." If you use this method, be committed to doing what you say, or your kids will learn that they can ignore you.

■ **Set them up for success.** Allow children to work in accordance with their skills and talents by letting them figure out how best to complete a job. Be certain that assigned chores are appropriate to their capabilities, and give them a hand if necessary.

■ **Offer limited choices.** "Do you want to put the toy on the top shelf or the bottom shelf?"

■ **Be flexible.** Don't be so rigid about chore time that you miss out on other opportunities. If children want to trade or rotate chores, allow them to do so.

- **Be careful about asking older children to supervise younger siblings.** Older children may not have the skills or patience to work with new learners, and young ones can get frustrated.

- **Always praise a child's sincere efforts, no matter the outcome.** Don't worry about efficiency: Thank them, then take the opportunity to help guide their efforts in the future.

- **Recognize the importance of a child's contribution to the team effort.** "Thanks, Noah, for helping me chop the vegetables. Your work helped me serve dinner on time."

- **Break out the gold stars.** These little rewards go a long way, and a chart or checklist is a handy way for kids to keep track of their assignments.

- **Provide special rewards for the accomplishment of big tasks.** "When the trash is taken out and you've raked the lawn, we'll all go out for ice cream."

Here are just a few ideas of what kids can be expected to do, according to age (with your direction and supervision):

- **Age 2–3:** Pick up and put away toys, feed pets, sweep the floor, place clothing in the washer and dryer, stir ingredients.

- **Age 4:** Empty wastebaskets, pick up around the house, scrub vegetables, get the mail, sort laundry.

- **Age 5:** Set the table, take out garbage, vacuum, fold clothes, strip beds.

- **Age 6:** Clean vegetables, rake leaves, put away groceries, hose walkways, empty dishwasher.

Bright Idea
So you think your household has descended too far into chaos? Start with a plan to clean thoroughly one room a day, or, if the budget allows, consider hiring someone to do a one-time thorough cleaning.

Timesaver
Give everyone a watering container and a section of the garden or house to water. Do this together, and you'll be done in no time.

Watch Out!
Be careful not to assign tasks to follow traditional gender roles. Boys can iron and fold clothes, just as girls can wash cars or take out the trash. They will need all of these skills if they ever live alone, even for a short time, as an adult.

- **Age 7–8:** Take phone messages, water the garden, clean refrigerator, wash the dog, help plan menus.

- **Age 9–10:** Mop and polish floors, weed garden, cook from simple recipes, paint, change bedding.

- **Age 11 and up:** Supervise younger children, clean bathrooms, mow lawn, iron, shovel snow, perform basic home repairs. (While their chores around the home may be expanded, many teens also start to earn their own money outside the home.)

Reality check

Doing too much housework may be just as damaging as too little. Don't go overboard with assignments, and always assign only those tasks that are age-appropriate.

First and foremost, remember to keep it all in perspective. While you should be able to maintain some level of family standards, realize that it won't all ever get done. With so much going on in the house—fascinating projects and works in progress—real learning, it seems, is not a neat process. So, for now, embrace your home's "lived-in" look.

Everybody into the kitchen!

While the family may balk at doing the laundry or other duties, you may find it easier to get them involved in the kitchen. Children love engaging in an activity where they have power over the process and the product. They also enjoy the camaraderie of the kitchen and the feeling that they are contributing to the group. In addition to practical cooking skills, children learn other things, such as where applesauce comes from, what makes bread rise, and

"
A homeschooling discussion board post: "I would really love a clean house but I just can't bring myself to completely do it since we like to do so many other things. My family is difficult to motivate in this area and I still struggle with it all the time.
—Anne Heerdt-Wingfield
"

how to make healthy choices. A recent study published in the *Journal of Nutrition* found that preschoolers who were more involved in food-related activities had significantly higher nutrition awareness scores.

Cooking can help teach:

- **Math skills.** Even younger children can learn the basics through measuring, weighing, sorting, and estimating ingredients.

- **Science.** Young cooks make observations, experiment, and draw conclusions. Let their questions—why are there bubbles in bread?—direct an exploration of food processes.

- **Language skills.** Read and follow recipes and charts in sequential order, share books about food and cooking, expand vocabulary.

- **Creativity.** Allow children to make choices about foods and how to arrange and combine them. Select recipes that allow children to be creative.

- **Nutrition.** Use recipes that exemplify healthy eating, and use a cooking project to discuss how nutrition relates to health.

- **Life skills.** There's value in letting them participate in other aspects of the process, such as meal planning and selecting recipes. Grocery shopping, for example, can exercise skills in money management.

Living a moral life

With little guidance from adults, the decline of moral literacy is reflected in our youth, many of whom are growing up not knowing the difference between right and wrong or understanding what

This is a constant struggle for me too, but it is getting better...Try just keeping the living room clean—or for me, I care more about the bathrooms and kitchen. Realize you are doing something very important for your child and let that be your focus.
—Stephanie Holland

Watch Out!
Safeguard your kitchen for any cooking that will involve young children, and always supervise. Face pot handles toward the center of the stove; have children sit while cutting; and put them in a higher seat or lower the work surface, so they can participate with ease.

conscience is. While school systems grapple with administering "morality education," experts acknowledge that children learn these values primarily from the most important models in their lives: their parents.

Children gain "moral intelligence," not so much through formal instruction, but rather from the day-to-day interaction with and observation of their parents. "You can read Kant and Hegel and the latest expert on child morality," says psychologist Robert Coles, "but the ultimate test is not what people preach, it is how they act. It is one thing to talk a good line; it's another to live a good and honorable life."

In addition to setting a good example, you can help your child develop moral intelligence in a number of ways, including the following:

- Praise and reward your child for exhibiting hard work, perseverance, kindness, or other attributes.

- Take action with bad behavior (for example, rude requests will be ignored).

- Allow children the opportunity to make moral choices of their own accord, before directing them.

- Take the opportunity to reinforce virtues even in difficult situations. When your child confesses to causing a stain on your new sofa, reward his honesty and his assuming responsibility for his actions.

- Share and discuss moral issues as they occur in your lives.

Tell your children stories that involve characters who exemplify and encourage emulation of desirable traits of character, such as honesty, civility, courage, perseverance, loyalty, self-restraint, compassion, tolerance, and fairness. Sources can include history, fiction, current events, or stories from your personal experience. Use these tales as a springboard for further discussion. What choices did the character have? What challenges did the character face? Consider the consequences of the opposite choice. Which is helpful, and which hurts? Help your children imagine themselves in the same situation. Continue your discussion of moral issues as they relate to daily life.

Extending care and concern beyond the home

The values of responsibility and concern, passed on through the family, should flow naturally through the rest of life

As we keep our commitments, make amends for our errors, and help maintain our environment, day to day we are modeling the Golden Rule for our children. Even a very young child will come to understand and exemplify consideration for others, despite the selfish behavior that occurs around him.

Volunteering

Much of our society depends on the philanthropic spirit of its citizens. Today, however, the concept of charity is challenged by our capitalistic culture, and many, particularly the young, are being excused from making sacrifices or otherwise responding to the needs that surround them.

Homeschoolers are keeping alive the tradition of volunteerism, with many families implementing service as an integral part of their curriculum.

Unofficially...
A recent poll found that experiences in a person's youth influenced their adult volunteering behavior. A majority of those who give as adults participated in youth groups and religious organizations, and one or both of their parents set an example by volunteering when they were young.
—Independent Sector, 1999 survey

The benefits of service

Volunteering provides opportunities to:

- Put into practice the ideas and skills your child has been learning at home. If, for example, your child is learning about measurements, take your child to a charity resale shop to help size used clothing.

- Gain experience outside the home. Volunteering expands your opportunities for learning. Teens in particular can learn valuable new skills and explore a future field of employment. If your child is interested in social work, for example, putting in two mornings a week at the office of a nonprofit organization is a good introduction to that arena. Such an experience can help your child to decide if the field is or isn't the right work for him or her.

- Earn important credentials. Volunteering may lead to letters of recommendation or contribute to a resume. This is particularly important when homeschoolers seek a job or admission to college.

- Meet and work with a variety of people. Unifying as a team working toward a common goal can be a rewarding social experience that will serve children throughout their lives.

To maximize the volunteer experience parents may wish to consider their child's personality and level of maturity in choosing an appropriate volunteer job. For example, those planning to work in a shelter for the needy must be prepared to deal with homeless people who have not bathed and who are suffering. Also help your child maintain realistic goals of what they are to accomplish, and what they can expect to receive in the exchange.

So many ways to help

If your community has a Volunteer Center, you can start by visiting this office to find out about local nonprofit agencies and current volunteer needs. You can also find volunteer opportunities through local community centers and religious communities, or listings in your local newspaper or on the Web.

You can find nonprofit agencies in the phone book or in the newspaper. If you find one that interests you, call and ask to speak to the volunteer coordinator. Tell this person about your interests. If your child is interested in volunteering, set up a meeting between the volunteer coordinator and your child. Support your child's volunteer work by making sure that your child understands his or her responsibilities while volunteering. Help your child to evaluate his or her volunteer experiences after they happen so that you can help your child see the value of the work and make future experiences more meaningful.

Consider your family's schedule before committing any time. But remember, giving just two, three, or four hours a week is a great contribution. While many volunteer opportunities require little or no experience, you may wish to offer any special skills that you have, such as a craft or hobby you or your child can teach to preschoolers.

It isn't necessary to join an existing program or organize your own. Look around and you'll find ways to contribute. Pick up litter along the shoreline or at your local park. Do you sing or play a musical instrument? You might perform for residents at the hospital or a nursing home. Or reach out on a personal level and offer to help a family new to the

You're either part of the Solution, or part of the Problem.
—Eldridge Cleaver

neighborhood. Perhaps an elderly neighbor might need some assistance with shopping. There are so many ways to help.

Volunteer vacations

Teens or adults looking for some adventure might consider international voluntary service projects, which welcome individuals from different countries to participate in a variety of projects around the world. While a few programs recruit highly skilled professionals (such as medical personnel), most require no previous experience.

Volunteers may devote as little as two weeks or up to several months assisting with the construction of houses or schools in underprivileged communities, renovation of historic places, or preservation of parklands and natural resources. Generally, volunteers are expected to pay their travel costs and possibly a nominal administration fee. Room and board are usually provided by the host organization.

Organizations in the United States that sponsor these programs include the Council on International Educational Exchange (CIEE), Service Civil International, and Volunteers for Peace. International service projects are also directed by churches and other religious organizations.

Still other exciting opportunities include field research and archaeological digs. Participants get to visit unusual settings, where the excitement of new discoveries is always a possibility. These experiences usually don't come cheap. In addition to covering their traveling and living expenses, volunteers are expected to pay an additional fee, which represents a share of the project's overall costs. These expenses, however, are usually tax-deductible.

Timesaver
With time-efficient schedules, which are also more flexible, home-schoolers are well-positioned to adapt a range of service activities.

Those interested can contact Earthwatch, Archaeology Abroad, or The Archaeological Institute of America, which produces an Archaeological Fieldwork Opportunities Bulletin.

Growing a garden

What form of recreation is enjoyed by 68 million Americans? Today, more people than ever are digging in the dirt, planting seeds, and tending flower beds. In fact, for the last two decades it has been America's number one hobby.

The act of gardening is a treat to the senses. To crumble good soil between your bare fingers, hear the glorious sound of birds greeting the spring, take in the rich sight and smell of a garden in full bloom—it is pure pleasure.

Gardening is a worthwhile activity for its own sake, but it has the added benefit of producing something to show for your efforts, whether it be a display of beautiful flowers or a season's worth of fresh, healthful produce for your family's table. Beyond your own home, a garden can help beautify your neighborhood, which will be particularly appreciated if you live in a city. Plantings also create a haven for butterflies, birds, and other fun-to-watch wildlife.

Cultivate learning

Gardening is not just a pleasurable hobby, but a terrific learning opportunity for all ages. By growing plants, you can cultivate:

■ **Inquiry and problem solving.** Even failed experiments give gardeners opportunities from which to learn.

■ **Persistence and patience.** These traits are a natural outcome of the activity, which is a process.

> **❝**
> To own a bit of ground, to scratch it with a hoe, to plant seeds, and watch the renewal of life—this is the commonest delight of the race, the most satisfactory thing a man can do.
> —Charles Dudley Warner, 1870
> **❞**

Bright Idea
If you grow your
own food, you
will no doubt
have surplus,
which you can
share with
neighbors or take
to a food bank
for distribution.

- **Living demonstrations of how plants function, survive, and interact with other elements of the ecosystem.** Children can learn other core life science concepts as well. Gardening, like all hands-on activities, makes it easier to understand "big concepts," which are also made more meaningful.

- **Learning over a range of levels.** An eight-year-old, for example, might become aware of the diversity of seed shapes and sizes; while a teenager can understand how seeds have evolved over millions of years to survive in a wide range of environmental conditions.

- **Therapeutic and healing benefits.** Horticultural therapy has been proven effective in treating many people with a range of disabilities, including developmental and physical disabilities and sensory impairment.

- **Awareness of the environment.** The act of gardening demonstrates the impact of human intervention, and offers choices in the methods and materials that we use. Resource management is achieved through composting and recycling waste.

- **Enrichment over the spectrum of curricular subjects.** An international garden, for instance, could link to an exploration of cultures, foods, and crops of other countries, and makes geography study more meaningful. Growing herbs might inspire a study of medicinal plants.

All gardeners are attuned to the weather. Take the opportunity to examine the change of seasons, how climates vary throughout the world, and how shifts in sunlight, warmth, and moisture affect living things.

Suggestions for growing things

For optimal success, start with a small project. Try a container garden or planter, for example, before attempting a full-scale garden, if you've had little previous experience. You can also do the following:

- If you have an existing yard or garden, devote a little space to the kids. Allowing them to just poke around in the dirt or work alongside you may spark their interest.

- Use appropriately sized equipment. Scaled-down gardening tools are available at any garden center. Another must: properly fitting gloves.

- Plant children's favorites: huge sunflowers; bean-pole teepees; plants that grow underground, such as peanuts and potatoes; and fragrant flowers and herbs, such as chocolate or pineapple mint.

- Compost with worms. Kids love these wriggly "pets." Feed them kitchen garbage and use worm castings to fertilize your plants.

- Grow around a theme. Plant a garden to attract butterflies or feed birds—this can introduce the study of plant reproductive strategies or plant/animal interdependence. In a "three-sisters" garden (corn, beans, and squash) children can learn how a particular culture devised this planting system to maximize crop and food production.

- Explore your horticultural heritage. Interview your relatives and gather other information about the plant foods significant to their culture. Research your local area and learn about the food crops that were grown by early settlers.

Timesaver
The National Garden Association offers a variety of helpful resources, including a teacher's newsletter, "Growing Ideas: A Journal on Garden-Based Learning"; a Youth Garden Grant Program; and a catalog of teaching tools, from worm bins to hydroponics kits.

Moneysaver
Fancy bins aren't necessary for successful composting. Instead, dig a hole or nail together a few scrap boards to form a frame. Throw in all organic waste: grass clippings, leaves, and all kitchen scraps, except meat. The finished compost, black and crumbly, is the best fertilizer for your garden.

- Study history through plants. Did you know that the humble potato helped fuel the Industrial Revolution? Discover how plants influence culture, social structure, and other major events in world history.

- Join a community garden, or start one. Begin with your homeschool group or cultivate partnerships with other members of the community, such as garden clubs, schools, businesses, and individuals.

Grow a famous or historic tree

Would you like to grow a seedling from the white oak tree that shades the birthplace of Abraham Lincoln? How about planting a sycamore linked to Susan B. Anthony, or an offspring of George Washington's holly tree?

In a unique program, American Forests, a non-profit organization dedicated to the preservation of American trees, is offering authentic, direct offspring grown from original "parent" trees that are living links to historic events and famous people. By placing an order, you become a member of American Forests. You can reach the American Forests Famous & Historic Trees program by writing to P.O. Box 2000, Washington, DC 20013 or by calling 202/955-4500. To view a catalog of seedlings or place an order for a complete tree kit, see their Web site: www.amfor.org/index.html.

Kids at Work

Many home-educated children engage in some form of industry. Work, even on a small scale, is a great experience that instills responsibility and self-confidence and develops a range of skills, such as money management, vocational training, and

Unofficially... The National Science Education Standards suggest that early elementary grades focus on what can be observed in the immediate environment, concerning individual organisms, their needs, and basic associations.

experience interacting with others. Such an experience will also serve well on a college or job application. Some kids participate in their family's home business, and others start up their own enterprise.

Many times a hobby or interest will inspire a youngster's entrepreneurial turn. Or perhaps a youngster has an entrepreneurial spirit but needs help finding a specific project, such as:

- **Offering services:** Tutoring, party planning, Web page design, errand service, golf caddy, mowing lawns and other yardwork, dog-walking, pet care, bike repair, word processing, baby-sitting, housecleaning, shoveling snow.

- **Selling goods:** T-shirts, lemonade and cookies, old toys and clothing, homegrown vegetables and flowers, handmade jewelry and crafts, handmade greeting cards, birdhouses.

Consider these issues before giving the go-ahead to youthful entrepreneurship:

- Will this activity infringe on their studies and other activities? It's easy for anyone to take on more than they can handle. Help your kids establish some method for anticipating their schedule and managing their time.

- Is this really something they're interested in? Kids can latch onto an idea that may not hold their attention in the long run.

- Can they handle the responsibilities involved? Help your child research the idea thoroughly, and consider his or her level of maturity and skills.

- How will their business impact the family? Perhaps this activity implies extra work and time expenditure for other family members.

Will this business leave Mom and Dad legally vulnerable?

Avoiding burnout

It may seem difficult to manage at times, with so much going on. Before you find yourself completely overwhelmed, take some precautionary measures against burnout.

First, veterans recommend avoiding a very structured approach to learning; it's simply too difficult to maintain such a regimen over the long haul. Here are some other ideas:

- Encourage independent learning.
- Continue to let your child's temperament and personality guide your teaching. Be flexible and responsive to your child's interests.
- Allow yourselves an occasional off day. Recognize that over the course of your program, there will be good days and not-so-good days, for parents and kids alike.
- Encourage everyone's participation in managing home affairs.
- Explore all available resources to support your course of study—novel ideas and activities can inject new life into your homeschooling.
- Find support from fellow homeschool parents.
- Take time to enjoy your successes.
- Drop whatever's not working.
- Vary your methods (use software, a correspondence course, videotape). If you've invested in a program, try alternating one week with the program, the next engaging in hands-on activities.

- Prepare your child for doing his own research (introduce library skills).

- Learn alongside your child and model lifetime learning.

- Take your act on the road: Refresh yourselves by changing the scenery. Look at some new faces. Take lessons, have Dad lead some of the learning, join a team-taught class through your co-op.

- Take care of yourself.

Finally, remember to allow everyone a little downtime. New homeschoolers, especially, may feel the need to have everyone engaged in activities every hour of the day. Allow yourselves the chance to step back to observe, ask questions, and evaluate how it's going. Provide opportunities to daydream and relax for you as well.

Just the facts

- With more time spent living and learning at home, it's helpful to install some organizational method to household management. Encourage even the youngest family members to do their share through empowerment and appropriate incentives.

- Charity, honesty, compassion, courage, and other qualities all begin at home. Lectures and theoretical arguments don't work; narratives, observed behavior, and relevant discussion do.

- A philanthropic spirit should be encouraged in youngsters, but make sure there's an appropriate outlet that fits their abilities and level of maturity.

Bright Idea
Even little ones can get into the entrepreneurial act. At your next garage sale, let them sort through their toys and belongings and choose some things to sell. Have them help make signs, price items, set up, or make change for customers. Let them keep some of the profits.

- Gardening is an ideal outdoor, hands-on activity that can be enjoyed by the whole family. Beyond the hobby aspect, gardening can link to an exploration of science, history, and culture.

- Micromanaging your household, along with too many activities, can easily lead to burnout. To maximize successful homeschooling over the long haul, vary your program, and allow time to just hang out.

School's in Session

PART V

GET THE SCOOP ON...
Learning through play with your preschooler
- The lowdown on reading theory
- Encouraging young writers of all levels
- How to make math fun

"Preschool" and the "Primary" Grades

Chapter 13

The basic skills of reading, writing, and 'rithmetic—still affectionately known as the three Rs—continue to be the focus in a child's early years, because they form the basis of future learning. Children must read well, for example, in order to access information on science, history, geography, and other subjects.

Understanding their importance, parents often feel anxious about their ability to instill these skills. Teaching a child to read is frequently thought to involve secret techniques or even magic that only a "real" teacher could possess. Parents also contend with any baggage left from their own educational pasts—you might say to yourself, "I was a terrible speller," or maybe you struggled to understand New Math.

In fact, homeschooling provides you and your children a unique opportunity for learning the basics. Research has shown that language arts and math concepts are best learned in the context of experiential learning and real-life problem solving.

259

In a society that is increasingly technological and complex, the basic skills of education are being redefined. Beyond the three Rs, students must be able to communicate effectively, reason logically, utilize technology and understand its limitations, make informed value judgments, and recognize and use their full learning potential. In this chapter, I'll examine the basic skills, including the early introduction of these concepts and information on supporting your child's evolving skills in the years ahead.

Preschoolers: Too early to teach?

> **"**
> Young children are natural mathematicians and scientists because of their curiosity and desire to explore and experiment.
> —Education experts at the National Science Foundation
> **"**

To foster a love of learning in your preschooler, try these activities:

- **Read to your child as often as possible.** Telling and reading each other stories forms the basis for reading and writing.

- **Engage your child in conversation.** Talk about what you see, and encourage your child to ask questions.

- **Expose your child to a variety of experiences.** Before an excursion, read about the things you are going to see. Discuss the experience with your child and follow up with further reading to reinforce learning.

- **Involve your child in your daily activities.** Something as easy as a shopping trip or sharing in your everyday duties can be an opportunity to stimulate your child's mind.

- **Play with your child.** Young children learn primarily through play. Your own playful attitude helps foster the joy of learning. So have fun!

- **Limit television and video viewing.** Teach your children to make intelligent choices when they do watch.

"I find that in the early years especially, homeschooling is the same as good parenting," said Patty Tanner, a mother in Texas who is homeschooling boys ages six, five, three, and nearly one. "Play is learning for wee ones."

Teri Stettnisch, another homeschooling mother, agrees. "On the other hand," she adds, "I couldn't resist enriching that play by offering my kids just one 'preschool' activity a day. There's no reason that you can't start now using [their] interests as springboards to the world.

"I recently tried a 'unit study' with my four-year-old daughter. I was reading her a biography of Helen Keller, which fascinated her. We read books on human and animal ears and eyes, built crawl-through models of the ear, eye, and nose out of cardboard boxes and big blocks and strings and whatever else was lying around, practiced finger spelling, played a game of identifying one tree out of several after feeling it blindfolded, added a card to our homemade map game ('What state did Helen Keller live in?'), looked at pictures of Helen Keller with Alexander Graham Bell, and discussed the invention of the telephone. We both had fun!"

Reading

One of the liveliest debates in education focuses on how children learn to read and the best methods for teaching the skill.

Bright Idea
Consider everything you read in a typical day— from newspaper headlines to your personal e-mail. Then, look for ways to creatively involve your children with this real-life reading material. For instance, "We read the Bible daily and discuss God's word," says one homeschooling mother. "Lately we have read from Psalms." Afterward, she says, "the children take their art journals and draw pictures of what the psalm means to them."

Watch Out!
Homeschooling support groups may not be appropriate for parents homeschooling a preschooler. Group activities (Math Olympiads, and the like) are often geared for older children, and parent discussions may revolve around academics and subject curriculum rather than preschool concerns.

Two approaches to reading: Phonics and whole language

In years past, two schools of thought sparked "the reading wars": phonics and whole language. Phonics emphasizes word analysis. Children learn letter sounds (c = *cuh*) and then blend them (cr = *cruh*) to form words. Employing phonetic strategies, they can figure out words they don't know. Whole language emphasizes literature and word meaning. As budding readers learn in context, they are encouraged to use invented spelling to write their own stories.

Critics charge that phonics programs tend to use low-interest reading material and too many boring worksheets. Critics of whole language programs say that too little emphasis is placed on word analysis or phonics. When that's left out, young readers may guess or skip over words they don't know, and some children may not learn how to read.

Conclusions on reading by the experts

Current research has determined that the most effective way to teach reading is an integration of the two methods. Children cannot learn to read without an understanding of phonics. All children must know their ABCs and the sound that each letter makes in order to communicate verbally. The question is not whether to teach "phonics" or "whole language," but how to teach phonics in context, rather than isolation, so that children make connections between speech sounds and the alphabet. "Of course reading good literature is also important," adds Jeanne Chall, reading expert and Professor Emeritus at Harvard University.

Reading, in practice

The task of teaching a child to read may cause great anxiety for parents. Adequate progress in reading, after all, is key to comprehending math, science, English, history, and all other subjects.

"I was a little hesitant at the thought of having to teach my child to read," homeschooler Giovanna Gomez recalls. "Surely there had to be some kind of 'magic' performed in schools all across the country. Kids walked in one day and came out reading the next, it seemed. Could I do the same at home? This was one area I wasn't so sure about. But my son learned and now my daughter is learning. There wasn't any 'secret magic.'"

For preschool-aged children, you can encourage language development, which connects to future reading skills, in several ways:

- At just a few months of age, an infant can look at pictures, listen to your voice, and point to objects on cardboard pages. By drawing attention to the pictures and associating the words with both the pictures and real-world objects, your child will begin to learn the importance of language.

- Continue to encourage conversation based on varied experiences, trips to the library, and other excursions, which will lead children to ask questions and inspire them to recount their experiences. Ask your child questions that require more than a yes or no answer.

- Read at least once a day, and more often if you can. Expect your youngster to favor one book and request repeated readings. When hearing *Goodnight Moon* for the hundredth time, children are not just memorizing the words, but learning to understand their meaning and how words tell a story.

Unofficially... "Reading and writing develop simultaneously and interrelatedly in young children, rather than sequentially. Children learn about written language as they actively engage with adults in reading and writing situations; as they explore print on their own; and as they observe others engaged in literacy activities." —Idaho Center on Developmental Disabilities

Once your child begins to read, you can do much to support this exciting early stage:

- Starting out with books that are manageable for beginning readers will help build confidence. Brief rhyming poems with repeated phrases are good choices.

- As their skills develop, provide more challenging titles, and ones that align with their interests. On regular trips to the library, encourage them to make their own selections.

- If your child has trouble reading words, you can help by telling them to skip over the word, read the rest of the sentence, and ask what word would make sense in the story. Help them use what they know about letters and sounds and then supply the correct word. This all can be very frustrating. Remember to offer encouragement and always praise their efforts.

- Provide some follow-up activity to reading, such as acting out a line of a poem or asking them to reflect on some aspect of the story. Discussing what you've read will instill greater comprehension.

Even after your child has learned to read independently, it's still important to read aloud together.

- Try taking turns: You read one paragraph, and your child reads the next one. This will help your child stay focused, and you'll be on hand to assist with any difficult words or passages.

- Post-reading discussions will help them make sense of the story; children often relate what they've read to real-life situations.

- As children become more adept, they will begin to increase their vocabularies, encountering new words through reading. Older children may sound out words without knowing their meaning. They'll have to look them up. Show them how to use a dictionary and other references, and introduce library skills they'll need for doing future research.

While older children may be selecting books on their own, parents can still exert a positive influence on the reading habits of adolescents:

■ Continue to set a good example of reading as a fun, worthwhile activity. Share what you're reading and encourage them to do the same. Discuss the newspaper together. Speaking, listening, reading, and writing are all parts of language skills that continue to build on one another.

■ To support their studies, encourage them to look for primary sources across a range of disciplines. The excellent biography of President Harry Truman by David McCullough, for example, would support a study of the Cold War. In your home library, include references and other titles within their areas of interest. Make time for sustained, solitary reading.

■ Those looking ahead to college can seek out recommended reading lists for college preparatory students. Some are designed for pre-college reading, while others are drawn from freshman literature and writing courses or other university undergraduate programs.

Reading difficulties

Reading is a learned skill that doesn't occur naturally, as talking does. In fact, it's a rather complex process, requiring simultaneous skills of visual

Moneysaver
Newspaper publishers frequently provide an accompanying study guide or other educational materials. Inquire at your local paper.

focusing across a page, comprehending letters and their associated sounds, understanding grammar, and comparing new ideas to information already known.

Again, experts believe the best results come from an integrated teaching approach that should be introduced early on. Parents must remain alert to any difficulties and take steps to help their children, and if necessary, seek assistance with remediation. About 10 million children have difficulties learning to read, according to the National Institutes of Child Health and Human Development. Ten to 15 percent eventually drop out of high school; only 2 percent complete a four-year college program.

Reading problems can affect a child's self-esteem, and in later years, can prevent them from exploring science, history, literature, and a wealth of other information. As they grow older, reading-impaired individuals may quickly become lost in a society that is largely text-based.

Dyslexia and other reading impairments

Reading disabilities affect an estimated 2 to 8 percent of elementary school children. Dyslexia, perhaps the most widely known disability, is characterized by an inability to distinguish or separate the sounds in spoken words, a skill fundamental to learning how to read. Other reading impairments may be linked to deficiencies in the way that the brain processes letter sounds.

Reading remediation techniques have been developed to help children acquire the necessary skills. These include various phonetic methods in which children are taught that words are comprised of segments of sounds. After this step, students are led to relate these sounds to representative letters.

Unofficially... Half of the young adults with criminal records have reading difficulties. Similarly, about half of the youths with a history of substance abuse have reading problems, according to the National Institutes of Child Health and Human Development.

Once the child can read words on a page, he or she can be exposed to literature.

If steps are not taken to compensate for this defect, reading disability will persist through life. Research has shown that from 90 to 95 percent of reading-impaired children overcome their difficulties if they receive appropriate treatment at an early age.

Other types of disorders, such as developmental writing disorder, or problems with reading comprehension, can appear in later years.

Are reading problems learning disabilities?

Whether or not poor readers are "learning-disabled" is controversial. Approximately 80 percent of those children diagnosed with an LD (learning disability) have reading problems. According to the Council for Exceptional Children, all but a few have been misdiagnosed. Wrongly identified as having a neurological or processing disorder, these children may not receive appropriate support and may suffer the stigma of the LD label.

Most reading difficulties, in fact, stem from poor instruction or lack of reading readiness, which can be overcome with early intervention and intensive reading instruction. According to Harvard professor Jeanne Chall, "Dyslexic kids may simply take longer to get it."

Here are some common signs of dyslexia:

- delayed spoken language
- lack of awareness of sounds in words
- poor sequencing of numbers
- problems with reading comprehension
- difficulty with handwriting
- similar problems among relatives

Watch Out!
Research shows that reading disability affects boys and girls at roughly the same rate. Reading-disabled boys tend to be referred for treatment, however, because they often draw attention for misbehavior. Reading-disabled girls may escape detection, as they may quietly withdraw.

Individuals with dyslexia require different instructional methods, including systematic phonetic instruction. You may wish to consult a reading specialist or an organization, such as the International Dyslexia Association, which can provide educational information.

Bright Idea
Explore the techniques of your favorite writers. Did you know that Robert McCloskey kept ducks in the bathtub of his Greenwich Village apartment while writing *Make Way for Ducklings,* or that E.B. White, author of *Charlotte's Web,* would sit on a bale of hay and watch a spider spin its web?

Writing

According to traditional theory, children must progress through a sequence of clearly defined skills—first reading, then the mechanics of writing, such as grammar—before they begin to write.

Today, researchers and parents understand that children in the early stages of literacy compose before they have much knowledge of writing conventions. Moreover, they have a lot to write about, and they take pleasure in the process. As they come to understand the usefulness of writing, they are encouraged to develop related skills.

In the kindergarten years, children write freely, scribbling or drawing, in an effort to relate their thoughts and experiences. Rather than view these early efforts as mistakes, adults should encourage youngsters to "write" without worrying about the mechanics of writing. In fact, too much skill and drill practice in early years may affect the ability of children to develop a pleasurable association with writing. With the support of good literature, children will continue to develop these skills as they progress to using language in various forms.

How to encourage young writers

These simple suggestions will help you support your budding writer develop overall language skills.

During the preschool years:

- Provide appealing writing supplies like markers and fun notebooks and a comfortable space where they can write. Put a chalk or dry erase board on the wall at your child's eye level.

■ "Writing" projects—making notes, creating lists, and the like—will help them see the relationship between spoken and written language. Have your preschooler dictate a story to you, perhaps a description of a family outing or experience. Have them illustrate the story.

■ Another good long-term project is a letter dictionary that you create yourselves. Take a notebook, and have your child devote a page to each letter in the alphabet. Cut out images that start with the letters from old magazines and paste them on the appropriate pages. Have your child create labels.

Elementary years:

■ In the early years, children may begin to experiment with phonetic spelling and move closer to conventional forms. Encourage them to create illustrated stories and keep a journal. A quick writing exercise is greeting cards, which they can illustrate and send.

■ Praise these early efforts, and avoid overemphasizing spelling errors or grammar.

■ When appraising their writing, don't focus on a single piece; instead, review a week's worth of projects. Have they explored more than one topic? Are they trying out other forms, such as poetry? What is their developing writing style? Discuss their work with them and prompt them with questions. What will you add to your story? What are some other topics you might like to write about?

- Letting them see you write can set a good example. From time to time, read aloud what you've written and ask your children for their opinion. Making changes in what you write helps establish revision as a natural part of writing.

- Continue to find occasions to involve them in daily writing, such as helping with grocery lists, writing thank-you notes, or taking phone messages.

Middle years:

- Continue to encourage independent reading. Engage them in a discussion about what they're reading, their favorite writers, and specific themes. Offer your recommendations for books based on their interests.

- To get into a regular routine of writing, try this: Set aside a certain period during your day, perhaps as often as twice a week, when you and your children communicate only through writing. Make correspondence a habit. Start writing regularly to relatives and friends. Treat letters as special events, reading them aloud to the entire family. Encourage them to use e-mail and chat online with friends. Keeping a diary or journal is another idea. But don't push too hard. We all have days when we feel like writing more than others.

- Provide a good dictionary as well as other references appropriate for the age. Nicely illustrated ones often act as a springboard for the study of other topics.

Reading, reading, and more reading will teach children of all ages about sentence structure, grammar, and vocabulary. Good readers become good writers.

Always praise your children's efforts and help them find the inspiration to continue. As their skills develop, encourage the discipline that will help them produce their best work. In a 1998 national writing assessment—which determined that three-quarters of students in the grades tested were not proficient in writing—those students who scored higher took time to plan and outline their ideas. The assessment also found that above all else, the more students practice writing, the clearer and more sophisticated their prose becomes.

For other writing projects, see Chapter 11.

Build a climate of words at home. Go places and see things with your child, then talk about what has been seen, heard, smelled, tasted, touched. The basis of good writing is good talk...
—The National Council of Teachers of English

Teaching the conventions of writing

Research indicates that studying grammar in isolation (that is, completely separate from a student's own writing) actually has a negative impact on these skills. Standard usage and other conventions are most effectively taught in the context of real writing problems.

When a young writer struggles to find meaning in an early draft, conventions are less important. Again, don't insist on accuracy in the first stages. When they are clear on what they want to say, demonstrate how conventions can enhance their meaning.

Consider providing mini-lessons on each topic: the semicolon, organization, use of verbs, and so forth. Point out how conventions are used in their favorite books.

How to help your child become a better speller

To help your child become a better speller, try one or more of the following suggestions:

- Encourage reading, which helps spelling.
- Continue to write regularly.

Unofficially...
Homeschooler Rebecca Sealfon won the 1997 Scripps Howard National Spelling Bee by correctly spelling the word "euonym," meaning an appropriate name for a person, place, or thing.

- Help your child get in the habit of checking his or her own writing for misspellings. Have your child examine the part of the word that is spelled wrong and keep a list of commonly misspelled words.

- Assign weekly spelling words. Have them select words they think will be useful for future writing.

- Look for spelling patterns and think of other words that have the same pattern. Look for words within words (such as "eat" in the word "treat"), or other words in the same family (such as *like:* "alike," "liking," "dislike"). Work on spelling the base word before adding the prefix or suffix. Also consider other words with the same derivative ("engage," "engagement," "disengage"). Make lists of spelling patterns, and have your child identify and underline the pattern, such as *ea* in "bead," "read," "treat."

- Help them find spelling patterns in their own writing, and take the opportunity to reinforce a particular rule. What do you notice about what happens to the base word when *-ed* is added? Try out these rules on other words: add *-ing, -er,* or *-est.*

- Games are great for reinforcing language. Younger children will enjoy rhyming games or songs—you can make up your own. With older children, encourage games such as Scrabble or Boggle, and introduce them to crossword puzzles.

The value of self-assessment

As opposed to traditional assessment methods such as unit tests or worksheets, writing lends itself to self-evaluation, which encourages the development of critical thinking skills.

Through a portfolio, a popular tool of home-schoolers, a student can establish criteria for evaluating his or her own work (for example, "my handwriting's better in this one"), analyzing progress over time, and helping to define future goals.

Challenges to writing: Dysgraphia

Some people struggle to produce neat, expressive writing, whether or not they have accompanying physical or cognitive difficulties. When the mechanics of writing become a barrier to learning, accommodations and remediation may be in order.

The signs of writing-related disabilities, or dysgraphia, include:

- Generally illegible writing (despite adequate time and attention given the task), as well as slow or labored writing

- Inconsistencies: mixtures of print and cursive, upper and lower case, or slant of letters

- Unfinished words or letters, omitted words

- Inconsistent position on the page with respect to lines and margins

- Inconsistent spacing between words and letters

- Cramped or unusual grip, or strange positioning of the wrist or body

- Content that does not reflect the student's other language skills

Experts recommend the following methods of accommodation:

- **Modify or change existing assignments or expectations to meet individual needs.** Allow more time for written tasks and reduce the amount of written work. For example, instead of a complete set of notes, ask for an outline. Alternative formats, such as an oral report or visual project, can also be used.

- **Change tools.** Allow student to choose cursive or manuscript, whichever is most legible, or alternative materials, such as graph paper, or writing instruments with different-sized grips.

- **Remediate.** Provide handwriting instruction, including alternative methods, such as *Handwriting without Tears*, a handwriting instruction program. Severe problems may benefit from occupational therapy or other special education services.

Mathematics

Moneysaver
Having trouble with math? You can save on tutoring by consulting online sources such as S.O.S Mathematics at www.sosmath.com/.

As with other subjects, children best learn math concepts when they relate to real-life problem solving and through hands-on activities. A child's first experience with addition, for example, may occur when putting together two sets of interlocking toys. A parent might then illustrate on paper how the groups of objects were joined together. This prepares the child for writing the addition using numbers and symbols.

Through active problem solving, children begin to experiment, record, and analyze their results and develop conclusions. They are developing the skills they'll need for the workplace of the future, which will require organization, analysis, and interpretation.

Even as older children progress to more complex material, they will still benefit from working with hands-on material before going to pencil and paper.

Things to consider when teaching math

You can help your children learn math skills by:

- Helping them understand the normalcy of math and the necessity of comprehending math concepts.

- Pointing out mathematics as it occurs every day. This will help your child relate bookwork to real-life applications. During play, for instance, experiment with joining sets of objects, or "take away" an object and model subtraction. If your child gets an allowance, have him or her keep an accounting. Use the calendar to determine dates and plan activities. "How many days is it until your birthday?"

- Using food preparation and cooking to introduce a variety of concepts. Use kitchen containers to measure liquid volume. Introduce fractions by letting children help slice a pizza or divide a dish into servings. Use prepackaged items to introduce multiplication. Juice boxes come in threes, soda comes in packs of six. "If we buy two of these packages, how many cans do we get?" Have younger children count out silverware and napkins before supper.

- Using counting songs to help them learn to skip count (counting by twos, fives, or tens). Challenge them to see patterns, including those that occur in nature. Use beading or other craft projects to create their own patterns.

- Playing card or board games that involve number concepts. Other toys that encourage math skills are dice, puzzles and blocks, and the games Tangrams (see Chapter 11) and Othello.

Timesaver
With so many math software programs, how do you choose? Seek recommendations from one of the many Web sites that provide software reviews, such as The Educational Software Review page at the SuperKids Web site: www.superkids. com.

- Accepting the struggle as a normal part of doing math, just as you accept the struggle to attain other skills, as in sports. Help children face up to any difficulties and find ways to overcome them.

- Looking beyond scores and other assessments for true understanding of the concepts.

- Integrating math lessons with other subject areas, including geography, music, science, and language arts. Read children's literature that relates to math, including books by Mitsumasa Anno and Steven Kellogg, and magazines such as *Zillions*. In the upper grade levels, the interpretation of data and statistics can help children comprehend social issues.

- Practicing and memorizing equations and other math processes to gain skills.

- Knowing that wrong answers can be helpful. Help them examine incorrect answers to determine their understanding of the question and the underlying concepts.

- Using a calculator to help children explore number patterns and assist in complex math problems. They still need to learn the facts of arithmetic, but calculators can make solving math fun.

- Using the computer for spreadsheets, math software, CD-ROM reference material, as well as the many math resources on the Internet (see Appendix B for suggestions).

- Modeling a positive attitude toward learning math.

In sum—no pun intended—effective math programs demonstrate that math is a dynamic process

Moneysaver
Need a calculator? Call up the Web site Calculator.com (www.calculator.com). For online flashcards, see www.edu4kids.som/math/.

through the use of manipulatives, math games, or other hands-on materials. Interesting exercises in problem solving should also enable children to discover that they can find an answer using more than one method.

Finally, always allow for more than one approach. Not everyone can grasp every math concept through the same method of teaching. Consider other available tools, such as computer software.

Math subjects

Today, young children are tackling other math elements beyond the basic four of arithmetic (adding, subtracting, multiplying, and dividing), such as problem-solving and probability. Traditionally upper-level mathematics, such as algebra and geometry , are being introduced to students as early as the fourth grade.

These are some of the key mathematical concepts adapted from the Department of Education publication *Helping Your Child Learn Math:*

- **Number sense:** Understanding the relative sizes of numbers and how to use them, whether doing arithmetic, estimation, measurement, or classification. Children in the early years begin to grasp number sense and the concept of place value.

- **Arithmetic:** The ability to add, subtract, multiply, and divide whole numbers and fractions. Children in the early elementary grades learn arithmetical operations, and apply these to problem-solving. In the middle years, children can be introduced to ratio, proportion and percent.

"
Do not worry about your difficulties in mathematics, I assure you that mine are greater.
—Albert Einstein
"

- **Geometry:** An area of math that deals with the properties of points, lines, angles and surfaces. Children first begin to recognize the properties of geometric figures, employ geometry to solve problems in the middle years. Upper grade students engage three-dimensional geometry and apply it to real-world situations.

- **Probability:** Determining the likelihood that something will happen, often expressed as a fraction or a ratio. Young children may be introduced to the concept of chance. Older children create theoretical models of situations involving probabilities.

- **Algebra:** A generalization of arithmetic in which letters of the alphabet represent numbers or a specified set of numbers, and are related by operations that hold for all numbers in the set. In the middle years, children engage variables, expressions, and equations. Upper-level students apply algebraic theory to real-world problems.

- **Trigonometry:** The study of the properties of triangles and trigonometric functions, and their applications (upper grades).

Students of math also engage the concepts of measurement, reasoning, and statistics. For math resources and math programs, see Appendix B.

Difficulties in math

While most of us have had our struggles with math, serious deficits in the subject are actually more common than we may think. An estimated 6 percent of school-aged children are affected, yet seldom do math difficulties lead these children to be evaluated.

Bright Idea
Family Math is a six-week, community-based course in which families learn a variety of math games they can enjoy at home. Parents, teachers, and community members take turns leading the program, which promotes positive attitudes about math. For information about Family Math, send e-mail to equals@uclink. berkeley.edu.

Within many schools, special education services are provided almost exclusively for reading disabilities.

There are different types of disabilities in math, which can range from mild to severe, with different adaptations and methods proscribed to treat them. One of the most common situations is when a child has persistent trouble memorizing basic number facts in the four operations. These children rely on counting fingers, or pencil marks, and seem unable to develop sufficient memory strategies on their own. In this case, experts say, it's crucial not to hold them back until they know their facts. Rather, they should be allowed to use a handy facts chart to assist them with more complex computation and problem solving. Having the full set of answers in view will help the student learn these facts, which can be blacked out when each is mastered. Other effective techniques include interactive games and short 15-minute sessions daily, rather than less frequent, longer sessions.

Some children have difficulty calculating in the earlier years but have an excellent grasp of higher math concepts that employ their conceptual talents. Still others simply require alternative teaching methods to help them learn specific procedures in math. Once again, concrete materials are particularly effective at teaching number relations, such as computation, fractions, geometry, percentage, and other concepts. You can also try other methods, such as dictating problems for students to translate in pictorial form or simply allowing more time for them to grasp these connections.

Mathematics learning disabilities are not often well-defined. They can be combinations of difficulties that include language processing problems, visual spatial confusion, memory difficulties, and

66
I hear and I forget. I see, and I remember. I do, and I understand.
—Chinese proverb
99

anxiety. Through careful observation, parents can intervene at an early stage, with alternate methods, understanding, and support.

Watch Out!
The prevailing social myth has led us to believe that it's okay to be rotten at math, when, in fact, math illiteracy can seriously handicap both daily living and vocational prospects. In today's world, mathematical knowledge, reasoning, and skills are no less important than writing ability.

Math competitions

National math programs, such as MathCounts and Math Olympiad, are fun group opportunities that feature achievement in math. Student "mathletes" are fostered in MathCounts, a national math coaching and competition program for seventh- and eighth-grade students founded in 1983 by the National Society of Professional Engineers and the National Council of Teachers of Mathematics. To get involved, the organization produces a Math-Counts School Handbook and kit, which provides everything you need to start a local program. The competition registration fee is $50 per school.

After several months of coaching, registered schools select four students to compete as teams and individuals in one of 500 local competitions, followed by state-wide events, and culminating in the top four individuals advancing to the national final. MathCounts also sponsors an alumni program to continue participants' interest in mathematics. For more information, contact the coordinator in your state, listed on the Web site at http://mathcounts.org/.

Just the facts

- While it's too early to formally "teach" preschoolers, you can find plenty of creative ways to stimulate your budding learner.

- Researchers have learned a lot about how children learn to read. When it comes to phonics versus whole language, combining aspects of both methods is an effective approach.

- Reading difficulties are very common. Often misdiagnosed as a learning disability, a reading problem must nevertheless be addressed and remediation sought, the earlier the better.

- Learning to write, along with the other basic skills, can easily frustrate youngsters. Always praise their efforts and prepare to change the method or activity if it's not working for them.

- Math is no longer the dreary, rote subject it once was. Today's manipulatives, math games, and other fun tools make a game of it.

GET THE SCOOP ON...
Bringing history to life through primary sources
▪ Getting excited about geography and science
▪ Studying the arts and foreign language
▪ Establishing goals for physical fitness

Homeschooling, by Subject

Chapter 14

A child's interests can flourish in homeschooling, especially as he or she begins to explore specific subject areas. "Home schooling gave me more time and flexibility to study spelling," said Rebecca Sealfon, National Spelling Bee champion, whose passion led her to study the subject up to three hours each day.

"I chose to homeschool in order to sustain my daughter's creativity," says Nancy Pistorius, a homeschooler in Kansas. "I didn't feel her creativity could be sustained in a classroom situation." Her daughter, Alyssa Buecker, exhibited an early talent, winning art contests at age 3.

At age 11, Alyssa attended a filmmaking class at a local arts center, where she made her first film, "Hazel the Guinea Pig's Package." After winning several film prizes, Alyssa, at the age of 15, recently completed her fifth guinea pig film commissioned by HBO.

This chapter will help you and your child begin to explore various subjects. While it is beyond the

283

scope of this book to dictate a specific course of study or commerical curriculum, the information herein details learning concepts and teaching ideas that will maximize excitement within each subject, and, perhaps, spark your child's passionate interest.

What should the children study?

Those who don't use a packaged or otherwise prescribed curriculum may just as readily design their own learning program. (For more on curricula, see Chapter 8.)

To determine what you'll be covering for each subject, you'll probably find it helpful to refer to some sort of framework. You can obtain curricular guides from a variety of sources, which can help you design your own list of goals and plan ahead for the coming "school" year. See Chapter 8 for more information.

What if I need teaching support?

As I've shown in previous chapters, you don't have to go it alone in home education. You can find assistance in every subject. Choosing the best tools for your children may involve a little trial and error as you become familiar with their learning styles. Varying your methods can also help break up a routine that's gone stale; engaging in a science-by-mail program or a museum workshop, for example, can help punctuate your days. Working with other people will also refresh both parent and child, who will be exposed to new, exciting perspectives.

Be careful not to go overboard on teaching helpers, such as online programs. Experts agree that no student should rely completely on such courses for their education, as a substitute for in-person instruction.

> " My schooling not only failed to teach me what it professed to be teaching, but prevented me from being educated to an extent which infuriates me when I think of all I might have learned at home by myself.
> —George Bernard Shaw "

Whatever you do, it's vitally important that you assess your children's progress throughout the course of your program, considering their emotional and spiritual growth as well as their academic achievement.

History

Many recall history class as a bland recitation of facts, figures, dates, and other meaningless trivia. In fact, the traditional history curriculum, according to one high school teacher, could substitute as a cheap form of anesthesia. But history doesn't have to be boring. When brought to life through primary sources, lively storytelling, and other creative techniques, history engages students with the fascination of events, personalities, and outcomes, revealing the full-scale drama that has been the human experience.

Why study history?

Learning history enables young people to understand where people have been, from which they can gain new perspectives on where people may be going in the future. Without historical knowledge, young people cannot comprehend the political, social, and moral issues of the world. Examination of the choices of the past prepares them to make informed decisions on the problems of today. Thomas Jefferson understood the importance of the common memory: He prescribed the study of history for all who would take part in self-government.

Historical memory enables young people to see their own significance in the stream of time and connects them with society and the core values that unify people. Students can recognize their own rela-

Moneysaver
Network with other home-schoolers and discuss your needs. Perhaps you can team up and share a tutor, or engage a music teacher for group lessons.

tionship to history, and they can see how their own lives and actions can influence future generations.

Studying history also extends young people beyond the boundaries of their own lives and culture to see a fuller picture of human experience, including different viewpoints. When fully engaged in the subject, students may gain an expanded global perspective and an appreciation of the world's diverse cultures, as well as the common humanity that binds us all.

Key elements in teaching history

With a more in-depth and dynamic approach, research has shown that students develop real insight into the past and greater enjoyment of the subject.

Here are some other issues involved in learning history:

- **History is big.** It has numerous dimensions, with a corresponding number of ways to teach it. Political history, including the story of wars, peace treaties, and changes of government, may be most familiar, but you can also engage in the study of social history, learning about how average people lived, worked, and played. The history of religion, ideas, art, and music are other important aspects of human life and should be included in the study of any historical period.

  Trying to tackle all of world or U.S. history in one year is both impossible and ineffective. Again, in-depth study of smaller segments is the better approach. Homeschoolers have the flexibility of extending their study of major periods or themes beyond a single "school" year.

Watch Out!
National youth programs like MathCounts welcome homeschoolers; but others, like the National Science Olympiad, exclude them. Still others, like the President's Challenge Physical Fitness Program, have certain restrictions—to win a State Champion Physical Fitness Award, your child must be in a homeschool co-op of at least 50 students.

■ **History is a sequence of events that occurs over time.** Children need to understand history as a chronology of events. They need to learn the measures of time, such as a year, decade, generation, century, and millennium. They need to be able to place and reconstruct events and trace their relationship over time, or, when taken together, show how they tell the story of a particular period. Without a sense of chronological order, events and figures will convey little meaning.

■ **History isn't just a bunch of facts.** Emphasis should be placed on a true understanding of history, rather than rote memorization of dates, battles, and simple conclusions. Broad themes and ideas should be examined, including an analysis of cause and effect. The story of Columbus, for example, is not simply the discovery of the "new world." It is a richer story of the Columbian exchange, human migration, transatlantic trade, and the exchange of plants, animals, diseases, art, and technology between the Eastern and Western Hemispheres.

■ **Engaging tools can bring history to life.** Primary sources and active learning experiences present history in such a way that learners can relate it to their lives and find meaning in it. Lessons may be enhanced through a rich variety of materials, including historical fiction; biographies; alternative media, such as videotapes and films; and by "doing" history, from reenacting the Constitutional Convention to chronicling your personal history. (See "Make history personal," a little later in this chapter.)

> **❝**
> We need a history that encourages humane values and hell-raising, a history filled with colorful characters and great stories, a history that doesn't sugar-coat the past or dispense false optimism for the future, a history that creates a greater interest in studying history.
> —Randolph T. Holhut, journalist
>

Bright Idea
A debate requires students to critically analyze a certain historical problem and is an excellent way to demonstrate both sides of the story.

■ **Don't stay inside a textbook.** Textbooks and curricular programs provide useful guidelines for what to study, but don't let them restrict your learning. Always consider your child's interests, which may take you in another direction. A study of the democratic process, for example, may spark their interest in exploring the women's suffrage movement. Examining the life of Leonardo da Vinci or Benjamin Franklin can become a cross-disciplinary study of history and science.

■ **There are many versions of history.** A good history program will expose a student to the many ways in which history can be viewed and how our understanding of history changes over time. Help them think systematically and critically about the strengths and weaknesses of differing views. Children must also be able to distinguish historical evidence from biases, propaganda, and opinion.

■ **The study of history can begin early in life.** New research suggests the capacity for formal historical thinking arises much earlier than the age at which history is traditionally introduced in schools. An ideal way to introduce young children to history is within the familiar context of family and community. Tracing a timeline or researching your family tree will help them recognize their own relationship to history and lay the groundwork for future inquiry. (See "Make history personal," a little later in this chapter.)

"Doing" history

Special experiences can pump life into children's history learning. Try the following:

- Field trips to museums and historical sites
- Simulations
- Craft- and model-building
- Oral history projects
- Family genealogies
- Reenactments
- Timelines

Homeschooler Liz Pike has created her own version of a timeline, using 4 × 6 index cards contained in file boxes, with sections divided into 100 years. As her family reads or learns about "something significant, we add a card to the appropriate century," says Pike. Such a project enables children to gain a real sense of time and make connections between events.

Primary sources and how to use them

Historical novels and other primary sources are vastly underused in the traditional classroom. Here are some examples of these other resources—most are readily available—and how they can enhance your child's learning:

- Diaries, newspapers, documents, and speeches from the period bring events to life and provide a context for understanding. For example, the writings of Elizabeth Cady Stanton illuminate the early women's movement, while the speeches of Dr. Martin Luther King, Jr., and Malcolm X help explain civil rights.

- The newspaper enhances the study of history and aids children in making informed judgments about the world.

Bright Idea
Create a personal timeline: Draw a vertical line on a sheet of paper. Mark this line in even intervals for each year of your child's life. Help your child label years with significant events, starting with your child's birthday, then add corresponding local, national, and world events.

Bright Idea
Look for "living" museums or sites where volunteers who are dressed in clothing of the period perform the tasks and practice the crafts of the past.

- Discuss the news regularly—perhaps daily—with older children. Take note of any references to past events and discuss the links you find between these references and the current news story. How have issues evolved over time, across decades, centuries? Do you see any historical patterns? Compare several accounts of a major news story from different news shows or magazines, and consider differing points of view.

- Feature films—including *The Grapes of Wrath, A Man for All Seasons,* and *JFK,* to name a few—can spark interest in historical subjects. However, they must always be viewed with a critical eye toward historical truth.

- Television programs and documentaries can also support historical study. A good example is Ken Burns' series on the Civil War. But be careful not to rely too heavily on such "visual aids."

- Historical artifacts, such as a reproduction of the Declaration of Independence, are exciting for kids to handle. To enhance your exploration of regional history, visit state historical bureaus or libraries to view original diaries, letters, photographs, or maps.

For recommendations on what to read, see the annual list Notable Children's Trade Books in the Field of Social Studies, sponsored by the Children's Book Council and the National Council for the Social Studies. Also check the *Annotated Bibliography of Historical Fiction for the Social Studies, Grades 5–12,* by Fran Silverblank, published for the National Council for the Social Studies.

Make history personal

To trace your family's past, you can employ formal genealogical techniques and sophisticated software, or you can just as effectively devise your own from scratch. For more information on doing a family history, including sample interview questions, see Chapter 11.

Widen your scope and explore the history of your community or region. Pick a local site or area that has always intrigued you and your children. Find any defining marks, dates, or designs to direct your search of local archives (ask for the librarian's help). Look for major events that took place there, and interview long-time residents, who might provide some insight.

One homeschooled child was reluctant to study history until he became curious about the local cemetery. This inspired a search at the local historical society, which then tied into national and world history.

An oral history project

Collecting and analyzing oral history is a recommended activity for students of all levels. Collecting oral history is a dynamic means of exploring a recent historical period as viewed through the eyes, experiences, and memories of people who lived during that time. Sample topics include World War II, the assassination of JFK, or the Vietnam War.

Using interview techniques—including audio- or videotaping—students learn that history is, in essence, the collective memories of actual events that have directly affected the lives of their friends, acquaintances, and relatives. Students experience history firsthand, placing local events within the

Moneysaver
A treasure trove of material is in the public domain. The National Digital Library Program of the Library of Congress has created American Memory, an online collection of digitized versions of millions of items in its United States history collections available to the public on the Internet (www.loc.gov).

overall context of national history. The project promotes other skills, including interviewing, writing, and organization of material.

What to study: The debate over the history curriculum

Concern over the decline in the educational achievement of American students prompted the creation of new standards in history education in the mid-1990s. A torrent of controversy ensued, with critics calling the standards offensive for de-emphasizing Western civilization for a more globalist approach. The authors were also accused of too much emphasis on social science and not enough on simply telling the facts of historical events. Opposing sides argued over the coverage of American history, and whether or not its purpose should be rooted in teaching values and instilling patriotism in students. (Other curriculum guides, such as Core Knowledge, are accused of leaning too heavily toward Western culture.)

The debate rages on. Parents should view any history guidelines with a critical eye, understanding that no guide to teaching history is completely neutral.

Geography

According to a recent [1997] report of the Commission on Geosciences, Environment and Resources, young American adults knew the least about geography of any age group in any country. About one half could not point out South Africa on a map, or identify even one South American country. Only 55 percent could locate New York.

Beyond simple location of physical places, geography enriches the understanding of people and cultures worldwide as well as the interaction among populations and their relationship with the environment. Integrating concepts from several areas— science, social science, and the humanities—the study of geography helps foster critical thinking skills necessary for understanding and dealing with current issues of local, national, and international importance. With the world's economies increasingly linked in an international network of trade and change, a thorough geographic education will help children assume their place as citizens of the world.

Children should be exposed to the tools of geography and how they are used. In addition to maps, geographers use different kinds of statistical information, photographs, and a variety of other methods, classifying the earth into regions in order to draw generalizations about the complex world in which we live. Geographic evidence also provides important clues to the past, with landforms and climate related to human migration patterns, the use of natural resources, and the rise and fall of civilizations.

As with other subjects, geography education is most effective when you integrate it into a child's learning in interesting ways. Try these ideas:

- **Acquire maps and other geographer's tools.**
  Display a map of the world, the United States, or another place that appeals to your family. A good, up-to-date atlas is another worthwhile investment, containing valuable information on population, climates, economies, and other important keys to understanding the world. Atlases, almanacs, and geographic databases

Unofficially...
Homeschooler David Biehl, from Saluda, South Carolina, won the National Geography Bee in 1999. Among the people he most admires is Seyi Fayanju, the 1996 winner

Moneysaver
A standard globe can cost hundreds of dollars. The National Council for Geography Education recommends an inflatable globe—available from most toy stores for under $10—as equally effective for helping a child see the proper shape and relationship of the earth's features.

are also widely available in CD-ROM and electronic formats.

- **Become a student yourself.** Approach the subject with a positive attitude and be a role model. Consult maps yourself or look up information in an atlas or almanac. These references should be readily available to your child.

- **Speak geography.** What's a peninsula? Inject your vocabulary with geographic terms and discuss the meanings of these words. Refine your description of places and destinations with proper terms, such as continent, border, plain, or plateau.

- **Travel in your armchair.** Refer to maps when you encounter names of countries, cities, or other places in television programs, novels, or when discussing the news.

- **Let your child navigate.** When planning a trip, obtain a road map or highway atlas and have your children help plan the trip or trace your route. Encourage them to suggest points of interest that might be found along the way. Have them log your daily mileage.

- **Make a game of it.** A variety of entertaining board and computer games promote geography skills. With map puzzles of the United States, younger children can begin to learn the shapes and relative positions of the states.

Maps are readily available for free from:

- The Government Printing Office. Contact the Superintendent of Documents, GPO, Washington, D.C. 20402; 202/512-1800.

- The U.S. Geological Survey, which also offers free teacher packets: Map Adventures (K–3) and What Do Maps Show? (upper elementary and middle school). Call 1-800-USA-MAPS.

- The National Park Service publishes maps of natural areas and trails, battlefields, and historic sites. Contact the specific site or write to the U.S. Department of the Interior, P.O. Box 37127, Washington, D.C. 20013-7127.

- State departments of tourism, or tourist agencies of foreign countries. Local transit authorities provide free maps of public transportation routes.

Science

A recent Louis Harris survey commissioned by the American Museum of Natural History revealed an astonishing lack of basic science knowledge among American adults; for example, 65 percent do not know how many planets are in the solar system, and 35 percent believe that humans lived at the same time as dinosaurs.

American youngsters don't fare much better. According to a recent national assessment, most students have a basic grasp of certain scientific facts by the end of high school, but they are unable to apply scientific knowledge to other situations, design an original experiment, or explain the reasoning behind their answers. Moreover, traditional teaching tools are both uninspiring and insufficient. According to the American Association for the Advancement of Science, none of the most widely used middle-school science textbooks are adequate to teach students fundamental concepts.

Everybody starts out as a scientist. Every child has the scientist's sense of wonder and awe.
—Carl Sagan, astronomer

As advancing technology continues to change our lives, all students will need a solid foundation in science and related concepts to ensure their success in an increasingly complex world.

Science as process

Science is much more than absorbing facts. Children must learn how to think critically, synthesize information accurately, and solve problems creatively.

Students engage in the process of inquiry by:

- Considering what is already known.

- Asking questions, which lead to hypotheses.

- Testing predictions through investigation under controlled conditions.

- Recording their observations.

- Making sense of those observations through analysis.

The process of inquiry itself becomes a learning tool, which can then be applied to other subjects. Students also must adapt new skills, such as proficiency with computers.

Science is best learned:

- **By "doing" science.** Hands-on learning allows children to fully engage in the process of scientific inquiry: to ask and answer questions, do investigations, and apply problem-solving skills. Allow them to help select these activities, which often result in boosting confidence in their ability to solve problems.

- **From a young age.** Children are natural investigators, examining and sorting things since infancy. By five or six years of age they are applying the basic concepts of collecting and organizing data.

Timesaver
Read any good science lately? Check out the annual list Outstanding Science Trade Books for Children, produced by the National Science Teachers Association and the Children's Book Council at the Science & Children Web site, www.nsta.org/pubs/sc/ostblist.htm.

- **With content and learning experiences appropriate to their age and cognitive level.**
  Inappropriate methods leave children unable to find deeper meanings within the content, and their interest in science will likely diminish.

- **Within the context of their own questions.**
  Children have a natural sense of wonder concerning the physical world. Encourage opportunities for them to express their own ideas and ask questions.

- **When information can build on existing knowledge.** For example, by maintaining a garden and caring for plants, a young child can observe and learn what organisms need to survive. These concepts can then be applied to life in another setting, such as the local park or the rain forest. In the middle years, these early ideas help promote an understanding of life at the cellular level, as well as the nature of the environment. The understanding of cellular structure progresses at the high school level with the additional concept of molecular genetics. Each level deepens a student's understanding based on what was learned earlier.

What should they be studying?

Science is generally divided into three categories: physical science, life science, and earth and space science. The National Standards in Science Education incorporates the additional categories of science and technology, science in personal and social perspectives, and history and nature of science.

Again, most guidelines for learning science stress the understanding of scientific concepts

Bright Idea
Is your child's interest in science lagging? Meeting people who have interesting careers that use science can help motivate kids. Pharmacists, biologists, and researchers are good role models.

and developing inquiry skills rather than learning subject matter for its own sake. Specific subjects and concepts designated for each grade level may be referenced from a variety of sources (see Appendix B).

How to promote science at home

In addition to curricular materials and science texts, these simple ideas can get your family excited about science:

- **Stimulate them with interesting environments.** A field trip to the shore, a wildlife sanctuary, a local park, or your back yard present opportunities for observing and discussing science. One homeschooler visited their local landfill, which provided her family with an educational tour, along with information about recycling. They then went home and conducted an experiment, creating a mini-landfill in their backyard.

- **Provide appropriate hands-on activities.** Choose varied and educational playthings that promote creativity and activities that stimulate young minds.

- **Identify your child's science interest and go with it.** Are they intrigued by snakes? Read books on snakes, discuss various species of snakes, construct models or draw pictures of snakes, and visit the zoo or the herpetology section of the museum.

- **Discover how science relates to your life.** Whip up an experiment in the kitchen and discover the science involved in cooking. Do you or any of your friends have a science-related job or hobby? Share it with your children.

- **Use the Internet.** Numerous sites relate to science, and many feature interactive activities.

- **Use other media as a springboard.** Television documentaries and news stories can lead to further investigation of science topics.

The arts

Parents continue to support art as an important part of their families' educations. In a recent poll, 90 percent of parents said that they want their kids to have more experience with the arts than they did as children.

Yet, public funding for education in the arts is diminishing, resulting in devastating losses for many children. Almost the entire generation regularly sits in front of computers or televisions, bombarded with visual images rich in symbolism or laden with marketing manipulations, and they have few tools with which to view these images critically.

The arts are an essential component of education. In addition to learning the various disciplines—visual arts, dance, music, and theater—art actively engages children in learning in general, and studies show positive effects on student achievement overall.

Students learn important life skills through the arts. Singing or playing an instrument enhances listening skills. Dance teaches a child about body and space. The study of folk and traditional art as well as the great masterpieces enhances an appreciation of history and understanding of various cultures. Production activities promote attention to detail, self-discipline, and creative problem solving, habits that stay with students and help them succeed in other areas of life and work.

> 66
> Great Nations write their autobiographies in three manuscripts: the book of their deeds, the book of their words, and the book of their art.
> —John Ruskin, English author, art critic, and social reformer
> 99

Unofficially...
Arts classes have been shown to significantly improve attitudes relating to self-expression, trust, self-acceptance, acceptance by others, self-awareness, and empowerment.

Integrating art with other academic subjects

For more information on studying art at home, see Chapter 11.

Art can support the study of other subjects. Integrating art with social studies, for example, can provide insight into human experiences, extending understanding beyond dry facts and abstractions. One can also learn tolerance for religions and systems of government other than one's own. And studying artwork of the past can reveal the values of a particular historic period. In fact, all that we know of some ancient cultures comes from their artistic records.

Other cross-disciplinary studies link the arts with other subjects, such as music and math.

Music

Of all the arts, music in particular gets short shrift in traditional education, which is geared toward linguistic and logical-mathematical skills. At the elementary-school level, more than half of all school districts in the United States have no full-time music teacher.

Beyond its intrinsic value, music offers other intellectual benefits (despite challenges from the debunking of the Mozart Effect, which claimed that passively listening to music could improve children's spatial-reasoning skills).

Studies define clear benefits from music:

- High school music students have higher grade point averages than non-musicians.

- Instrument practice can enhance coordination, concentration, memory, improvement of eyesight, and hearing acuity.

- Musical games can help teach fundamental academic concepts.

- The therapeutic effect of music promotes significant gains among disabled students.

- Young children taking music lessons are better able to grasp concepts that are also essential to math and science.

- Accomplishment in music inspires confidence to take on future challenges.

- Data from the College Board Profile of College-Bound Seniors consistently shows that students who participate in arts education courses score higher on the SATs than those who do not.

Encouraging music at home

To promote a love of music, you should:

- **Surround your children with music.** Start in their infancy by singing lullabies and nursery rhymes. Provide musical toys, and listen to a variety of music on tape or CD. Take them to hear live performances. If you aren't particularly musical yourself, you might consider taking private lessons or participating in music-related group activities.

- **Make music a family affair.** Sing along in the car, take lessons along with your child (as recommended in the Suzuki method), or enjoy performances together. Performances by other children may be particularly inspiring. Listen to popular music with your children, and give musical gifts such as instruments or concert tickets.

- **Foster participation in music.** When a child is old enough to ask for music lessons, one teacher advises, they are usually old enough to have them. Formal instruction can begin

Unofficially... Country singer LeAnn Rimes homeschooled with the help of a tutor, who accompanied the teen on road trips. She studied one course at a time for two to three hours a day.

Moneysaver
Private music lessons can be quite costly. Try bartering, in which home-schoolers commonly exchange goods or services for lessons. Also consider group lessons, a fun and less expensive alternative.

as early as age six. Follow their interests in choosing the instrument or type of music they'll pursue. Experts recommend starting with simpler instruments such as the piano or violin (as opposed to an instrument like the trumpet, which requires a sufficient degree of lung power). To maximize success, the style of lesson or activity should also suit the child's personality. A gregarious child, for instance, might enjoy the fellowship of a choir over the solitude of clarinet lessons. Try to provide a quiet and regular time for practice, and never use music practice as a form of punishment.

Foreign language

Most people know that learning a foreign language is best begun in the early years. Scientific study, including Magnetic Resonance Imaging (MRI) of the brain, has proven the unique cognitive capacity that allows young children to absorb a language more readily than adolescents or adults. New sounds are physically easier for a child to imitate, and young ones tend to be less inhibited.

Learning a foreign language opens up new worlds to a child, and in later years translates to greater job and career opportunities. Bilingualism also promotes:

- Increased achievement, including higher standardized test scores
- Greater cognitive development
- An understanding of other cultures, and a global perspective
- Increased confidence

The ins and outs of learning another language

When tackling another language, consider the following:

- Language experts believe the best approach involves immersion, in which a large part of course work is taught in the foreign language. In the total immersion method, students hear nothing but the foreign language.

- When choosing a language, consider what your child is interested in studying. But be aware that they may not stick with that choice. Having a parent or another adult with background in the language can help shore up their interest.

- Integrate the language in your overall course of study. Thematic units can be quite successful. One could, for example, incorporate lessons in Portuguese with a unit on Brazil. Study can include other cultural aspects, such as food and traditions.

- Support your learning with lots of practice. Many homeschoolers creatively access local tutors, such as native speakers of the language. You can also view appropriate foreign language films.

- Learning a language requires consistent instruction over a long period of time. If a student studies language for two years—as prescribed in public programs—then doesn't use it for two years, the student will forget it. Homeschooling can accommodate continuity in foreign language study. Still, families must realize that becoming proficient in a language takes many years.

Unofficially...
Students with at least four years of foreign language tend to score higher on the verbal section of the SAT. Moreover, they'll have an easier time acquiring a third language in adulthood.

Foreign language software

Software and audio programs are popular tools for teaching language. A range of such products is currently offered on the market, but how do you choose? Start by asking other homeschoolers what they use, or consult review media.

Different programs employ various methods, including the immersion approach. Many feature appealing activities, dialogue of native speakers, songs, and interactive games, which provide immediate feedback.

Do your research to find the best program, and be careful to select the appropriate level for your child. Intermediate levels, for example, assume some understanding of grammar. Traditional workbooks, employing the grammar and translation method, are also an option, although they may not be the best for promoting conversational ability.

As appealing as the programs are, don't rely exclusively on software. Learning another language requires lots of practice and study.

Technology skills

Computer skills should be an important component of any child's basic education. These are the general recommended areas of study:

- Operational proficiency in the use of technology
- Ethical, cultural, and societal issues related to technology, including personal responsibility
- Employing technology tools to enhance learning and creativity
- Using various media to communicate ideas
- Using technology to locate, evaluate, and collect information

▪ Using technological resources to solve problems in the real world

Physical education

Despite common awareness of the benefits of exercise, the U.S. population is softer than ever in this regard. A recent report from the Surgeon General states that only about half of all Americans aged 12 to 21 exercise regularly; one-quarter get no exercise at all. Among school-aged children, between 15 and 25 percent are overweight, increasing their risk of heart disease, diabetes, and high blood pressure.

The physical education curriculum

The National Standards for Physical Education specifies that programs foster:

1. Mastery of basic skills related to a variety of physical activities

2. Regular participation in physical activity

3. Physical fitness

4. Understanding of the role of fitness activities in maintaining physical health and well-being

What's involved in physical fitness? Here are the related benefits:

▪ Fat loss

▪ A healthier heart

▪ Heightened self-image

▪ Better posture

▪ Better athletic performance

▪ Support of emotional health

▪ A strengthened immune system

To determine fitness, consider participation in the President's Challenge Physical Fitness Program, described next.

The President's Challenge

The President's Challenge Physical Fitness Program is a physical fitness awards program for children ages six through 17, including students with special needs. Call 800/258-8146 for an information packet that describes the award levels that can be achieved, the tests, and the correct techniques for performing all components.

Homeschoolers can administer the program by qualifying as a Presidential award winner under the guidance of a certified physical education teacher or specialist. Your homeschool group may have specific information on how to get involved in your area, or contact the Presidential Challenge program at the number above to locate a nearby school that is taking the President's Challenge.

Everyone off the couch!

Fitness activities can easily be made into a family affair. First, be a good role model; engage in regular sports or workouts that help meet the recommended 30 minutes of daily exercise for adults. Emphasize safety: Engage in adequate stretching or warm up prior to any physical activity, and start slowly. Provide for any safety measures, such as appropriate headgear or pads for cycling or skating.

Let your child's enthusiasms direct a favorite activity that everyone can join in. Add any entries for fitness or sports in your homeschool journal. This is a good way to begin gauging your fitness goals and can motivate you to schedule a regular time for exercise. (Of course, jumping rope, working out to a home exercise tape, playing tag in the backyard, or other fun activities also count toward fitness.)

Finally, think of promoting lifetime sports or fitness activities, such as cycling, golf, swimming, yoga, or squash. Football and baseball are terrific sports, but they may not contribute to fitness over the long haul. There are also potential drawbacks to competitive sports, such as an overemphasis on winning. Other considerations include your child's physical and emotional maturity and the values that are being promoted within the program. (For more information on organized sports, see Chapter 5.)

Just the facts

- In addition to learning the facts of history, students can engage the subject through lively reading, hands-on projects, and other methods that make historical events come alive.

- Stimulating interest in current events, world culture, and physical geography will help prepare our youngsters for the global community.

- Unlike conventional education, home-schooling allows interested youngsters to actively engage subjects. A backyard expedition, for example, is a fun way to reinforce science concepts.

- Software and other products are useful tools for tackling difficult subjects, such as foreign language. (See Appendix B for a listing of resources by subject.)

- Competitive sports are only one option for promoting physical fitness. Also consider lifetime sports and those activities that the family can enjoy together.

High School
and Beyond

PART VI

Homeschooling Teens

Chapter 15

B y the end of the seventh grade, Trever Gilkerson, according to his mother Kysa Kohl Gilkerson, "was very bright and very bored." Short and skinny, he was targeted at school, where a bully struck him in the face with a book, breaking his glasses. Before he entered the eighth grade, Kysa took him out of school.

At home, Trever "relaxed into the person he used to be," says his mother, who enrolled him in a high school correspondence course. "Trever took the syllabi and did most things on his own," says Kysa. "He only came to me for questions in math and chemistry." After four hours of schoolwork in the morning, he would go outside to 'play.' He built a greenhouse that first year, followed by a second. Working with his father and grandfather, these efforts grew into a commercial garden business. Now a junior in college on two academic scholarships, Trever also runs the greenhouse at the school. He netted $5,000 this summer on his greenhouse and garden business. His mother says, "I have never met a happier young man."

In this chapter, I'll show you how homeschooling can be a viable alternative to high school, with information on designing your course of study, nurturing self-directed learning, and discovering the world of work.

Weighing the pros and cons

Homeschooling a teenager presents its own unique challenges, but the potential rewards make it an intriguing proposition. You'll have to weigh the issues involved—briefly summarized below—from the perspective of your own situation.

The advantages include:

- Lack of exposure to negative peer influences in the high school environment.

- Independent learning.

- Family unity at an age when relationships may be challenged.

- Support of family members readily available to your teen.

- A flexible schedule that can accommodate choices about what your teen will study and when.

- Greater opportunities for positive peer interaction through church, the Y, music clubs, and other youth groups.

- An opportunity to get a head start on college coursework.

- More discretionary time to follow interests, engage in work/volunteering, and travel.

- Early definition of career or occupational path as teens follow their interests and engage in hands-on, "real-life" activities.

The disadvantages include:

- Challenges to maintaining motivation levels, especially for individuals who need more direction.

- Conflict over course of study.

- Strain on family relationships as your teen's increasing need for independence emerges.

- Limited access to school activities, such as clubs, sports, chorus, or band.

- Lack of such special celebrations as prom and high school graduation. If these aspects of campus life are important to you, they may factor into your decision to homeschool. (Although homeschoolers are now creating these opportunities for themselves.)

- Finding ways to address the challenge of advanced coursework, and if necessary, seek assistance.

- Lack of a guidance counselor, leaving you to be completely responsible for the college application process and career direction.

- The expense (advanced science, for example, will involve the cost of labwork, either at home or through a community college course). Consider any added fees and materials. A quality microscope, for instance, can cost up to $500.

How you make your decision depends on the issues that have the most priority for you and the amount of commitment you and your teen are willing to make to the effort.

Unofficially...
Recent reports claim that adolescent girls' self-esteem diminishes in their high school years. In her book, *A Sense of Self: Listening to Homeschooled Adolescent Girls,* Susannah Sheffer interviewed 55 subjects whose self-confidence is strikingly different from that of their peers in school.

The culture of high school

Incidents of school violence have focused our attention on the treacherous atmosphere negotiated by children on high school campuses nationwide. While statistics seem to support that schools in the United States are generally safe, anecdotal evidence supports the opposite conclusion, at least for some. Many parents I encountered while researching this book cite specific incidents of actual or threatened violence involving their children, which prompted these families to consider leaving school.

Beyond physical violence, youngsters risk exclusion, humiliation, and other cruelty that can impact their self-confidence and emotional well-being for years to come.

Immersed in the high school peer group, teens also encounter pressures to experiment with drugs, alcohol, and sex. While the greater culture will continue to challenge families with the wrong messages, homeschoolers have the opportunity to address these issues within the supportive family environment, providing their children with information and guidance that will help them make the right personal choices.

Peer pressure and a bad environment may not in and of themselves constitute a reason for homeschooling. Depending on your personal circumstances, however, they may contribute to your decision.

Although homeschoolers are spared the direct effects of a toxic peer environment, certain issues remain to be dealt with, even if you take away high school. Teens are still subject to negative aspects of our modern culture. The media is saturated with images of violence and sex, and consumer products target teens using objectionable methods.

They still face the inevitable changes that come with adolescence. Surging hormones, hair-trigger emotions, and the challenge to adult authority can contribute to family stress. Again, homeschooling is not a magic panacea to cure all problems. It will take all your parenting skills to help you through this challenging stage. (I discuss how to maintain communication with your teen, along with other parenting tips, later in this chapter.)

As I've emphasized throughout this book, homeschooling is a sizable commitment, and neither parents nor their children should make such a decision without fully understanding what's involved.

A flexible program

The flexible nature of homeschooling is possibly the greatest advantage to a teenager. If teens gain competency in following their own interests in order to learn and achieve their goals, the freedom of homeschooling opens up a much richer learning experience. Too often in school, staid, traditional teaching methods leave students bored in subjects that have no meaning in their lives.

As you'll see in this chapter, homeschooled teens engage in varied experiences. In terms of work, their flexible schedules often enable them to get better volunteer and paying positions. The greater efficiency of homeschooling also gives them more discretionary time, with which they can further expand their interests, such as travel or setting up a home business. Or they may wish to advance more quickly to college-level coursework, which can earn them advanced credits, thus saving time and money.

Flexibility can also enhance family unity. Teens can stretch their wings outside the home, yet still have immediate access to the security and

Unofficially...
In the month following the April 1999 shootings at Colorado's Columbine High School—which claimed 15 lives—the Colorado Department of Education fielded 68 inquiries about home-schooling, about 60 percent more than usual.
—*Education Week*

guidance offered by their parents, as homeschooling facilitates both.

Those who homeschool successfully describe a less confrontational nature to their relationships, in which parent and child stay "plugged in" to each other, as the child evolves toward independent adulthood.

When older children leave school

While many children are homeschooled from an early age, you can choose this option after your child has been attending school for years. The deschooling process, however, in which children decompress from school, may be more involved. Learning to follow your child's interests toward a goal of self-directed learning will take time. Keep in mind that homeschooling will be radically different from traditional education, which conditions students to do what they're told. Make sure to encourage your child's involvement—which topics would they most like to explore?

Still other youngsters need time and support to regain their emotional health, if they have suffered from a negative peer situation or other stress. Although they may be unaccustomed to time spent alone, your teenager will benefit from some solitude.

Realize that this is a major transition for your child and for the entire family. Keep your expectations realistic, and have patience with the process. To help you make the transition to homeschooling:

- Get acquainted with other homeschooling families.

- Research teen-based activities (like church groups and Scouting), and share this information with your teen.

- Begin a homeschool journal.

- Encourage your teen toward self-directed activity. (Remember, let it be his or her choice.)

- Encourage your child to read up on homeschooling. A sampling of titles appears in Appendix C, or you can visit a homeschooling discussion board or chat room for teens.

Self-directed learning

The ability and motivation to learn independently, self-directed learning is especially critical for older children to achieve, no matter what your homeschooling style. If they don't have the motivation or haven't developed personal tools for learning, they will find it very difficult to manage their own education.

Self-directed learning may evolve from years of homeschooling. But for those just starting out, it takes real effort on everyone's part to break out of the traditional educational mode, which emphasizes a highly directed, top-down approach to learning.

In particular, students who take on a correspondence or distance learning course will achieve the greatest level of success if they are firmly committed to achieving their goals and able to gauge their own progress.

To find out whether you're fostering self-directed learning in your children, ask yourself the following:

- Do you encourage your children to take a leading role in their education?

- Are they helping set their own goals? Or are they consistently depending on those of a prescribed program?

66

The first year was VERY difficult for all of us. We had to deprogram our daughter. She kept saying "in school, we did it this way," or "my teacher taught us this way." We worked through these and progressed.
—Barbara Cooper, homeschooling mother

99

- Do they follow through in meeting those goals? Do you follow up?

- Are you in the habit of doing things for your children, rather than letting them do it themselves?

- Do you involve them in other decision making, such as meal planning, family vacations, or configuring their study area?

- Are their activities directed by your interests, or theirs?

- Do activities stimulate problem solving and critical thinking skills?

- Are they able to keep themselves motivated?

- Are you setting a good example and learning alongside your children?

- How much TV are they watching?

- Do they have any consistency in their schedules?

- Do they write regularly?

- Are references and other learning tools readily accessible in your home?

- Do your children know how to use the library?

- How do they participate in evaluating their own work?

- When momentum bogs down, does your child take the initiative in getting things going again?

It's helpful to have some method to track your progress, such as a journal or formal list of goals. Journal entries, especially, can be quite illuminating, demonstrating your children's initiative in tackling subjects, whether or not they followed projects

Bright Idea
Be a model for lifelong learning. Homeschool parents have learned to play the violin; flip-turn in a swimming pool; write a new language, HTML; joined a blues/funk band; tried yoga; raised Angora goats; joined a Bible study group; and started a home-school resource center. Are you still learning?

through to completion, and their progress toward long-term goals. Once set on the path of self-directed learning, your children will reap the rewards in their college years and beyond.

What about teenage rebellion?

Anticipating rebellion, mood swings, and other challenges attendant to the age has most parents keeping their fingers crossed. Homeschoolers may fear that these issues will overwhelm the family and make learning impossible.

However frustrating, recognize this period as a natural and legitimate part of your child's transition to independent adulthood. Parents can do much to smooth the way by maintaining communication and otherwise nurturing their child's development. Here are some suggestions for helping your teen:

- Remain accessible. While adolescents may take a bold stand for greater independence, they still need the loving support of their parents. Be proactive in addressing their fears or insecurities, and let them know you'll be there.

- Don't deliver a lecture. Teens are especially sensitive to harsh criticism. When you talk to your teen, be a good listener. While certain issues remain non-negotiable—such as matters of health and safety—allow them to express their viewpoints, even if they differ from your own.

- Break up the intensity of the one-on-one or solitary experience of homeschooling with group activities, such as interest-oriented societies or clubs or homeschool teen groups. Employ the help of your spouse, a relative, or other trusted adult.

Timesaver
Looking for advice on homeschooling teens? Consider posting your question on an electronic message board—you're sure to get some thoughtful answers, responses are almost immediate. There are several appropriate boards, including the High School HomeSchooling Board (http://vegsource.org/wwwboard/hschool/wwwboard.htm/).

- Adjust your schedule to optimize their best hours. If they're not quite alert at 9am, for example, arrange academic work for the afternoon. Parents may not realize that teens aged 14 to 16 need more rest than at any time since infancy.

- Shake off the doldrums by staying active. Sports and other fitness activities help teens develop a good self-image and provide opportunities for achieving excellence.

- Apply the concept of self-evaluation to other aspects of their lives. The principles of self-directed learning can help teens analyze their strengths and weaknesses, and establish personal goals.

"I have gone through some turbulent years with my teens," says Deborah Dow, a Maine mother who has successfully homeschooled four children. "Mostly they need[ed] to push against something (me) to find out who they were. Homeschooling is a wonderful alternative to traditional school, but it doesn't guarantee there won't be teen hassles. One thing that it did do was help them discover who they were and what they stood for, therefore defeating the peer pressure monster."

Kathy Ward, a mother from California, describes some tough days as a homeschooler: "Some weeks I felt like I was hanging on by my fingernails. But hang on I did. There wasn't any real frightening 'rebellion' with [my oldest son], but things weren't as comfortable or smooth as I had expected. What has been driven home for me is the importance of maintaining as nonadversarial an approach as possible with the teens and listening to them closely, sometimes laying aside my own previous notions of how things oughta be and really hearing them."

The high school curriculum

In considering what to study, homeschoolers at the high school level should begin by first defining their goals:

Watch Out!
In some areas, underage teens and non–high school graduates may be restricted from taking classes at community colleges. Instead, look into a distance learning course.

- Is your child preparing for college entrance or entry into a trade or vocational school?

- Does your child have a special talent or area of interest that he or she wishes to pursue?

- Is your teen planning to go directly to work after high school?

For those planning to attend a four-year college or university, expect these minimum requirements for high school work:

- **Language Arts:** Four years.

- **Math:** Three years, including algebra I and II and geometry. Students may also take advanced algebra, trigonometry, pre-calculus, or calculus.

- **Science:** Three years. Typical requirements are biology, physics, or chemistry with lab experience.

- **Social Science:** Two years or more of social science or history.

- **Foreign Language:** Two years. Most colleges prefer more.

You'll need to check with the institution of your choice for its specific requirements. Colleges expect able students to challenge themselves with more advanced courses in these subjects. Additionally, students are expected to engage the arts and have a functioning knowledge of computer skills. Some colleges even require applications to be filled out and sent in online.

A high school scope and sequence (a formal outline of what to study) can provide a helpful framework for you to use to start planning your program. Many homeschoolers actually find themselves speeding through the traditional high school curriculum in as few as two to three years. In this case, homeschoolers may choose to take on college classes or consider early entrance to college.

Students planning to enter college must acquire a certain breadth of reading experience. For sources on reading lists, see Appendix B. Different institutions also produce their own college-prep reading lists.

Homeschoolers should, of course, maintain their own list of books. In their book, *Homeschooling for Excellence* (see Appendix C), David and Micki Colfax list "One Hundred (More or Less) Favorite Books Remembered." Among the titles read by their four sons—three of whom entered Harvard—are such classics as *The Old Man and the Sea,* by Ernest Hemmingway as well as some lesser-known, nonfiction works, including *The Double Helix,* by James D. Watson.

Joanne Ward and her daughter Jenny are unschoolers. Here's how they devised their high school plan: "We sat down in the summer before sending in our notice of intent and brainstormed the kinds of things Jenny wanted to do that year so we could figure out a manner of attack and resources to line up. Sometimes she did some of what we'd come up with, but other times she changed horses in mid-stream or started a new interest. Jenny's activities (and therefore her 'curriculum') were arranged around her participation in a number of interest activities (creative writing club,

Unofficially...
Winston Churchill was a nonreader until age 13–14. Through home-schooling, he became well-versed in the classics and world history. In his mid-teens he was sent to a military academy where he caught up, reading and writing well enough to become a war correspondent at age 19.

book discussion club, math club, geography club, Latin club, science-by-mail, art club, young astronauts, Shakespearean theater, and more). So our planning took in what kinds of activities she wanted to participate in and the topics she planned to explore. Rather than doing much planning ahead, I recorded what actually took place as we lived our busy lives and took advantage of opportunities that came up."

In addition, Jenny took courses at their local community college. A National Merit finalist, Jenny was offered full scholarships from a number of schools, including Stanford University, the University of Florida, and the University of Rochester.

Handling advanced math and other tough subjects

Fears over difficult subject matter prevent many parents from considering homeschooling in the high school years. There are actually several ways to handle advanced coursework, including outside assistance. The key is meeting these issues head-on and getting help when you need it.

You can handle tough subjects by:

- Following a complete curriculum (available for specific subjects, curricular packages may include all supplemental materials and teacher support).
- Enrolling in a correspondence or distance learning course.
- Taking courses at a local college.
- Hiring a tutor.
- Securing a mentor.
- Employing software (particularly effective for teaching foreign languages).

- Supporting study with supplemental materials, such as lectures on tape or video instruction.

- Learning alongside your child.

Ideally, your teen should be taking on this coursework independently, perhaps in the form of self-instructional programs, as described in the following section.

Correspondence courses or distance education programs

These programs present terrific opportunities to enhance your learning. But like any consumer, you'll need to choose the product carefully. Also, make sure this is something your child is ready to take on. No matter what the program, the level of success depends primarily on their self-motivation and the ability to work independently.

When considering such a program, ask yourself the following:

- Does the school have a particular philosophy or orientation?

- Will participation in the program comply with local homeschool regulations?

- How flexible is the program? Can you incorporate other resources (work experience, independent projects, and other activities)

- Is it textbook-based?

- Are their credits accepted? (Before enrolling, it's a good idea to contact the school to which you plan to transfer these credits.)

- What administrative services are handled by the school? Do they provide student transcripts?

- What methods of assessment are used?

- Are students involved in the evaluation process?
- What is the background of the administrators and teachers?
- Are the teachers subject specialists?
- What kind of feedback can we expect to receive?
- How accessible are the teachers?
- Is tutoring available?
- How long does it take for work to be returned?
- How does one determine which level course to enroll in?
- What are the course requirements for graduation?
- What is the enrollment period?
- How long does the student have to complete the program?

Distance learners need to be familiar with computers, e-mail, and the Internet. Consider the following questions:

- Is your child comfortable with this technology?
- How is your computer proficiency?
- How much material is sent via the Internet? (Some send all instructional materials electronically, others use textbooks.)
- How much interaction is there with the teacher?
- How effective are the parent/study guides?
- Do online courses provide appropriate links to other resources?
- What is the required hardware?

Unofficially...
Further evidence of the distance learning explosion: American colleges and universities have doubled the number of these course offerings and enrollment in them between the 1994–95 and 1997–98 academic years.
—National Center for Education Statistics

- How much does it cost (including any additional fees)?

- Are materials all-inclusive, or are supplemental purchases required?

For more on distance learning, see Chapter 6.

Engaging the world

Homeschooling facilitates a teen's efforts to extend beyond the home. Unrestricted by a defined school day, homeschooled teens have greater opportunities to seek an apprenticeship, learn a new skill, or explore a subject in depth by engaging a related activity.

Looking up to a mentor

Mentoring is an opportunity to connect a young person with a suitable adult who can provide inspiration, advice, and support. Through a sustained relationship, mentors can introduce a career path, teach a vocational skill, assist with academic work, and help your teen deal with problems.

How does one find a mentor?

Teens can start by considering their existing relationships. Perhaps they have a relative or other favorite adult who is already performing this function on an informal basis. Discuss other possibilities with parents and consider approaching a relative, friend, neighbor, coach, youth club leader, your minister or rabbi, or a neighbor.

Mentorships are also available through programs such as Big Brothers/Big Sisters or Boys/ Girls Club of America. Religious institutions foster mentor relationships, and some corporations and social organizations may also involve their employees and members in formal programs.

To find a mentor, your teen should:

- Outline his or her ideas on paper. What is the purpose of this relationship?

- List the people he or she knows who might act as a mentor, or help find a mentor.

- Think of how the relationship will benefit the mentor. Will the teen provide the mentor with labor or other assistance?

- Rehearse the proposal. How much time will this require? How often will they meet? Consider proposing a trial period, or at least a few sessions, for getting acquainted.

- Understand that not everyone will be able to accept such an arrangement. In one case, an auto mechanic had to decline a young trainee for insurance reasons. Others simply will not have the time. If a prospective mentor is unable to perform in this capacity, encourage your teen to ask if that person can suggest someone else.

Once your teen enters a formal mentorship, make sure he or she is aware of the responsibilities that go along with it. Your teen should dress appropriately, arrive promptly for appointments, and keep to the allotted time. Your teen should also introduce you to the mentor.

Mentorships often evolve into lasting friendships and may possibly lead to a job.

Joining group activities

Without the built-in activities of school, home-schooled teens have to find other opportunities for getting involved with sports, academic clubs, musical or theatrical performances, or other activities.

> **"**
> All men who have turned out worth anything have had the chief hand in their own education.
> —Sir Walter Scott
> **"**

While the flexible nature of homeschooling helps accommodate these activities, take care not to overdo. Overscheduling may put a strain on your child and the entire family. While your child's enthusiasm may lead him or her to try many things, you want to avoid encouraging dilettantism. Moreover, your child should understand that membership in certain groups might involve a commitment of ongoing participation.

Participating in your local school

Many homeschoolers wish to participate in on-campus programs, such as band or orchestra, clubs, or other activities. Generally, a school's openness to this type of proposal is decided on a case-by-case basis, depending on the administrators involved, both at the school or district level. See Chapters 5 and 6 for more information.

The world of work

A teen can gain work experience through several paths. Some are paying, while others, such as internships or apprenticeships, provide valuable experience and skills. Teens may consider:

- Taking a part-time job
- Launching their own business
- Participating in a parent's work or job
- Assisting a mentor
- Apprenticing with a craftsperson or other professional
- Volunteering
- Interning

Again, keep an eye on how much your teen can handle. A job, particularly their own business, may become all-consuming. Expectations of career fulfillment or abundant profits may discourage your teen when they don't pan out. Make sure their goals remain realistic.

Apprenticeship/internship

These positions enable teens to expand their learning base, working among adults in an authentic work setting. Homeschoolers have an advantage over school kids in that their flexible schedules can be adapted to suit a variety of arrangements. For instance, a local radio station or community center may only need an intern in the morning, during school hours.

Internship guidebooks are useful for getting ideas about the type of arrangements available in your area of interest. But you can just as easily seek your own opportunities closer to home. A family friend or neighborhood business, may, in fact, offer greater opportunities to gain "real" work experience. Help your teen understand that any entry-level worker should expect to do a certain amount of grunt or "go-fer" work.

As with mentorships, it's important to first define your needs. When your teen finds an interesting opportunity, these are questions your teen should be asking:

- Will they require a personal interview and/or a resume?
- What is the duration of the position?
- What will be the work schedule?
- What precisely will be the duties?
- Is it paid or unpaid?
- What qualifications or skills are required?
- Are there other requirements, such as a driver's license and car?

Unofficially...
About 80 percent of teenagers work at some time during the school year during their junior or senior years. Seventeen-year-olds put in 18 hours of work on average per week during the school year, and 26 hours per week during the summer, according to *Education Week.*

- What will the sponsor provide (work materials, housing)?

- What skills will be gained?

Before you approach a prospective sponsor with your original proposal, make sure your plan is well thought out. When you've covered all the bases, you increase the likelihood that your plan will be accepted. In addition to proposing a trial period, it's helpful to demonstrate your interest with previous experience or study related to the field.

For example, one maker of musical instruments, deluged with requests from potential apprentices, instated a prerequisite. Applicants were asked to first build a simple lidded box for hand tools before he would consider taking them on.

Volunteering

Volunteering is another excellent way to gain experience, explore a field of interest, learn to work with a variety of people, and help support others in the community. Acts of service also help teens get outside themselves during an age when it's easy to become self-involved. Volunteer experiences are a great way to introduce even younger children to the concepts of work and service. And it's something the whole family can participate in together.

As with apprenticeships and internships, volunteer opportunities are open to anyone, and young people shouldn't encounter any barriers because they homeschool. However, certain jobs may have minimum age restrictions.

To learn more about volunteering, see Chapter 12.

Get a job

As with all endeavors, teens should think creatively and seek experiences that truly interest them when pursuing paid employment. While babysitting or shoveling snow are fine jobs, don't limit yourself to typically teenage work.

Most teens are eager to earn their own money, and paid employment engenders a sense of pride and responsibility. Parents can help teens decide if a particular job is right for them and how many hours are appropriate. Make sure that the work schedule doesn't undermine their learning, and any other aspect of their emotional or social development.

Both federal and state laws apply to teenage workers. Basically, 16- and 17-year-olds can work unlimited hours, but 14- and 15-year-olds are restricted to a certain number of hours per day and per week. There are also regulations on hazardous jobs. Contact your state labor office for details and for information about securing a work permit.

The young entrepreneur

Homeschoolers have established a tradition of creative entrepreneurship. Kids and adults alike enjoy the challenge and pride of having their own business. Kids, however, don't have the pressure of having to support themselves or the family and simply engage their enterprise as another creative learning experience.

Here's a sample of what homeschooled kids have done:

- Owned and operated an antique clothing business
- Run a nursery
- Taught guitar
- Designed and built treehouses
- Offered a word processing service
- Entertained at parties

Moneysaver
If your teen is starting work, this is a good opportunity to instill money management skills. They might prepare a budget, one that includes saving as well as spending. Perhaps they could take responsibility for their entertainment expenses, or if they drive, pay a portion of your car insurance.

- Designed gardens
- Trained and worked as a clown
- Assisted in the family bicycle repair business
- Designed products for people with disabilities
- Taught karate
- Bred tropical fish

Travel

Homeschoolers looking to venture further afield have the freedom to explore a variety of travel opportunities. One homeschooling family traveled all together on a year-long sail around the world. A self-educated teen, after studying the rain forest, took an extended tour of Panama.

Your teen can devise his or her own plan or participate in a formal program. These include:

- International or residential volunteering
- Foreign exchange programs
- Homeschool or other organized youth tours
- Language study programs
- Research programs that welcome volunteers, such as archaeological digs

Participation in these programs may earn academic credits, in some cases.

"Graduation"

Some homeschoolers plan to enter high school, or consider part-time enrollment, before graduation. (If this is the case for your teen, you'll need to plan at least two years ahead. See "Entering school," a little later in this chapter.) Other teens continue a home program to completion. In this case, if your teen desires a diploma:

Bright Idea
A high school diploma may not be an essential document; nevertheless, you might like to have one to present to your graduate. You can easily obtain a diploma from a commercial printer or office supply store, or create one on your computer.

- He or she can create one.
- Your teen may seek equivalency by taking the GED exam.
- Umbrella schools or programs may issue a high school diploma.

Keep in mind that a diploma is not a requirement for college admissions. This process is covered in depth in the following chapter. Joanne Ward, a homeschooling mom from Virginia, describes a graduation ceremony planned for a small group of homeschoolers: "The four teens who will be going off to college in the fall and their families planned what they thought would be meaningful. They have known each other for a number of years and have been in several enrichment/interest activities together (creative writing club, book discussion club, and math club) throughout their high school years.

"They have gotten caps and gowns (different colors representing different homeschools). We are using a local church, invited friends and families as well as the homeschooling community, will have a commencement speaker, and will have a reception afterwards in the fellowship hall. The parents will award a diploma to their own child. A band (composed of homeschoolers) will play during the reception.

"Afterwards, the graduates and their families are planning to go out for dinner at a local French cafe (three of the four grads have been studying French for several years)."

Your homeschooling progress report

In previous chapters, I've covered methods for assessing your child's academic progress. Beyond these measures, you'll need to simply step back on occasion and consider your homeschooling overall. How are your children doing? Are they happy and consistently excited about learning? While it is less tangible than a test score, your child's level of motivation is, nonetheless, a critical element to homeschooling success.

Your child's motivation

Children are naturally curious, interested, and eager to learn. Motivation issues, however, may confront you at some point during your homeschool journey and interrupt learning. So you need to remain vigilant regarding the bug-a-boo of motivation. Here are some tips:

- Maintain an environment conducive to learning. Eliminate TV and other distractions while you and your teen are engaged in learning. Interesting books and activities—appropriate to what your child's doing right now—should be readily available.

- Is there an area devoted to their projects? Concern over neatness might stifle your child's exploration of projects or endeavors they might fear are too messy.

- Remain responsive to your child's interests. While this is the most commonly heard piece of advice on homeschooling, it should serve as a reminder to even the most veteran parents. It's difficult when you're gung-ho on a new curriculum, let's say, and it proves to be ill-suited to your child's learning style.

- Emphasize your child's achievements. Gold stars or another appropriate reward go a long way toward bolstering a positive attitude. Create a special place to display their work.

"
My older son told his grand-mother he learns more at home than he ever did at school! He has told me he wants to learn Japanese this year... He would never have wanted to do this if I had tried to force him!
—Jole Reinhardt, homeschooling mother
"

Take the time to give yourself a pat on the back, too.

- Reflect on your attitude. Do you get impatient, are you anxious about whether you're covering everything? Are you stressed about money? Kids pick up on this sort of thing, and consciously or not, it may influence their own attitude.

- Is someone else's influence undermining your homeschooling? The resistance that you may have encountered when you first decided on this option may continue to haunt you. Are disapproving relatives or friends sending signals to your family? Be careful to handle this in a calm way. An emotional outburst could do further damage to your relationships and your homeschooling, not to mention make you appear as a bad model for your kids.

- Reinforce your support network. Maintain your connections with other homeschoolers. Arrange regular social opportunities; your active relationships with other committed homeschoolers will help boost everyone's motivation.

Make an honest appraisal of how it's going. Perhaps you might have to set aside a certain subject, scrap a curriculum that's not working, or seek help. Try to be proactive in addressing any problems.

A homeschooler reflects on her experience

"It is sometimes hard to be different," says Sarah Covington, a homeschooling mother. "Our oldest child wanted to go to school this year, because we are in a rural area—no neighbors with children—and wanted more social interaction. There is also a lot of pressure [for homeschoolers] to do far better than the average student in school, because it is assumed you *can't* do as well. Ryan, our oldest, is in sixth grade, although he is fifth-grade age. I wonder if I pushed him too much when he was younger because I felt that pressure. He is doing well academically, which has been an ego booster for us."

Entering school

Whether you've chosen to homeschool for a limited period or have decided to end homeschooling for other reasons, entering school is generally a straightforward process. Certain states may have related policies, such as Oregon, which considers homeschool students who return to public school as transfer students. The school will have to determine your child's grade level by considering your records, any formal coursework, and test results.

Homeschooler Kathy Ward's son (whose experience is described below) entered a private school, which requested transcripts, but they were hesitant about accepting homeschool documents. "They also gave him a battery of achievement tests and some essays to write," says Ward. "Our son was happy to comply and they accepted him readily after he jumped through these hoops."

High school students may have problems with earning credits that accrue toward graduation, unless they are enrolled in a program recognized by your state. Talk to the school as soon as possible (as much as two years in advance) if you want your high school student to return to public school and graduate.

"Two of our eight children have chosen to go to school at one time or another," says Kathy Ward, a homeschooling mother. "In each case, both of them began talking about it for a year or so before it happened. We parents sat down with the kids and discussed why the kids wanted to go and looked at possible alternative ways to meet their needs and to address the issues that concerned the kids. One of the children, a 16-year-old son, made a list of pros and cons to each of three options: continuing to homeschool, public school, and the local private school [He was not interested in enrollment at the local community college.] We discussed each option and gave him our input, but in the end, the choice was up to him. He chose to attend private school." [Ward's 13-year-old daughter chose to go to the local public school, where she is now enjoying her first year, eighth grade.]

"Our son went to school for the last year and a half of his high school years and did well," Ward says. "He enjoyed the chance to interact with a large pool of kids, he enjoyed learning from some of his teachers, and he liked participating in some of the school theater productions, and in some of the sports. He graduated with honors.

"He views his homeschooling years fondly, especially the freedom he had to explore his environment (we lived in a small mountain community and he was outdoors a lot) and the opportunities he had to work and play with his younger brother, with whom he is still close friends today."

Beverly Mastroianni from Ozark, MO, describes her family's return to school:

"I have no regrets although I get frustrated with the public school sometimes, but then I got frustrated homeschooling at times also. The kids all enjoy school, and they are progressing nicely. I do plan on supplementing with some math and of course lots of reading and a touch of history

Unofficially...
Reformers may look to homeschooling for ways to improve education for all children. Homeschooling supports the case for greater parental involvement, and the use of diverse methods matched to individual learning styles.

this summer. My 13-year-old son would love to homeschool again, but he is the one I had trouble with completing his assignments daily and applying himself to his work, so I feel the structure of public school is best for him right now. I may homeschool again in the future; I've kept all the books, etc. I don't want to close any doors, but for right now, things are going well."

Just the facts

- The drawbacks of traditional school are magnified in the teen years, when harmful peer influences make homeschooling that much more attractive.

- A goal of all home educators, self-directed learning is especially important for teens. Without a certain level of self-motivation and enthusiasm for the enterprise, homeschooling will have limited success.

- While homeschooling can optimize learning, you'll still need to face the emotions and conflicts that go with parenting a teen, and things can get very intense when they're at home. During these turbulent years, communication is key.

- Correspondence and online programs are great resources, but with so many available you'll have to shop carefully. Once you sign up, you may be reluctant to drop out, so make sure it's the right fit.

- With their flexible schedules, homeschooled teens are freer to pursue internships, part-time work, and other extracurricular activities. Take care, however, not to spread yourselves too thin.

GET THE SCOOP ON...
Preparing for college admissions
▪ How admissions officers view homeschoolers
▪ A checklist for the college-bound
▪ Alternative life choices

College and Beyond

Chapter 16

R esearchers estimate that approximately 30,000 homeschooled students are now applying to college. Over the next decade, as many as one million of these students may be knocking on college doors across the country.

Homeschool advocate Karl M. Bunday maintains a list of more than 910 selective colleges that have admitted homeschooled applicants. Among these institutions are Amherst, Boston University, Brigham Young University, Caltech, the College of William and Mary, MIT, Northwestern University, Oberlin, Princeton, Rice University, St. John's, Swarthmore, West Point, The U.S. Naval Academy, the U.S. Air Force Academy, the University of Pennsylvania, and Yale. Outside the United States, Oxford and Cambridge Universities in the U.K. and York University in Ontario, Canada, have also admitted homeschoolers.

While homeschoolers are indeed making their way, they may face unique challenges during the college admissions process. In this chapter I'll give you the lowdown on preparing for college from a homeschool perspective, from creating your own transcript to the ins and outs of college admissions testing. I'll help you consider whether college is right for you and explore other alternatives to a fulfilling and successful adult life.

Homeschoolers and college

The Colfaxes, along with many other homeschooling pioneers, have blazed the trail into college institutions, from state universities to the Ivy League. These institutions have realized that the self-motivation, emotional maturity, and diverse experience of homeschoolers offer a unique contribution to their student communities.

Of course, most colleges first require candidates to have a solid foundation in the basics: a prescribed number of years or credits in English, science, mathematics, foreign language, and other subjects, as well as strong reading and critical thinking skills. But beyond a core curriculum, according to the College Entrance Examination Board, "Colleges seek to put together a community of young people who are alive—who think, create, interact, share, and care." A homeschooler's uniqueness can work in their favor in college admissions, as most schools are looking to assemble a freshman class consisting of a broad range of backgrounds.

Hundreds of homeschoolers have entered college, many without a high school diploma or official transcript. As these admissions have become more common, many schools now welcome homeschoolers.

Many Christian schools and others, such as Oklahoma State University, send recruiters to interview homeschoolers. Other prestigious schools,

Unofficially...
Sixty-nine percent of homeschooled graduates go to college, only 2 percent less than public school graduates, according to a study by Dr. Brian D. Ray.

such as Stanford University and the U.S. Air Force Academy, have instated policies to deal with home-schooled applicants, while most other institutions evaluate each application on an individual basis. The most competitive schools, ironically, are often the most flexible.

Nevertheless, those homeschoolers who are college-bound must plan years in advance, work diligently toward their long-range goals, and be prepared to meet any additional requirements. According to the College Entrance Examination Board, "homeschooled students face special challenges when it comes to planning for and applying to college."

The challenges

Some of the challenges homeschooled applicants may face include:

- Some institutions may have additional requirements for homeschoolers, such as the GED, or SAT II Subject Tests, not required of other applicants.

- Despite the most careful documentation some officials may view a home transcript with suspicion. Test scores, and other elements of the application, therefore, become more important.

- Many students, unfamiliar with standardized testing and the formal classroom environment, will have to take an extra measure of preparation.

- Some admissions officers will be concerned about socialization.

- Homeschoolers must remain organized and self-motivated throughout the application process, keeping track of important dates and deadlines.

- Students must seek out and obtain unbiased evaluations.

Bright Idea
Consider attending a residential summer college program. A nice introduction to campus life, such a program can also prove a homeschooler's ability to function in a classroom setting.

Get a head start on college admissions

Homeschoolers should start exploring college admissions earlier than traditional students, beginning in the ninth grade. Begin researching specific colleges or universities, their course requirements, whether they have admitted homeschoolers in the past, and if they maintain a specific policy regarding homeschoolers. An early start is particularly important if your child is considering competitive institutions.

College-bound homeschoolers must:

- Engage in a college-prep academic program (see the minimum course requirements listed in Chapter 15).

- Acquire good study skills.

- Maintain systematic documentation of all activities.

- Compile a transcript, which may include grades and credits, or acquire a transcript through an umbrella or cover program.

- Consider taking advanced-level or college courses.

- Prepare for college-entrance exams.

- Maintain quality portfolio materials, including research papers or other demonstration of writing ability, and other exemplary work.

- Establish a financial plan to pay for college.

Once you've identified the schools your child is interested in, contact their admissions offices as early as possible.

Earning college credit in high school

With the benefits of time-efficiency and self-directed learning, many homeschoolers are able to take on advanced coursework during their high school years.

Advanced Placement (AP) courses

Homeschoolers with the ability can participate in Advanced Placement classes and can get a jump on earning college credit. In addition to the opportunity to study a subject in depth, AP courses prepare homeschoolers for college-level work and help them adjust to being in a classroom environment, making formal presentations and taking tests. Additionally, AP courses look very attractive on a homeschool record when it comes to college admissions. A passing grade in an AP exam may allow the student to bypass a lower-level required class in college, therefore saving time and money.

Advanced Placement subjects include art, computer science, economics, English, environmental science, government and politics, music theory, psychology, U.S. history, and statistics.

Homeschoolers interested in AP courses should contact their local high school. If you wish, you may take the exam without enrolling in a course. According to the College Board, many of these homeschoolers perform well on these exams, provided they have engaged in appropriate coursework and in-depth study.

CLEP exams

Homeschoolers can demonstrate college-level knowledge through CLEP (College-Level Examination

Watch Out!
Planning to apply for college scholarships? Examine the eligibility rules carefully—a student may be disqualified for earning too many college credits while in high school.

Program) exams. This allows them to accumulate credits toward a degree, earn exemptions from taking introductory courses, and determine placement, such as in foreign language courses. Approximately 2,900 institutions award college credit to those who perform well on the CLEP exams.

There are 34 CLEP exams. They include general exams (such as English composition, humanities, college mathematics, natural sciences, social sciences, and history) and subject exams in college-level French, German, and Spanish, freshman college composition, American government, college algebra, and trigonometry. Subject exams are also offered in business topics, such as principles of marketing and introductory business law.

Find out if the college your teen plans to attend grants credit for CLEP exams. Many of these schools administer the exams at their own CLEP test centers (for test locations, check College Board Online).

Choosing a college

It's beyond the scope of this chapter to advise your family on how to choose a college. Basically, though, teens should identify the institutions that are the right match for them, their subject interests, and their career goals. You will also have to evaluate the school's:

- Academic offerings
- Size
- Cost/availability of financial aid
- Ranking (overall and in the area of interest)
- Academic environment
- Religious orientation

- Quality of student body
- Facilities
- Innovative programs (like study abroad)
- Location

Consider what your son or daughter is looking for in the overall college experience.

By and large, homeschoolers research schools in much the same way as other college-bound students: by reading guidebooks, reviewing college catalogs, and attending college fairs.

What admissions officers look for in homeschoolers

While many institutions specify course requirements for all incoming freshmen, Stanford University does not. Their letter to homeschool applicants reads: "We do not have a required curriculum or set of courses for applicants to Stanford...Primarily we want them to be able to demonstrate that they have successfully undertaken a serious, rigorous course of study." They also mention that a prescribed or approved homeschool program is not necessary. Instead, Stanford looks for broader evidence of "intellectual vitality."

Within the homeschooler's written application, Stanford is interested to learn why the family chose homeschooling, how the learning was organized, and what benefits the student derived from the experience. Other schools request applicants to describe their home education, including Rice University in Texas and Wesleyan University in Connecticut.

While many schools will accept a home-generated transcript, they may still be concerned over academic ability. Therefore, standardized test

Timesaver
To view a listing of more than 940 selective colleges and universities that have accepted home-schoolers, see Karl M. Bunday's Web site, "School Is Dead; Learn in Freedom" (http://learninfreedom.org/colleges_4_hmsch_html).

scores take on more significance in a home-schooler's application and may result in additional requirements. Southern Methodist University in Texas and Rhodes College in Tennessee, for example, require additional SAT II Subject Tests from homeschoolers that are not required of other applicants. Three SAT II Tests are required of home-school applicants to the University of Texas. Other state universities may require as many as four to eight SAT II Tests of homeschoolers. Stanford does not require any SAT II Subject Tests; nevertheless, they strongly recommend them for homeschooled students. (I describe college admissions tests, including the SAT II Tests, later in this chapter.)

Colleges also seek well-rounded individuals, and admissions officers may be concerned that homeschoolers will be limited in this regard. They may also be looking for evidence that a home-schooler will be able to function socially within the campus environment. Stanford has found home-school applicants "are often involved in sports, community service, religious life, drama, local politics, or work with a dedication and energy that we find very attractive, and easily comparable to conventional high school activities…" Other institutions are on the lookout for equivalent experience, so make sure your record documents the breadth of your activities.

Another potential sticky point is recommendation letters, which are traditionally provided by teachers. Institutions may naturally suspect a glowing recommendation from your mom. Some schools, including Stanford, will allow one recommendation from a parent, but they suggest that you seek other unbiased sources. (I'll also cover recommendation letters a little later.)

Still other institutions have no policy and treat homeschoolers largely as they would other applicants. Such is the case at Harvard University.

Gaining admission to the college of your choice

Bear in mind that beyond the issues specific to homeschoolers, other factors determine college admissions. For one, each college and university has its own specific goals in determining the makeup of its incoming freshman class. Another important factor is the size and quality of the applicant pool, which has grown larger, making college admissions increasingly competitive.

This may not necessarily leave homeschoolers at a disadvantage. Generally, the more selective the institution, the more other factors besides grades play into an admissions decision. At Dartmouth College, for example, the admissions office considers essays first. In addition to demonstrating the student's writing ability, the essay also enables the reader to get a sense of the student's individuality. This, of course, is an area where homeschoolers can really shine.

To maximize successful admissions, students should apply to several schools where they feel they are a good match, giving each application their best efforts. They should also understand that there is never just one college that's the best for them. Another option to consider is to enroll in a two-year college and then apply as a transfer student to a four-year institution.

In the end, whether the college admits or rejects you is not a reflection on your worth or, for that matter, homeschooling. It's about how you fit in with the other students competing for the same slots in a freshman class.

Watch Out!
Most states have a minimum age requirement for taking the GED, usually 18. You may need to secure special permission if you wish to take it earlier.

What about a high school diploma or GED?

Generally, a high school diploma is not required for college admission. Certain institutions, however, ask homeschoolers to take the GED, the examination for high school equivalency. One such school is Southern Adventist University, which states that homeschoolers must pass the GED exam if they have less than one year of formal high school education and if they have not received an official high school diploma.

Homeschoolers looking to obtain a diploma or some "proof" of completing high school may believe they need the GED. However, when it comes to college admissions, taking the GED may adversely affect your record, as it is commonly associated with students who have dropped out, and conveys only basic competency. So, make sure the GED is required before you take it.

Homeschool transcripts

Many institutions, including the most competitive, have admitted homeschoolers based on home-generated transcripts. However, this policy varies widely among schools.

For example, U.S.News Online related the case of homeschooler Rio Benin from Berkeley, California, who scored a perfect 1600 on his SATs and won a $20,000 scholarship in the 1999 Intel Science Talent Search. Yet he could not gain admission to the University of California San Diego without a high school transcript. Benin was eventually accepted to Harvard, Berkeley, and Cambridge University, England, and chose to attend Harvard.

So, again, it's important to research your schools and learn early on of any special requirements that will affect you.

How to create your own

Effective transcripts are easily generated from your homeschool records. You should have in place a solid organizational system; many homeschoolers find the computer streamlines record keeping. You can find software programs with templates for homeschool records, or you can create an effective system on your own, using a standard spreadsheet program. You may wish to view an actual high school transcript for an idea of the traditional format.

Wheaton College, a Christian institution in Wheaton, Illinois, recommends providing a syllabus with a home transcript. This helps the college determine the content of the course. It helps to begin creating transcripts as early as the ninth grade year, updating them periodically. These documents are also helpful for your children to review, as a transcript helps them evaluate their program as they look ahead to college.

Translating homeschool activities to your transcript

Homeschoolers are attractive college candidates because of their diverse experience—they travel, work, and volunteer in their communities; interact with family, friends, and other homeschoolers; participate in hands-on projects; and read widely. This activity makes an impression on college officials, so make sure your record shows the fullness of your homeschool experience.

A journal is a good tool for detailing all activities, from field trips and internships to sports and special hobbies. Periodically, you can revisit these records and average the time spent on many of the activities. Then assign broad subject categories (English, science, math, social science) to each. To streamline your entries, you can employ a coding system that corresponds to course headings. For example, when the student writes a piece for your community newspaper, mark the entry "E" for English.

While extracurricular activities do help your record, it's worthwhile to note that, for college admissions, dedicated participation in one or two projects looks much better than a list of numerous, unrelated activities.

Computing credits and your GPA

Unofficially
Homeschooler Michael Kearney became the youngest person to earn a master's degree when he graduated in 1998 from Middle Tennessee State University with a degree in biochemistry at age 14.

From a college admissions perspective, grades are used primarily to compare students applying from the same or similar large high schools. You may, however, wish to apply traditional grades in your child's home transcript and compute a GPA (grade point average).

Generally, one credit corresponds to a one-year high school course. Clonlara School, a home-based correspondence program, awards Carnegie Credit units, with one unit equal to 180 hours of work. Other homeschoolers award credits for fewer or more hours. It might be helpful to include an explanation of your credit system.

A GPA is determined by the traditional grade scale: A = 4.0, B = 3.0, C = 2.0, D = 1.0. F = 0. To determine the grade points for each course, multiply the course credit by the grade points. For example, A 1-credit course with an assigned grade of A would earn four grade points. Add the grade points and divide the total grade points by the total number of credits to obtain your GPA.

Other important elements of your homeschool record

Admissions officers are usually willing to work individually with homeschoolers to evaluate their high school documentation. In lieu of an official transcript, other items can help support your record.

A portfolio

Always popular among homeschoolers, the portfolio has gained plenty of attention in recent years, being touted among traditional educators as a more accurate reflection of learning.

A college-bound homeschool portfolio may include:

- Standardized test scores
- Reading lists
- A writing sample (recommended by the College Entrance Examination Board)
- Research papers
- Featured work from courses in which the student excelled
- Pages from a logbook recording daily learning activities
- Self-tests
- Solved math or scientific problems
- Essays
- A resume or work experience
- Volunteer work
- Awards or honors
- Travel experience

Homeschoolers may adapt a portfolio for college admissions; however, the acceptability of this form depends on the particular institution. Schools

Bright Idea
A college admissions portfolio is an opportunity to showcase your unique strengths and experience. Demonstrate any special concentration with examples of your work, activities, or volunteer work related to that subject.

that accept portfolios include Kansas State University and Colorado College. Homeschool applicants to Kansas State University, for example, may submit a portfolio of their work in place of an accredited diploma; however, they must also submit a record of their high school program of study. This can be a transcript from an independent study high school program or a home-generated transcript. The makeup of an admissions portfolio would be up to the student's discretion.

Many institutions, though, particularly larger ones, may simply not have the time to evaluate a portfolio. Inquire with the schools you are interested in to learn their policy regarding portfolios.

Letters of recommendation

As I mentioned earlier, some colleges accept recommendations from a parent, but admissions officers may view these recommendations as biased. Have your child think of other adults that know him or her well, such as:

- The professor of a college course
- An employer
- Your pastor
- A coach
- A leader of a volunteer organization or other group in which he or she has been active
- A teacher of a workshop
- A tutor
- A mentor

If children don't have such contacts, they need to become more involved. Incorporate varied activities into your home program and find out more about how to participate in the community.

(To learn more about volunteering, see Chapters 12 and 15.)

The college interview

A personal interview is beneficial to homeschoolers, as it gives them a chance to present their full potential as a candidate. Find out if the college your child is considering provides for an interview as part of the application process. If so, make sure to schedule the appointment well in advance of your campus visit.

Most larger institutions, however, cannot accommodate interviewing and decide admissions solely based on submitted criteria. Speak to the admissions office, and, if possible, see if you can arrange an interview.

College admissions testing

In addition to a transcript, the most common requirements are the Scholastic Assessment Test (SAT) or the American College Testing Program (ACT). Both tests are intended to predict a student's performance in college, as well as provide a common yardstick for comparing students from a wide range of educational backgrounds. As I mentioned previously, these test results may take on more importance in the college application of a homeschooler.

Until recently, the SAT was required by schools in the northeast and on both coasts, while the ACT was traditionally the test for colleges in the Midwest. Today most schools accept results of both the SAT and ACT.

It's important to prepare for these tests within your high school program. For example, you must be competent in math concepts—arithmetic,

Moneysaver
Test preparation courses are costly, and they may not help that much. According to the College Board, studies have shown that 20-hour test courses improve scores on the average only about 10 points on the verbal section and about 15 points on the math section.

algebra I and II, and geometry—in order to perform well on these tests. Secure practice materials at your local high school or from the test publishers. Study guides are widely available from a number of other sources. Software programs can provide more practice. If both tests are accepted by your prospective school, take the one you best perform on. (See the following two sections for more on the SAT and the ACT.)

Early preparation is especially important for those homeschoolers who have little or no experience with testing. Students need to become comfortable with the entire process before taking these formal exams.

Before scheduling testing, consider application deadlines of the colleges and scholarship agencies that are of interest to your child. Many selective colleges begin to process applications as much as 10 months in advance. It will take up to eight weeks after the test for your child to receive the scores, so you'll need to factor in at least that amount of time.

Both the SAT and ACT can be taken at the end of the junior year or the fall of the senior year of high school. Consider the summer or fall before you begin applying to colleges. Administered by independent agencies throughout the country, the tests are given five or six times throughout the school year. Homeschoolers usually take tests at their local high school. You may retake the tests, but be aware that you cannot report only the latest or the highest scores.

The SAT

The SAT is designed to test critical thinking and problem solving. Compared to the ACT, the SAT tests vocabulary to a much higher degree. But unlike the ACT, the questions are not entirely multiple choice. What can you expect to find on the SAT?

Three types of verbal questions:

- Analogies (knowledge of word meanings, ability to see the relationship in a pair of words)
- Sentence completions
- Critical reading

Three types of math questions:

- Five-choice multiple choice
- Four-choice quantitative comparison
- Student-produced response

The ACT

The ACT is a content-based test that measures knowledge, understanding, and skills that reflect the student's education. As the test is based on curriculum, a solid high school program in English, mathematics, science, and social studies is necessary in order to do well on the test. Unlike the SAT, the ACT includes a science reasoning test, trigonometry within the math section, and grammar testing.

The 215 multiple-choice questions of the ACT cover these sections:

- English
- Math
- Reading
- Science reasoning

Compared to traditional students, homeschoolers on average score higher on the ACT. They do best in science and reading, while math scores tend to be lower than the national average.

Unofficially
In his recent study of home-schooled adults, researcher Gary Knowles asked his subjects, if they had to live their lives over again, whether or not they would wish to be homeschooled. Ninety-six percent answered yes.

Watch Out!
The PSAT is only given once a year, in October. Make sure to contact your local high school as early as June.

The PSAT/NMSQT

The PSAT (Preliminary Scholastic Assessment Test) is good preparation for the SAT I. It consists of five sections: two that test verbal reasoning skills, two that test mathematical skills, and one that tests writing skills. All those who take the PSAT (also called the National Merit Scholarship Qualifying Test), including homeschoolers, also have the chance to qualify for the National Merit Scholarship. (For more information about the scholarship program, contact your local school's guidance office or the National Merit Scholarship Corporation: 1560 Sherman Avenue, Suite 200, Evanston, IL 60201-4897.)

Homeschoolers must register for the PSAT/NMSQT through their local high school. (The test may also be administered by private schools.) Most students take the test during their sophomore or junior year. However, only scores recorded in the junior year can qualify for the National Merit Scholarship. Homeschoolers should contact their school in June to request the test for the following October.

You'll need to find out the day your school will administer the test—they have a choice of two possible days in October. Also inquire about the fees involved, which may include an administrative cost charged by the school.

The SAT II Subject Tests

Some colleges and universities also require homeschoolers to take SAT II tests, as required by some institutions.

The following subjects are covered in the SAT II:

- English: literature, writing
- History: American history and social studies, world history
- Mathematics level IC
- Mathematics level IIC
- Science: biology E/M (Ecological/Molecular), chemistry, physics
- Language tests: French, German, modern Hebrew, Italian, Latin, Spanish

Some of the more selective colleges and universities require one to three (or more) SAT II Subject Tests, as well as the AP exams. Ideally, your child should take these exams when related coursework is still fresh in his or her mind. If your child plans to take several, stagger the test dates to cut down on stress.

It's especially important for homeschoolers to stay on top of testing dates and deadlines—remember, you won't have reminders from a guidance office. You'll need to maintain a calendar with all critical dates, including test registration deadlines.

Financial aid

Paying for college is a concern for all families, not just homeschoolers. Procedures are largely the same as they are for traditional students. It's important that you:

- Contact the college's financial aid office for information.
- Explore all financial aid options available to you.
- Learn the requirements.
- Make sure you are qualified.
- Secure applications and observe deadlines.

Unofficially
In 1998, more than 70 home-schooled high school seniors were selected as semifinalists by the National Merit Scholarship Corporation.

Bright Idea
There are several scholarship databases available online. Check out Peterson's COLLEGEQUEST (http://216.33.117.163/plugin.nd/College_Quest/pgGateway) and College Board's Scholarship Search (www.collegeboard.org/fundfinder/html/ssrchtop.html).

Investigate the availability of scholarships from local, state, federal, and private sources. Make sure not to overlook scholarships provided by organizations, such as corporations, labor unions, professional associations, religious organizations, and credit unions.

There are three basic categories of financial aid: grants and scholarships, which do not have to be repaid by the student; loans, which must be repaid with interest; and work study, in which student employment is subsidized by the government and the college. You can obtain information about these programs through the college to which you are applying.

A college progress report

Well, your child has made it! But this is only the beginning of a new journey. For any student—not just homeschoolers—college is a big adjustment. Very often, students may find that first semester rough going, with the rigors of college-level coursework resulting in poor grades. So it's important for both students and parents to assess their progress. It's best to identify any problems early and seek help. Students should be proactive in addressing their weakest areas. They might try another approach, such as taking an introductory course, lining up a study partner, or finding a study group. They should also communicate with professors and classmates and let them know if they're having any difficulties. A peer or upperclassman may be available for tutoring. It's cheaper to pay for tutoring now than wasting a semester or more.

The college or university will also provide available assistance, which may include workshops in time management. Remember, you're a paying customer, so don't be shy about requesting help or accessing services. Their goal is for students to succeed.

Be as proactive with any personal issues as well. Encourage your teens to keep in close touch with you, and let them know you're there for them.

Alternatives to college

College is a major commitment in a young person's life, not to mention its tremendous financial impact on the family. Students should never invest time, money, and effort into earning a degree if they're not sure it's something they really want or need. As I've discussed throughout this book, homeschooling is about tailoring education to individual needs and interests, and this philosophy should extend to a decision on college.

It's worth noting that many homeschoolers have gone on to live productive and interesting adult lives without attending college. In many cases, homeschooling led them to follow their interests directly into a career. Some choose apprenticeship into a trade, while others channel their independent ways into launching their own business. There are many choices.

Students may need some time to decompress from coursework, explore career interests, and discover what they really want to do. During this period they can also explore the possibility of attending college.

If, after a time, a student decides on college, they will most likely need to submit a dated transcript demonstrating high school coursework, along with college admissions test scores, depending on the particular requirements of the institution. In addition to the overall academic record, admissions officers will also be interested in the student's experience, and how it relates to their intended course of study. A visual arts program, for example, will look for demonstrated ability and artistic development within the candidate's portfolio. Another option is to enroll in a two year college, earn credits and establish an academic record, and then transfer into a four-year program.

❝ There is life without a four-year degree

...if you go to college without ever thinking about the possibility of not going to college, it takes on many of the same negative qualities as 'compulsory' school. *Don't enroll just because it's expected of you.* —Grace Llewellyn, *The Teenage Liberation Handbook*

❞

Going to college provides no guarantees when it comes to employment. No one can be sure what the job market will be like 10 years from now. Someone with an MBA may have no more security than a chef or someone who drives a taxi. In fact, very few of the fastest-growing occupations, according to Labor Department statistics, require a four-year degree.

Consider the following job areas—none require a four-year degree:

- Forestry management and conservation
- Landscaping and gardening
- Design (industrial, interior, apparel, textile)
- Photography
- Fine arts and administration
- Construction trades
- Health care (emergency medical technicians, nursing, laboratory technicians, etc.)
- Food services
- Retailing and sales
- Real estate
- Mechanical trades
- Performing arts

- Woodworking and other crafts
- Sports and fitness
- Computer programming
- Drafting
- Paralegal

Entry into these fields may involve vocational training or attendance at a two-year college or professional program.

Be your own career counselor

What do I want to be when I grow up? Lots of adults still ponder this question, which can lead them to alter their career paths several times over the course of their lives.

Young people may feel extraordinary pressure in this regard, which may force them into a job or other decision before they can discover what it is they really want to do. Where should they start? Like a career office, they can begin exploring their options by developing a personal profile of their interests and talents.

To build a profile:

1. Start recording personal affinities in a notebook or diary.

2. Throughout the homeschooling experience, continue to explore interests through elective courses, special workshops, internships, service jobs, and other activities.

3. Seek out adults to discuss their work, why they love or hate their jobs, the path they took to their careers, and their future goals.

4. Begin to define personal interests. Do you like to work with people? Are you interested in the media and the arts? Are you very mechanical,

do you enjoy building things? What topics are of personal importance to you? Write these down as categories.

5. Brainstorm areas of work that relate to these categories. There are many ways for people to participate in the areas that interest them most. For example, you don't have to be a star performer to have an important job in the entertainment world. There are set and costume designers, electricians, administrative personnel, and a host of craftspeople that play an active role in the field.

6. Explore ways in which you can try out these fields, such as volunteering or taking a summer job. Discuss your findings with your parents.

7. Once the choice is down to a specific area or type of work, extend research to specific job opportunities. Explore resources in the community.

8. Prepare a resume.

College by mail

One alternative to college is to, in effect, continue homeschooling by taking college courses at home. There are numerous programs available, from correspondence schools to distance learning programs. This way you eliminate any concerns over a questionable college environment (campus safety, drinking, and other issues).

College by mail offers an incredible savings on tuition. Every state university, for example, has a correspondence program. Their four-year degree through home study may cost as little as 15 percent of the same degree earned on campus. Four-year degrees by correspondence may not be available in every subject major, and some degree programs specify on-campus requirements, such as completing at least a year or two on campus.

Of course, you don't have to stop there. Whether you pursue graduate school, launch a new business, learn a new trade or skill, or start some other life adventure (like homeschooling!), it is all a continual process of learning. I hope that this book has provided you with some ideas that will help you support the joy of learning in your family. Good luck!

Just the facts

- If going to college is your goal, it's vitally important to engage a rigorous course of study. Admissions officers will be on the lookout for any weak areas, particularly among homeschoolers.

- Homeschoolers can jump ahead and earn college credit through college or AP courses and/or CLEP exams. These efforts will impress admissions officers, and might save you money too.

- If you maintain good records, creating a transcript is relatively simple. Hundreds of homeschoolers before you have been admitted to college on the basis of similar original documents.

- Like it or not, test scores hold greater importance in the application of a homeschooler. Prepare early with a solid academic program, supplemented by test study and practice.

- College isn't for everyone; in fact, 50 percent of college students drop out before graduating. It's advisable to take some time to figure out what you really want to do.

Glossary

achievement test A test that measures the extent to which a person has acquired certain information or mastered certain skills, usually as a result of planned instruction or training.

ACT Assessment written and sponsored by American College Testing Inc. Along with the SAT, the ACT assessment is a major college admissions test used throughout the United States. *See also* **SAT.**

afterschooling Supplemental educational activities that take place outside of traditional school.

alternative assessment Any method, outside of traditional standardized tests, that measures a student's knowledge and abilities. Alternative forms of assessment include portfolios and performance-based assessments. *See also* **portfolio** and **performance-based assessment.**

AP Advanced Placement Formal advanced-level courses in several academic subjects, with exams given at the conclusion of each course. Students earning high scores on AP exams can be placed in upper-level college courses and may receive credit for introductory courses.

aptitude test A test designed to measure a person's ability to learn and the likelihood of success in future school work or in a specific career.

assisted homeschooling Homeschooling that incorporates any supplemental option, such as correspondence schools, umbrella schools, independent study programs, charter schools, co-ops, and the like.

attachment parenting A style of parenting that responds to an infant's need for trust and affection, especially during the first three years of life. Includes breastfeeding on demand; immediate response to a baby's crying; close physical contact, including the use of cloth infant carriers, and sleeping in a family bed.

authentic assessment A form of assessment that presents tasks that are significant and meaningful to students and that reflect the kinds of mastery demonstrated by experts. Authentic assessment both mirrors and measures student performance in "real-work" tasks and situations.

autodidact A self-taught person.

basic skills The traditional building blocks of a curriculum that are most commonly associated with explicit instruction in elementary language arts and mathematics.

CAI Computer-assisted instruction.

CAT California Achievement Test. A norm-referenced achievement test (one which compares students with a specified group of the same level) for grades K-12. Published by CTB/McGraw-Hill.

Charlotte Mason method Also called the Living Books approach. A teaching method based on the writing of Charlotte Mason, an early 19th-century British educator, who respected the abilities of children and advocated their involvement in real-life experiences, the reading of "living" books (primary sources), and the practice of narration.

charter schools Nonsectarian public schools run independently of the traditional public school system by groups, which may include parents, teachers, or foundations. These schools are established and run on the basis of a **charter**—a performance contract with the school board—which details the school's mission, program, and goals.

classical education A medieval form of education based on a three-part model called the trivium, which incorporates a grammar stage, logic or dialectic stage, and a rhetoric stage.

CLEP College-Level Examination Program. College-level equivalency exams that enable students who achieve a passing score to earn college credits at participating colleges and universities.

College Board (College Entrance Examination Board) A nonprofit organization that assists students in entering higher education. The SAT and AP programs are administered by the College Board. *See also* **SAT** and **AP.**

cover school See **umbrella school.**

CTBS California Test of Basic Skills. A norm-referenced achievement test (one which compares students with a specified group of the same level) that measures reading, language, and math in grades K-12.

curriculum A plan of instruction that details what students are to know and how they are to learn it.

deschooling The process whereby many of the negative experiences are "cleansed" from a child who is making the transition from public or traditional school to homeschool. A component of the unschooling approach.

distance learning   An alternative mode of education in which teacher and student(s) in different locations communicate with one another using technology such as electronic media or interactive television.

DOE   Department of Education (usually refers to the state department of education).

dual enrollment   Occurs when a homeschooled child enrolls in school on a part-time basis.

dysarthria   A disorder of the speech muscles that affects the ability to pronounce words.

dyslexia   Impairment of the ability to deal with language (speaking, reading, spelling, writing). A dyslexic may see letters, syllables, or words upside down, reversed, blurred, backwards, or otherwise distorted.

eclectic homeschooling   A form of homeschooling in which parents pick and choose various educational methods according to their children's needs.

ERIC   Educational Resources Information Center.

FAQ   List of frequently asked questions and their answers.

GED   General Education Diploma. Confers high school equivalency to students who pass a series of competency tests.

homeschool co-ops   Generally offshoots of support groups, co-ops are organized by homeschoolers who pool their efforts in order to share teaching responsibilities, materials, and other resources.

homeschooling   The practice of children being taught at home under the guidance of their parents, rather than sending them to public school.

home study program (HSP)   A public satellite program that involves instruction at home. Also public school independent study program (ISP). *See also* **ISP.**

HSLDA Home School Legal Defense Association

IDEA Individuals with Disabilities Education Act. A landmark 1975 federal law, which guarantees that all children with disabilities receive a "free, appropriate public education." The law has been amended several times but originally addressed children with disabilities who were kept out of the public schools, and were taught either at home or in institutions.

IEP Individualized education plan or program. A written educational prescription developed for each handicapped child. School districts are required by law to develop these plans in cooperation with parents.

inclusive When used to describe a homeschooling group, this implies that membership or participation is not defined by characteristic criteria, such as religion, ethnic background, or special interest.

interest-initiated learning Also child-directed learning. A philosophy in which educational activity is dictated by the child's own interest.

Iowa Tests of Basic Skills (ITBS) General achievement tests for grades 3 through 8. Along with others, such as the Comprehensive Tests of Basic Skills and the Stanford Achievement Test series, they are designed to measure how well a student has learned the basic knowledge and skills that are taught in elementary and middle schools, in such areas as reading and mathematics. *See also* **Stanford Achievement Test.**

ISP Independent study program. A formal educational program of institutional schools, public or private, which may enroll homeschoolers, and supervise their home study, provide coursework or curriculum, maintain school records, issue diplomas, or provide other services.

LEA   Local education agency.

learning disabilities (LDs)   Disorders of the basic psychological processes that affect the way a child learns. Many children with learning disabilities have average or above-average intelligence. Included are perceptual handicaps and dyslexia.

learning styles   Distinct cognitive styles in which an individual is believed to best process information. Based on studies by psychologist Howard Gardner, who proposed that all people possess seven distinct intelligences, or capabilities: spatial, bodily-kinesthetic, musical, linguistic, logical mathematical, interpersonal, and intrapersonal.

manipulative   Any physical object that can be used to represent or model a problem situation or develop a mathematical concept.

mentor   A mature person who gives advice or help.

modeling   Demonstrating to a student how to do a task with the expectation that the student will copy the model. Modeling often involves talking about how to work through a task or thinking aloud.

Montessori method   Founded in 1907 by Italian physician Dr. Maria Montessori, the Montessori approach to education emphasizes individualized learning through a choice of hands-on activities, education of the whole personality rather than the teaching of a specific body of knowledge, and a mixed-age setting, among other qualities. Applicable to children of all ages, Montessori is readily adapted into a home-based program.

Moore formula   An approach to homeschooling devised by Raymond S. Moore, the formula prescribes a balance of manual work and study, and daily service within the home and community.

notification   The process in which a child's parent or guardian formally notifies the school superintendent or district of their intention to homeschool the child.

outcome-based education (OBE) An education theory that guides curricula by setting goals for students to accomplish. Outcome-based education focuses more on these goals, or **outcomes,** than on "inputs," or subject units. This theory has drawn intense criticism from parents and others who fear that by focusing on outcomes, schools are inflicting values onto students.

performance-based assessment Requires students to perform hands-on tasks, such as writing an essay or conducting a science experiment. Such assessments are becoming increasingly common as alternatives to multiple-choice, machine-scored tests.

phonics An instructional strategy used to teach letter-sound relationships to beginning readers by having them "sound out" words.

portfolio A file of materials created by a student which displays and explains skills, talents, experience, and knowledge gained over a period of time.

PSAT/NMSQT Preliminary Scholastic Assessment Test/National Merit Scholarship Qualifying Test. A high school test that measures verbal and math skills and prepares students for the SAT I. It determines eligibility for the National Merit Scholarship.

relaxed homeschooling An approach that encourages interest-initiated learning in homeschooled children, along with gentle guidance from parents. For teaching basic skills (math and language), relaxed homeschooling advocates the use of more structured methods.

remediation Process in which an individual is provided instruction and practice in skills that are weak or nonexistent in an effort to develop/strengthen these skills.

Ritalin Trade name for one of several stimulant drugs often given to modify hyperactivity in children.

SAHM Stay-at-home mom.

SAT Scholastic Assessment Test (formerly the Scholastic Aptitude Test). A standard college admissions test published by the College Entrance Examination Board.

scope & sequence Curricular guidelines that outline what to study and when.

SEA State education agency.

socialization An issue that relates to homeschooling's capacity to provide appropriate social experiences for children, and whether this mode of learning promotes adequate social skills. Frequently cited by critics of homeschooling, socialization is disparagingly referred to among homeschoolers as the "s-word."

standardized test A test that compares a child's performance with the performance of a large group of similar children. IQ tests and most achievement tests are standardized.

Stanford Achievement Test A widely used test, also known as the Stanford 9, designed to measure achievement in the curriculum content taught in grades 1 through 9.

statement of intent A form submitted to state or local officials that provides formal notification of a family's intention to homeschool their child. Required in many states, this form may include information about the curricular program and other details, depending on local homeschooling regulations.

structured homeschooling See **traditional homeschooling.**

TAG Talented and gifted. The acronym that generally refers to those children formally identified in an education setting as academically talented, and related services.

traditional homeschooling A method that replicates the traditional classroom approach to education, in whole or in part. Sometimes referred to as "school at home."

transcript An official record of a student's educational progress; it may include course listings, grades, and credits earned.

umbrella school A term used to describe a program that oversees individual families involved in home education. Also called cover school.

unit studies A teaching method involving the intense study of a particular topic. Each "unit" integrates a variety of skill areas and learning tools, notably hands-on activities, and can be taught to several ages simultaneously.

unschooling A popular philosophy among homeschoolers, unschooling generally involves allowing a child's interests to determine the focus of learning, and openness to the educational value of nontraditional materials and experiences, rather than teacher-led instruction, textbooks, and other trappings of conventional school.

WAHM Work-at-home mom.

Waldorf The first Waldorf school was founded in Stuttgart, Germany, in 1919, by scientist and scholar Rudolf Steiner, with the purpose of nurturing the whole child, spiritually and physically, as well as academically. The Waldorf curriculum includes rhythmic movement, handwork, and learning math and other concepts through stories.

whole language An instructional strategy that emphasizes reading for meaning and in context. Although teachers may incorporate phonics instruction, the emphasis is on teaching students to look at the wholeness of words and text.

Resource Directory

Select homeschooling Web sites

These sites are recommended starting points for accessing information on homeschooling. For more on homeschooling in your area, visit the Web pages of regional support groups, which are accessible through many of the sites below. Also worthwhile are the many commercial sites of homeschool suppliers, correspondence schools, and educational Web sites.

A to Z Home's Cool: http://hometown.aol.com/anaise.homeschoolinfo.html

> Well-organized site by Ann Zeiss, informative articles, member area, recommended books by topic. "Regional and Worldwide Homeschooling" includes links to support groups.

Alternative Education Resource Organization: www.edrev.org

> Directed by Jerry Mintz, this nonprofit organization concerns education alternatives: community schools, alternative learning centers (public and private), and homeschooling. Site features e-mail discussion groups, a

magazine, radio talk show, and catalog on education news.

Homeschool-Teens-College: www.homeschoolteens college.net/

Support for homeschoolers ages 11–18, featuring articles, college admissions policies, sample homeschooler college application essays, a complete list of independent study programs, and more. By Cafi Cohen, author of *And What About College?*

The Caron Family's Homeschool Homepage: http://members.mint.net/caronfam/index.html

A Maine homeschooling family offers information on their homeschooling, with links to Maine resources and information on finding homeschool materials.

Christy's Garden: www.smokylake.com/Christy/

Christy Taylor, an unschooled teen, shares her favorite quotes on education, advice to parents of new homeschoolers, trigonometry using K'nex, and more.

Eclectic Homeschool Online: http://eho.org/

The online edition provides feature articles. Samples include the following: "How Do I Handle High School?" "Meet an Archaeologist," "FrontPorch History," and "Developing a Child's Faith"; also, articles on homeschooling in the news, unit studies, math, and other departments.

familyeducation.com: http://familyeducation.com/ home/

The FamilyEducation Network provides helpful advice by ages, grades and school subjects, educational activities, news affecting children and families, and homeschooling. Searchable by keyword.

Finding Homeschool Support on the Internet: www. geocities.com/Athens/8259/index2.html

An up-to-date site offering curriculum support, with links to grade level curriculum guidelines and educational search engines. The best resource is an annotated listing of message boards, newsgroups, and e-mail groups, with guidance on accessing on connecting to IRC chats and newsgroups.

The Graham Family: www.usatrip.org/

This homeschooling family traveled to all 50 states within a year.

Growing Without Schooling (GWS): www.holtgws. com/index.htm

GWS and Holt Associates is an information clearinghouse on homeschooling, largely dedicated to the work and teaching of education reformer John Holt, who founded the magazine *Growing Without Schooling* in 1977. In addition to a catalog of John Holt's Bookstore, the site includes links to the magazine and information on GWS seminars, conferences, and a homeschooling consultation service.

Heather's Homeschooling page: www.madrone. com/home-ed.htm

Homeschooler Heather Madrone's site with personal essays on her reasons for homeschooling, unschooling, and how she and her family approached specific subjects.

High School Homeschooling Board: www.vegsource. com/wwwboard/highschool/wwwboard.html

A highly visited bulletin board where homeschooling parents, and sometimes teens, exchange information on curricula, independent study programs, college applications, and other aspects of the high school experience.

Home Education Magazine: www.home-ed-magazine.com/wlcm_HEM.html

The *Home Education* magazine Web site includes articles and columns; a free online newsletter; popular discussion boards on a variety of homeschool topics; a homeschool information library, with e-mail files on starting out, high school, college, and working; fathers and homeschooling, and much more.

Homeschool Central: http://homeschoolcentral.com

A comprehensive menu of homeschool sites, study resources, and an online Homeschool Mall.

Home Schooling Daily: www.inifinet.com/~baugust

Large list of lesson plans available online; freebies, selected for homeschoolers and screened; and regional information for Columbus, Ohio homeschoolers.

Homeschool Fun: http://homeschoolfun.com/index.html

Monthly e-zine with articles, ideas, lesson plans, and educational resources and tips.

Home School Legal Defense Association: www.hslda.org/

This attractive Web site of the national legal organization features easily accessible summaries of applicable laws and homeschool statutes by state.

Homeschool Resource Guide: http://members.
home.com/ct-homeschool/guide.htm
> A comprehensive listing of homeschool
> resources, curriculum suppliers, and retailers.

Homeschool World: http://home-school.com/
> Christian site of *Practical Homeschooling* maga-
> zine, including articles and a list of home-
> school organizations.

The Homeschool Zone: www.homeschoolzone.
com/
> Offerings include the Zone newsletter; zone
> member center; homeschool yellow pages,
> listing support groups by state; book reviews
> and author interviews; helpful FAQs; global
> home-ed support; and distance ed links.

Homeschooling: www.life.ca/hs/
> Canadian site with articles on self-directed
> learning, measuring learning and "deprofes-
> sionalizing" education, by Wendy Priesnitz,
> homeschooling author.

Homeschooling at About.Com:
http://homeschooling.about.com/education/
homeschooling/
> Search capacity, comprehensive homeschool-
> ing coverage with weekly feature articles; up-
> to-date links to a host of related subjects, field
> trips, distance learning, homeschooling news,
> and more.

Homeschooling on a Shoestring: www.geocities.
com/Athens/4663/
> Crafts, recipes, unit ideas, and more for the
> homeschooler on a budget.

Homeschooling Today Magazine: http://homeschool
today.com/
> Online magazine.

Jon's Homeschool Resource Page: www.midnight
beach.com/hs/
> One of the largest homeschooling sites on
> the Web; annotated lists of resources; home-
> pages sorted by category and rating (secular,
> religious); discussion groups; links to home-
> schooling FAQs; listing of support groups by
> state; and more.

Kaleidoscapes: www.kaledioscapes.com
> Large discussion area for homeschoolers on
> science, monthly topics, unit studies, compli-
> ance tips, special needs, and other home-
> school issues.

National Home Education Network: www.nhen.org/
> The site of the recently formed national
> group, which seeks to encourage and facili-
> tate the grassroots network of state and local
> homeschooling groups, and disseminating
> homeschool information on a national level.
> Includes a comprehensive support group list-
> ing and a newsletter.

**National Home Education Research Institute
(NHERI):** www.nheri.org
> Homeschooling research organization with
> free fact sheets and online catalog for NHERI
> documents.

NPIN: National Parent Information Network:
http://ericps.ed.uiuc.edu/npin/
> A searchable site of the ERIC Clearinghouse
> on Elementary and Early Childhood
> Education, with helpful information for
> all parents on a range of education and
> parenting subjects.

ParentsPlace.com: www.parentsplace.com/
This parenting site hosts homeschooling
support group chats, parenting bulletin
boards with homeschool subjects. General
parenting information on health, pregnancy,
and developmental stages.

Pennsylvania Homeschoolers: www.pahomeschoolers.
com/
The site of the Richmans, a homeschooling
family in Kittanning, PA. Homeschoolers is a
newsletter and publisher of homeschooling
materials. A well-organized local site with
information on homeschool evaluators in PA,
support group activities, and a homeschoolers accreditation agency.

School is Dead; Learn in Freedom!:
http://learninfreedom.org/
Karl Bunday's substantial site (more than
40 pages), with extensive bibliographies,
socialization research, school issues, and a
list of more than 940 colleges that admit
homeschoolers.

The Teel Family Web site: www.teelfamily.com/
Appealing, well-organized personal site of this
Alaskan homeschooling family. Activities, education, and personal pages describe activities
around the seasons, "Kid's Snow Page," directions for making your own Athabascan Birch
Bark Basket, and the best times to see the
northern lights. Alaskan Cool Places for Kids.

The Teen Homeschooler: ww.eatbug.com/
homeschool/
The personal site of Alethia Price, with
humor and edification from a homeschooled
teen's perspective.

Unschooling.com: www.unschooling.com/
FAQs; essays; message board: sorted by sub-
jects, including Dealing With Reluctance,
Unschooling Specific Subjects, and How to
Explain Unschooling.

Windycreek Home School: http://windycreek.com
Home site of Nancy Lande, author *of Homeschooling: A Patchwork of Days,* and her family.

Resources by Subject

General educational supplies

Bluestocking Press (History)
P.O. Box 2030
Shingle Springs, CA 95682-2030
800/959-8586

The Education Connection
P.O. Box 1417
Tehachapi, CA 93581
800/863-3828
Web site: www.educationconnection.com

Genius Tribe (innovative catalog geared for
unschoolers)
P.O. Box 1014
Eugene, OR 97440-1014
541/686-2325

Home School Books and Supplies
104 S. West Avenue
Arlington, WA 98223
800/788-1221
Web site: www.TheHomeSchool.com

Social Studies School Service
10200 Jefferson Blvd.
P.O. Box 802
Culver City, CA 90232-0802
800/421-4246
Web site: http://SocialStudies.com

The Sycamore Tree
2179 Meyer Place
Costa Mesa, CA 92627
800/779-6750
Web site: www.sycamoretree.com
Zephyr Press
3316 N. Chapel Avenue
P.O. Box 66006
Tucson, AZ 85732-6006
800/232-2187
Web site: www.zephyrpress.com

Learning games and activities
Animal Town
P.O. Box 757
Greenland, NH 03840
800/445-8642
Aristoplay
450 S. Wagner Rd.
Ann Arbor, MI 48107
800/634-7738
Web site: www.aristoplay.com
Chatham Hill Games, Inc.
P.O. Box 253
Chatham, NY 12037
800/554-3039
Web site: www.ocdc.com/Chatham_Hill_games
Constructive Playthings
13201 Arrington Rd.
Grandview, MO 64030-2886
800/832-0572
Web site: www.ustoyco.com
Cuisenaire/Dale Seymour Publications
P.O. Box 5026
White Plains, NY 10602-5026
800/872-1100
Web site: www.aw.com/dsp/

Curiosity Kits
P.O. Box 811
Cockeysville, MD 21030
800/584-KITS
e-mail: Ckitsinc@aol.com
ETA (science materials)
620 Lakeview Pkwy.
Vernon Hills, IL 60061
800/445-5985
Web site: www.etauniverse.com
Lakeshore Learning Materials
2695 E. Dominguez St.
P.O. Box 6261
Carson, CA 90749
Web site: www.lakeshorelearning.com
Lego Dacta (Educational Division of Lego)
555 Taylor Rd.
Enfield, CT 95062
800/527-8339
Turn off the TV Family Game Catalog
P.O. Box 4162
Bellevue, WA 98009
800/949-8688
Web site: www.turnoffthetv.com
United Art and Education Supply Co.
P.O. Box 9219
Fort Wayne, IN 46899
800/322-3247

Audio sources
Chinaberry Books (books and tapes)
2780 Via Orange Way, Suite B
Spring Valley, CA 91978
800/776-2242

The Educational Record Center
3233 Burnt Mill Dr., Suite 100
Wilmington, NC 28403-2698
800/438-1637
Web site: www.erc-inc

Listening Library, Inc.
1 Park Ave.
Old Greenwich, CT 06870-1727
800/243-4504
Web site: www.listeninglib.com

The National Association for the Preservation and Perpetuation of Storytelling (NAPPS)
P.O. Box 309
Jonesborough, TN 37659
615/753-2171

Music and musical instruments

Anyone Can Whistle
P.O. Box 4407
Kingston, NY 12401

Lark in the Morning
P.O. Box 1176
Mendocino, CA 95460

Music for Little People
4320 Marine Avenue
P.O. Box 1720
Lawndale, CA 90260
800/727-2233

Software sources

Broderbund (children's software, including Carmen Sandiego series)
500 Redwood Blvd.
Novato, CA, 94948
800/474-8840
Web site: www.broderbund.com

Children's Software Revue
44 Main St.
Flemington, NJ 08822
800/993-9499
Web site: www.childrenssoftware.com
Davidson and Associates (the JumpStart and
MathBlaster series)
P.O. Box 2961
Torrance, CA 90503
800/542-4240
Web site: www.education.com
Edmark Corporation (software for preschool
through grade 8)
P.O. Box 97021
Redmond, WA 98073
800/362-2890
e-mail: edmarkteam@edmark.com
Web site: www.edmark.com
Educational Resources
1550 Executive Dr.
Elgin, IL 60123-9330
800/624-2926
Web site: www.edresources.com
Educorp (comprehensive CD-ROM offerings)
12 B W. Main St.
Elmsford, NY 10523
800/843-9497
Web site: www.educorp.com
The Edutainment Catalog
P.O. Box 21210
Boulder, CO 80308
800/338-3844
Web site: www.edutainco.com

The Learning Company
6760 Summit Dr. N.
Minneapolis, MN 55430-4003
800/685-6322
Web site: www.learningco.com
Scholastic New Media
2931 E. McCarty St.
Garland, TX 75041
800/726-3446
Web site: http://scholastic.com

Academic subjects

Language arts resources

Books

Choosing Books for Children by Betsy Hearne (University of Illinois Press, 1999)

Families Writing by Peter R. Stillman (Writer's Digest, 1989)

The Read-Aloud Handbook by Jim Trelease (Penguin Books, 1995)

Reading Lists for College-Bound Students by Doug Estell, Michele L. Satchwell, and Patricia S. Wright (IDG Books, 1993)

Teach Your Child to Read in 100 Easy Lessons by Siegried, Engelmann, Phyllis Haddox, and Elaine Bruner (Simon & Schuster, 1983)

Writing Because We Love To: Homeschoolers At Work by Susannah Sheffer (Heinemann, 1992)

The Writing Road to Reading: The Spalding Method of Phonics for Teaching Speech, Writing and Reading/Book and Record by Romalda Bishop Spalding and Walter T. Spalding (Quill, 1990)

Web sites

The American Library Association: www.ala.org/
The Children's Book Council: www.cbcbooks.org/
navigation/autoindes.htm
The Children's Literature Web Guide: www.acs.
ucalgary.ca/~dkbrown
Vandergrift's Children's Literature Page:
www.scils.rutgers.edu/special/kay/childlit.html

Suppliers

Ball-Stick-Bird Publications, Inc.
P.O. Box 592
Stony Brook, NY 11790
516/331-9164
(reading program)
Children's Book of the Month Club
Camp Hill, PA 17012-9852
717/697-1209
Chinaberry Books
2780 Via Orange Way
Suite B
Spring Valley, CA 91978
800/776-2242
Dick Blick Company
P.O. Box 1267
Galesburg, IL 61402
800/933-2542
(calligraphy supplies)
Great Books Foundation
35 E. Wacker Dr.
Suite 2300
Chicago, IL 60601-2298
800/222-5870
Web site: www.greatbooks.org

Hooked On Phonics
Gateway Educational Products
2900 S. Harbor Blvd.
Santa Ana, CA 92704-6429
800/616-4004

International Reading Systems, Inc.
1000 112th Circle N.
St. Petersburg, FL 33716
800/321-8322
Web site: www.singspell.com
(Sing, Spell, Read & Write phonics program)

Italic Handwriting Series
Portland State University
Division of Continuing Education
P.O. Box 1394
Portland, OR 97207

National Council of Teachers of English
111 W. Kenyon Rd.
Urbana, IL 61801-1096
800/369-NCTE
Web site: www.ncte.org

**The National Library Service for the Blind
and Physically Handicapped**
Library of Congress
Washington, DC 20542
202/707-5100
e-mail: nls@loc.gov
Web site: www.loc.gov/nls/

National Writing Institute
7946 Wright Rd.
Niles, MI 49120
800/688-5375

The Paradigm Co.
P.O. Box 45161
Boise, ID 83711
(Alpha-Phonics program)

The Writing Company
10200 Jefferson Blvd.
P.O. Box 802
Culver City, CA 90232-0802
800/421-4246
Web site: http://WritingCo.com/Writing

Math resources

Books

Anno's Mysterious Multiplying Jar (age 4–8) by Masaichiro Anno and Mitsumasa Anno. (Paper Star, 1999)

Beyond Facts and Flashcards: Exploring Math with Your Kids by Janice R. Mokros (Heinemann, 1996)

Elementary Algebra by Harold R. Jacobs (W.H. Freeman, 1995)

Family Math by Jean Kerr Stenmark (Lawrence Hall of Science, 1986)

Geometry by Harold R. Jacobs (W. H. Freeman, 1987)

How Much is a Million? by David M. Schwartz (William Morrow & Co., 1985)

The I Hate Mathematics! Book by Marilyn Burns (Little Brown, 1976)

Janice Vancleave's Math for Every Kid: Easy Activities that Make Learning Fun by Janice Pratt VanCleave (John Wiley & Sons, 1991)

Math for Smarty Pants (Grades 7–9) by Marilyn Burns (Little Brown, 1982)

Web sites

Ask Dr. Math: http://forum.swarthmore.edu/dr.math/dr-math.html

Family Math: www.lhs.berkeley.edu
Program developed by Lawrence Hall of Science (UC Berkeley)

Great sites for Math Teachers: www/clarify connect.com/webpage/terri/sites.html

Homeschooling message board: Reading and Math Support: www.vegsource.com/wwwboard/reading/wwwboard.html
Mega-Mathematics: Los Alamos National Laboratory: www.c3.lanl.gov/mega-math/
Mrs. Glosser's Math Goodies: www.mathgoodies.com/

Curricula and teaching materials
Cuisenaire/Dale Seymour Publications
P.O. Box 5026
White Plains, NY 10602-5026
800/872-1100
Web site: www.cuisenaire.com
Delta Hands-On Math
P.O. Box 3000
Nashua, NH 03061-3000
800/442-5444
Web site: www.delta-ed.com
Family Math
University of California
Lawrence Hall of Science, #5200
Berkeley, CA 94720-5200
510/642-1016
Web site: www.lhs.berkely.edu
Institute for Math Mania
P.O. Box 910
Montpelier, VT 05601-0910
802/223-5871
Key Curriculum Press
P.O. Box 2304
Berkeley, CA 94702-0304
800/995-MATH
Web site: www.keypress.com
(Miquon Math program)

"Math-It"
The Sycamore Tree
2179 Meyer Place
Costa Mesa, CA 92627
714/650-4466
Web site: www.sycamoretree.com
Math-U-See
6601 E. Mill Plain Blvd.
Vancouver, WA 98661
360/750-9050
Mortensen Math
Mortensen Math Academic Excellence Institute
2450 Fort Union Blvd.
Salt Lake City, UT 84121
800/338-9939
Saxon Math
Saxon Publishers
1320 W. Lindsey St.
Norman, OK 73069
800/284-7019
Web site: www.saxonpub.com

Science resources

Magazines
3-2-1-Contact
Children's Television Workshop
One Lincoln Plaza
New York, NY 10023
Cricket, the Magazine for Children
P.O. Box 52961
Boulder, CO 80322-2961
Discover
P.O. Box 420105
Palm Coast, FL 32142-0105
800/829-9132
Web site: www.enews.com/magazines/discover

Odyssey (astronomy for kids)
Cobblestone Publishing, Inc.
30 Grove St.
Peterborough, NH 03458-1454
800/821-0115
Web site: www.cobblestonepub.com
Quantum (magazine of math and science)
National Science Teachers Association
1840 Wilson Blvd.
Arlington, VA 22201-3000
800/722-NSTA
Ranger Rick
National Wildlife Federation
1412 16th St. NW
Washington, DC 20036-2266
Science Weekly
P.O. Box 70154
Washington, DC 20088-0154
SuperScience
Scholastic, Inc.
P.O. Box 7502
Jefferson City, MO 65102
800/325-6149
Web site: www.scholastic.com

Web sites

**Experimental Science Projects: An Introductory
Level Guide:** www.isd77.k12.mn.us/resources/cf/
SciProjIntro.html
Exploratorium: www.exploratorium.edu
Frank Potter's Science Gems: http://sciencegems.
com/
The Franklin Institute Science Museum:
http://sln.fi.edu/tfi/welcome.html
NASAKids: http://kid.msfc.nasa.gov/

The National Science Education Standards: www.
nsta.org

> The National Science Teachers Association
> 1840 Wilson Blvd.
> Arlington, VA 22201-3000
> 703/243-7100

National Wildlife Federation: www.nwf.org/kids
Online Guide to Meteorology: http://covis.atmos.
uiuc.edu/guide/guide.html
Science Fair Idea Exchange: www.halcyon.com/
sciclub/cgi-pvt/cifair/guestbook.html
U.S. Geological Survey: www.usgs.gov
Virtual Chemistry: www.chem.ucla.edu/
chempointers.html
Woods Hole Oceanographic Institution: www.whoi.
edu/index.html
You Can With Beakman and Jax:
www.beakman.com

Suppliers
Aves Science Kits
P.O. Box 229
Peru, ME 04290
Carolina Biological Supply Co.
2700 York Rd.
Burlington, NC 27215
800/334-5551
Web site: www.carolina.com
Delta Hands-On Science
P.O. Box 3000
Nashua, NH 03061-3000
800/442-5444
Web site: www.delta-ed.com

Edmund Scientific Company
101 E. Gloucester Pike
Barrington, NJ 08007-1380
800/728-6999
Web site: www.edsci.com

Science-by-Mail
Museum of Science
Science Park
Boston, MA 02114
800/729-3300

TOPS Learning Systems
10970 S. Mulino Rd.
Canby, OR 97013
Web site: www.topscience.com

Wild Goose Co.
375 Whitney Ave.
Salt Lake City, UT 84115
800/373-1498

Geography resources

Magazines
World **magazine: Pen Pals**
National Geographic Society
Dept. GeoMail Pen Pal Network
20 Academy St.
Norwalk, CT 06852-7100

Web sites
Geography at About.Com:
http://geography.about.
com/education/geography/index.htm
The Learning Web at the U.S. Geological Survey:
www.usgs.gov/education
Mapquest: www.mapquest.com
National Geographic Society: www.national
geographic.com
National Weather Services: www.nws.noaa.gov

Software

Carmen Sandiego Junior Detective Edition (grades Pre-K to 3) and Where in the World Is Carmen Sandiego (grades 4–12)

Cartopedia (ages 9 and up), DK Multimedia

Geosafari (ages 8 and up), Rand McNally

GeoMedia (grades 4–9)

History resources

Web sites

American Historical Association: www.theaha.org/

American Memory: Historical Collections for the National Digital Library (Library of Congress): http://rs6.loc.gov/amhome.html

Ancient Civilizations: http://tqd.advanced.org/2840/index.html

Askeric Virtual Library: http://ericir.syr.edu/virtual/

Biography A&E: www.biography.com/find/find.html

The History Channel: www.execpc.com/~dboals/boals.htm

> History/Social Studies Web Site for K–12 teachers (great site)

The National Council for History Education: www.history.org/nche/

The National Park Service Tools for Teaching (gateway site): www.cr.nps.gov/toolsfor.htm

National Trust for Historic Preservation Teaching with Historic Places; 800/766-6847): www.nthp.org/

The World's Largest Collection of History Links: www.ukans.edu/history/VL/

Historical fiction Web sites

Historical Fiction (**Tempe Public Library**): www.tempe.gov/library/youth/uthistfc.htm

The Scott O'Dell Historical Fiction Award: www. acs.ucalgary.ca/~dkbrown/odell.htm/
Young Adult Historical Fiction Reviews: www.ih. k12.oh.us/ms/woodring/hfsite/masterbl.htm

Suppliers

American Association for State and Local History
172 Second Ave. N.
Suite 202
Nashville, TN 37201
Greenleaf Press
1570 Old Laguardo Rd.
Lebanon, TM 37087
National Council for History Education
26915 Westwood Rd.
Suite B-2
Westlake, Ohio 44145
440/835-1776
Web site: www.history.org/nche/
National Register of Historic Places
Interagency Resources Division
National Park Service
P.O. Box 37127
Washington, DC 20013-7127
Pleasant Company
8400 Fairway Pl.
P.O. Box 620190
Middleton, WI 53562-0190
800/845-0005
Social Studies School Service
10200 Jefferson Blvd.
P.O. Box 802
Culver City, CA 90232-0802
800/421-4246
Web site: http://SocialStudies.com

Foreign language resources

Web sites

American Sign Language Browser: http://
commtechlab.msu.edu/sites/aslweb/browser.htm
Foreign Language Resources on the Web: www.
itp.berkeley.edu/~thorne/HumanResources.html

Programs and catalogs

Artes Latinae
847/526-4344

Audio-Forum
96 Broad St.
Guilford, CT 06437
800/243-1234

Muzzy, The BBC Language Course for Children
Early Advantage
P.O. Box 320368
Fairfield, CT 06432
888/327-5923
Web site: www.early-advantage.com

Power-Glide Language Courses
988 Cedar Ave.
Provo, UT 84604
800/596-0910
Web site: www.power-glide.com

Teach Me Tapes
9900 Bren Rd. E.
B-1 Opus Center, Suite 100
Minnetonka, MN 55343-9664
800/456-4656
Web site: www.wavetech.net/~teachme

Triple Play software series
Syracuse Language Systems
800/797-5264

Art resources

Books

Carpentry for Children by Lester Walker (Viking, 1985)

Doing Art Together: Discovering the joys and appreciating and creating art as taught at the Metropolitan Museum of Art's Famous Parent-Child Workshop by Muriel Silberstein-Storfer and Mablen Jones (Harry N. Abrams, 1997)

Drawing for Older Children and Teens: A Creative Method that Works for Adult Beginners Too by Mona Brookes (Tarcher, 1991)

Drawing on the Right Side of the Brain by Betty Edwards (J.P. Tarcher, 1989)

Drawing with Children by Mona Brookes (Putnam Publishing, 1996)

History of Art for Young People by H.W. Janson (Abrams, 1997)

Kids Knitting by Melanie D. Falick and Kristin Nicholas (Artisan, 1998)

Architecture books

The Architecture Pack by Ron Van Der Meer and Deyan Sudjic (Knopf, 1996)

Castle by David MacAulay (ages 9–12) (Houghton Mifflin, 1982)

Web sites

the @rt room: www.arts.ufl.edu/art/rt_room/@rtroom_home.html

ArchKIDecture: www.childmmc.edu/cmhweb/kidshome.html

The Art Room: www.arts.ufl.edu/art/rt_room/@rtroom_home.html

Artist Quest: www.angelfire.com/mo/sasschool/ArtQuest.html

> Linking geography and history through the study of artists' lives

Arts Education On-Line—The Incredible Art Department: www.artswire.org/kenroar/

ArtsEdNet: The Getty's Art Education Site (Getty Education Institute for the Arts): www.artsednet.getty.edu/

High School Art Lessons: www.edu-orchard.net/PROFESS/LESSON/ARTS/KR/krhigh.html

Learning About Leonardo: http://library.advanced.org/13681/data/davin2/shtml

Music Education Online: www.geocities.com/Athens/2405

National Standards for Music Education: http://camil40.music.uiuc.edu/Projects/tomi/teaching/standards/standards.html

Suppliers

KidsArt
P.O. Box 274
Mt. Shasta, CA 96067
530/926-5076
Web site: www.kidsart.com

S & S Arts and Crafts
P.O. Box 513
Colchester, CT 06415-0513
800/243-9232
Web site: www.snswwide.com

Music Programs

Suzuki Method: A Japanese program that stresses learning an instrument such as piano by ear and through memory. (www.Suzuki-Music.com)

Kindermusik: A program from Germany that stresses a range of music and movement activities to introduce musical concepts to groups of young children. (www.kindermusik.com)

Physical education resources

Books

Everybody's a Winner: A Kid's Guide to New Sports and Fitness by Tom Schneider (Little, Brown, 1976)
Home School Family Fitness: A Practical Curriculum Guide by Bruce Whitney (Home School Family Fitness Institute, 1995)

Web sites

Coaching Youth Sports: www.chre.vt.edu/f-s/rstratto/CYS/
National Standards for Physical Education: www.ed.gov/databases/ERIC Digests/ed406361.html
PE Central: http://pe.central.vt.edu/
SportsParents (companion journal to *Sports Illustrated for Kids*): http://sportsparents.com/index.html
Sports Illustrated for Kids: www.sikids.com/
Way Cool Running Kids' Page (for kids who love to bike and run): www.waycoolrunning.com/

Academic competitions

National Geography Bee: Annual competition for grades 4–8

National Geographic Society
1145 17th St. NW
Washington, DC 20036-4688
Web site: www.nationalgeographic.com/society/ngp/geobee/gasics.html

Odyssey of the Mind: An annual, international team competition, emphasizing program-solving skills, with long-term problems to work on over the school year.

> Odysssey of the Mind
> P.O. Box 547
> Glassboro, NJ 08028
> 609/881-1603
> Web site: www.odyssey.org/

Scripps Howard National Spelling Bee: For those in 8th grade and below.

> Scripps Howard National Spelling Bee
> P.O. Box 371541
> Pittsburgh, PA 15251-7541
> Web site: www.spellingbee.com/

Math Olympiad

> Math Olympiad
> 2154 Bellmore Ave.
> Bellmore, NY 11710-5645
> Web site: www.moems.org/

MathCounts

> National Society of Professional Engineers
> 1420 King St.
> Alexandria, VA 22314
> Web site: www.mathcounts.org

ThinkQuest

> Advanced Network and Services, Inc.
> 200 Business Park Dr.
> Armonk, NY 10504
> Web site: www.thinkquest.org/index.shtml

Recommended Reading List

Books

The following include titles that explore in-depth specific subjects, including learning differences, practical homeschooling methods, and perspectives on education and learning.

Armstrong, Thomas. *In Their Own Way: Discovering and Encouraging Your Child's Personal Learning Style.* New York: Tarcher/Putnam, 1987.

Beechick, Ruth. *Dr. Beechick's Homeschool Answer Book.* Pollock Pines, CA: Arrow Press, 1998.

——. *Language Wars and Other Writings for Homeschoolers.* Pollock Pines, CA: Arrow Press, 1995.

Bell, Debra. *The Ultimate Guide to Homeschooling.* Nashville, TN: Thomas Nelson, 1997.

Bendt, Valerie. *How to Create Your Own Unit Study.* Melrose, FL: Common Sense Press, 1997.

Blumenfeld, Samuel L. *Homeschooling: A Parent's Guide to Teaching Children.* New York: Citadel Press, 1997.

Boyer, Rick, and Marilyn Boyer. *Home Educating with Confidence*. Paperback edition. Elkton, MD: Holly Hall Publishing, 1996.

Clark, Mary K. *Catholic Home Schooling: A Handbook for Parents*. Front Royal, VA: Seton Home Study School Press Rockford, IL: TAN Books, 1993.

Cohen, Cafi. *And What About College?: How Homeschooling Can Lead to Admission to the Best Colleges & Universities*. Cambridge, MA: Holt Associates, 1997.

Colfax, David, and Micki Colfax. *Homeschooling for Excellence*. New York: Warner Books, 1988.

Dobson, Linda. *The Art of Education: Reclaiming Your Family, Community and Self*. Tonasket, WA: Home Education Press, 1995.

———. *The Homeschooling Book of Answers: 88 Important Questions Answered by Homeschooling's Most Respected Voices*. Rocklin, CA: Prima Publishing, 1998.

Duffy, Cathy. *Christian Home Educators' Curriculum Manual Elementary Grades*, 9th edition. Westminster, CA: Grove Publishing, 9th edition 1997.

———. *Christian Home Educators' Curriculum Manual Junior/Senior High*. Westminster, CA: Home Run Enterprises, updated edition 1997.

Farenga, Patrick. *The Beginner's Guide to Homeschooling*. Cambridge, MA: Holt Associates, 1995.

Gatto, John Taylor. *Dumbing Us Down: The Hidden Curriculum of Compulsory Schooling*. Gabriola Island, B. C., Canada: New Society Publishers, 1991.

Griffith, Mary. *The Homeschooling Handbook: From Preschool to High School, a Parent's Guide*. Rocklin, CA: Prima Publishing, 1997.

——. *The Unschooling Handbook: How to Use the Whole World as Your Child's Classroom,* 2nd edition. Rocklin, CA: Prima Publishing, 2nd edition, 1998.

Groll, Ron. *The Homeschool Resource & Supply Manual.* St. Louis, MO: Razzem Publications, 1998.

Guterson, David. *Family Matters: Why Homeschooling Makes Sense.* Orlando, FL: Harcourt Brace Jovanovich, 1992.

Hahn, Kimberly, and Mary Hasso. *Catholic Education: Homeward Bound: A Useful Guide to Catholic Home Schooling.* San Francisco, CA: Ignatius Press, 1996.

Hegener, Mark, and Helen Hegener, eds. *The Homeschool Reader: Collected Articles from Home Education Magazine 1984–1994.* Tonasket, WA: Home Education Press, revised edition 1995.

Hellyer, Janie Levine. *Homeschooling: The Teen Years.* Rocklin, CA: Prima Publishing, 1999.

Hendrickson, Borg. *Home School: Taking the First Step: The Complete Program Planning Handbook.* Sitka, AK: Mountain Meadow Press, revised. edition. 1994.

——. *How to Write a Low-Cost/No-Cost Curriculum for Your Home-School Child.* Sitka, AK: Mountain Meadow Press, revised edition 1998.

Hensley, Sharon. *Home Schooling Children with Special Needs.* Gresham, OR: Noble Publishing Associates, 1997.

Hern, Matt, ed. *Deschooling Our Lives.* Gabriola Island, B. C., Canada: New Society Publishers, 1996. [collection of essays]

Hirsch, Jr., E.D., ed. *What Your First Grader Needs to Know: Fundamentals of a Good First-Grade Education.* Revised edition New York: Dell Publishing, 1998.

——. *What Your Kindergartner Needs to Know: Preparing Your Child for a Lifetime of Learning.* (Core Knowledge Series). New York: Dell Publishing, 1997.

Hirsch, Jr., E. D., and John Holden, eds. *Books to Build On: A Grade-By-Grade Resource Guide for Parents and Teachers.* New York: Dell Publishing, 1996.

Holt, John. *How Children Fail.* Reading, MA: Addison-Wesley, 1995.

——. *How Children Learn.* Reading, MA: Addison Wesley, 1995.

——. *Learning All the Time.*, Perseus Press reprint edition. Reading, MA: Addison-Wesley, 1990.

——. *Teach Your Own: A Hopeful Path for Education,* 3rd edition. Cambridge, MA: Holt Associates, 3rd edition, 1997.

Hood, Mary. *The Home-Schooling Resource Guide and Directory of Organizations.* Cartersville, GA: Ambleside Educational Press, 1996.

——. *The Joyful Homeschool.* Cartersville, CA: Ambleside Educational Press, 1997.

Kaseman, M. Larry, and Susan D. Kaseman. *Taking Charge Through Homeschooling: Personal and Political Empowerment.* Stoughton, WI: Koshkonong Press, 1991.

Kealoha, Anna. *Trust the Children: A Manual and Activity Guide for Homeschooling and Alternative Learning.* Berkeley, CA: Celestial Arts Publishing Company, 1995.

Kenyon, Mary Potter. *Home Schooling from Scratch: Simple Living—Super Learning.* Bridgman, MI: Gazelle Publications, 1996.

Lahrson-Fisher, Ann. *Homeschooling in Oregon: The 1998 Handbook.* Portland, OR: Nettlepatch Press,

2nd edition 1998. [practical guidance for all homeschoolers]

Lande, Nancy, ed. *Homeschooling: A Patchwork of Days.* Wynewood, PA: Windy Creek Press, 1996.

Leistico, Agnes. *I Learn Better By Teaching Myself.* Cambridge, MA: Holt Associates, 1997.

———. *Still Teaching Ourselves.* Cambridge, MA: Holt Associates, 1997.

Llewellyn, Grace. *Freedom Challenge: African American Homeschoolers.* Eugene, OR: Lowry House, 1996.

———. *Real Lives: Eleven Teenagers Who Don't Go to School.* Paperback edition. Eugene, OR: Lowry House Pub, 1993.

———. *The Teenage Liberation Handbook: How to Quit School and Get a Real Life and Education.* Boston, MA: Element Books, revised edition, 1997.

———. *Freedom Challenge: African American Homeschoolers.* Eugene, OR: Lowry House, 1996.

Lurie, Jon. *Allison's Story: A Book about Homeschooling.* (Children's book.) Minneapolis, MN: Lerner Publications Company, 1996.

Mason, Charlotte. *Charlotte Mason's Original Homeschooling Series.* Rockland, ME: Charlotte Mason Research & Supply Company, 1993.

McClaine, L. S. *Physical Education for Homeschoolers: An Easy to Use, Low Equipment Cost Program for Homeschooling Families.* Moscow, ID: Nutmeg Publications, 1994.

McIntire, Deborah, and Robert Windham. *Home Schooling: Answers to Questions Parents Most Often Ask.* Cypress, CA: Creative Teaching Press, 1995.

Mintz, Jerry. *The Handbook of Alternative Education.* New York: Macmillan, 1994.

Moore, Raymond S. and Dorothy N. Moore. *Home-Grown Kids: A Practical Handbook for Teaching Your Children at Home.* Camas, WA: Moore Foundation, 1985.

———. *The Successful Homeschool Family Handbook: A Creative and Stress-Free Approach to Homeschooling.* Nashville, TN: Thomas Nelson, 1994.

O'Leary, Jenifer. *Write Your Own Curriculum: A Complete Guide to Planning, Organizing and Documenting Homeschool Curriculums.* (Family, High School, Primary, and Middle Grades volumes.) Stevens Point, WI: Whole Life Publishers, 1994.

Pride, Mary. *The Big Book of Home Learning.* Westchester, IL: Crossway, 1991; Vol. 2 Preschool and Elementary, 1999.

Priesnitz, Wendy. *School Free: The Home Schooling Handbook.* St. George, Ontario: Alternate Press, 1996.

Reed, Donn. *The Home School Source Book,* 2nd edition. Bridgewater, ME: Brook Farm Books, 2nd edition, 1994.

Rupp, Rebecca. *Good Stuff: Learning Tools for All Ages.* Cambridge, MA: Holt Associates, revised edition 1998.

———. *The Complete Home Learning Source Book: The Essential Resource Guide for Homeschoolers, Parents and Educators.* New York: Three Rivers Press, 1998.

———. *Good Stuff: Learning Tools for All Ages.* Cambridge, MA: Holt Associates, revised edition, 1998

Scheps, Susan G. *The Librarians' Guide to Homeschooling Resources.* Chicago, IL: American Library Association Editions, 1998.

Sheffer, Susannah. *A Sense of Self: Listening to Homeschooled Adolescent Girls.* Portsmouth, NH: Boynton/Cook Publishers, 1995. (Paperback edition: Heinemann, 1997.)

Soyke, Jean M., with Illustrations by Pattye Carlson. *Art Adventures at Home: A Curriculum Guide for Home Schools.* Baltimore, MD: M. J. Soyke, 1993.

Wade, Theodore, Jr. *The Home School Manual: Plans, Pointers, Reasons & Resources,* 7th Edition. Bridgman, MI: Gazelle Publications, 1996. (Also available on disk.)

Waring, Diana. *Beyond Survival: A Guide to Abundant-Life Homeschooling.* Lynwood, WA: Emerald Books, 1996.

Homeschooling magazines, newsletters, and e-zines

Countless newsletters are also available from various regional organizations.

Eclectic Homeschool Online Magazine: http://eho.org
> A complete magazine for creative homeschoolers, with feature articles, a resources section, and downloads of useful forms.

F.U.N. News
Family Unschooler's Network
Dept. W
1688 Belhaven Woods Ct.
Pasadena, MD 21122-3727
888/FUN-7020
Web site: www.unschooling.org
> "Learning can be fun for the whole family." Includes low-cost resources, reviews, and articles.

Growing Without Schooling
Holt Associates
2269 Massachusetts Ave.
Cambridge, MA 021400
617/864-3100
Web site: www.holtgws.com
> Bimonthly journal that includes news about the homeschooling movement in the U. S. and around the world; book and resource reviews; pen-pal listings, and information directories.

Home Education Magazine
P.O. Box 1083
Tonasket, WA 98855
800/236-2753
Web site: www.home-ed-press.com
> Bimonthly magazine featuring columnists and features, including political action, older kids, homeschooling fathers, and more.

Homefires: The Journal of Homeschooling
180 El Camino Real
Suite 10
Millbrae, CA 94030
888/4-HOME-ED
Web site: www.Homefires.com
> A bimonthly publication for homeschoolers in Northern California and beyond. With general interest articles on home education, learning differences, educational technology, family businesses, and more.

The Home School Digest
Wisdom's Gate
P.O. Box 374-www
Covert, MI 49043
e-mail: WisGate@characterlink.net

Christian quarterly with practical tips and thought-provoking articles.

HomeSchool Dad magazine
609 Starlight Dr.
Grand Junction, CO 81504
970/434-6946
Web site: http://users.acsol.net/~hsd/index.html
Online bimonthly whose stated goal is to "strengthen families and encourage husbands and wives to work together." Educational activity ideas, fathering book reviews, and home business.

Homeschooling Today
P.O. Box 1425
Melrose, FL 32666
904/475-3088
Web site: www.homeschooltoday.com/
Magazine with a Christian perspective favors the unit study approach, providing curriculum guides, software reviews, pull-out lesson plans, and reproducible pages.

The Link
587 N. Ventu Park Rd.
Suite F-911
Newbury Park, CA 91320
Web site: www.homeschoolnewslink.com/index.html
Free bimonthly national publication featuring columns, reviews, homeschool resources, and articles from "Discover Your Child's Learning Style" to "The Field Trip Lady."

NATHHAN News
National Challenged Homeschoolers Association
Network
5383 Alpine Road, SE
Olalla, WA 32666
>   Newsletter with helpful advice on home-
>   schooling special needs children.

Natural Life magazine
RR1, St. George
Ontario, Canada NOE INO
519/448-4001; 800/215-9574
e-mail: natural@life.ca
Web site: www.life.ca/index.html
>   A Canadian journal on natural living,
>   includes helpful articles on homeschooling.

Options in Learning
The Alliance for Parental Involvement in
Education (ALLPIE)
P.O. Box 59
East Chatham, NY 12060-0059
518/392-6900
Web site: www.croton.com/allpie/
>   Member's newsletter exploring the gamut of
>   public, private, and home-education options.

Practical Homeschooling
Home Life, Inc.
P.O. Box 1250
Fenton, MO 63026
800/346-6322
Web site: www.home-school.com
>   Christian perspective magazine, with product
>   reviews, teaching methods, and features, such
>   as the "Day at our House" diaries.

Important Documents

A homeschool checklist

The following outline may be helpful as you consider the issues involved in homeschooling. Photocopy these pages to create a handy list for jotting notes, ideas you might like to pursue, your goals for learning, important contacts, and more.

What are our educational goals?: _____

_____

Our education options: _____

_____

Could homeschooling work for us?: _____

Questions or concerns: _____

_____

RELATED ISSUES:

Personal: _____

Family:

    Scheduling: _____

    Work: _____

    Financial: _____

    Home management: _____

    Special needs: _____

413

Advantages of homeschooling: _____

_____

Potential drawbacks: _____

_____

HOMESCHOOL SUPPORT GROUPS:

State network: _____
Local support group(s): _____
Other (co-ops, resource centers): _____

_____

Important events: _____

_____

Key contacts: _____

_____

OUR STATE HOMESCHOOLING REGULATIONS:

Options: _____
Parent/teacher requirements: _____

_____

Curricular requirements: _____

_____

Supervision: _____
Notification: _____
    Date: _____
Assessment: _____
Testing: _____
Assessment dates: _____
Other related laws: _____
Key contacts: _____

_____

OUR HOMESCHOOLING MISSION STATEMENT:

_____

_____

OUR OBJECTIVES:

Teaching/learning: _____

_____

Operational goals: _____

_____

RECORD-KEEPING:

Legal requirements:_____

For our own purposes: _____

Methods of assessment: _____

OUR ESTIMATED HOMESCHOOLING BUDGET:

Curricula: _____

Miscellaneous materials: _____

Lessons: _____

Trips: _____

Other activities: _____

Savings: _____

HOMESCHOOLING ASSISTANCE:

Umbrella or cover programs:_____

Distance learning or correspondence courses: _____

_____

Community college courses: _____

Homeschool co-op: _____

Tutoring: _____

Other:_____

DEALING WITH LOCAL SCHOOLS:

Key contacts:_____

_____

Withdrawal: _____

Access by homeschoolers:

Academic program: _____

Services: _____

OUR ACADEMIC PLAN:

Yearly goals:

Reading: _____

Writing: _____

Mathematics: _____

History: _____

Science: _____

Foreign language: _____

The arts:

    Visual art: _____

    Music: _____

    Drama: _____

    Dance: _____

Religion/values: _____

Computer skills: _____

Life skills:

    Work: _____

    Service: _____

Other: _____

OUR FAVORITE RESOURCES/WEB SITES:

Reading: _____

Writing: _____

Mathematics: _____

History: _____

Science: _____

Foreign language: _____

The arts:

    Visual art: _____

    Music: _____

    Drama: _____

    Dance: _____

Religion/values: _____

Computer skills: _____

Life skills:
    Work: _____
    Service: _____
Physical education: _____
Other:_____

OUR PROJECTED PLANS FOR NEXT YEAR:

Reading: _____
Writing: _____
Mathematics: _____
History: _____
Science: _____
Foreign language: _____
The arts:
    Visual art: _____
    Music: _____
    Drama: _____
    Dance: _____
Religion/values: _____
Computer skills:_____
Life skills:
    Work: _____
    Service: _____
Physical education: _____
Other:_____

OUR LONG-TERM EDUCATION GOALS:

Homeschool (# of years):_____
College:_____
Vocational school or training:_____
Other specialized education:_____

Important Statistics

Homeschooling Regulations, by State

The following summaries are not be construed as legal advice. For information on the practical application of the law in your area, contact your state or local homeschool group or your local education agency. These laws are subject to change—make sure your information is current.

Alabama

Compulsory school ages: 7 to 16

Homeschoolers may either establish or enroll in a church school by providing one-time notification to the local superintendent and maintaining an attendance register; or use a state-certified private tutor (140 days per year, three hours per day), providing notification to the local superintendent of subjects covered and hours taught, and maintaining a register of the child's work. The private tutor option requires coverage of core subjects including Alabama history. No testing required.

Alabama Code 16-28-1 through 16-28-8

Alaska

Compulsory school ages: 7 to 16

Homeschoolers may establish and operate a homeschool, and be exempt from all requirements and regulations. They may (but are not required to) notify the local school, in case they wish to take some classes there. Alternatively, they may use a state-certified private tutor, enroll in a state-approved full-time correspondence program, request school board approval to provide an equal alternate educational experience, or qualify as a religious or other private school. Private schools must file an enrollment report by the first day of public school, provide a school calendar to the state Department of Education by October 15 of each year, maintain records (attendance, immunization, courses, testing, grades, and physical exams), and administer a standardized test in grades 4, 6, and 8. All options but the "homeschool" option require 180 days of attendance per year.

Alaska Statutes 14-30.010 and 14.45-120(a)

Arizona

Compulsory school ages: 6 to 16

Homeschoolers may establish a homeschool by filing an affidavit of intent (including a certified birth certificate) with the local superintendent within 30 days of the beginning of the school year the first year of homeschooling. No notice is required in succeeding years. If homeschooling is to be terminated, the local superintendent must be notified within 30 days of the end of homeschooling. Basic academic subjects are required. For homeschoolers, actual instruction may be deferred till age 8, as long as the affidavit is filed on time. There are no required teacher qualifications, testing, or record keeping.

Arizona Revised Statute 15-802 through 805, and 15-828

Arkansas

Compulsory school ages: 5 to 17 on or before September 15 of school year (may be waived from kindergarten by submitting state form)

Homeschoolers may establish and operate a homeschool by filing a written notice of intent with the local superintendent by August 15 (fall semester) or December 15 (spring semester), or with 14 days notice (mid-semester), and then re-filing the notice annually at the beginning of the school year from then on. They must also sign a waiver releasing the state from any future liability for the education of their child. (If students wish to re-enter public schools, they must take a test to determine placement level.) Must be tested at 5th, 7th, and 10th grades (same as public schools); district pays for testing materials, but if parents use approved alternate testing procedures, parents pay costs of testing (other than materials). District will get administrative summaries of tests (for reporting purposes only) with no personally identifiable information. There are no minimum teacher qualifications or required record keeping.

Arkansas Statute Ann. 6-18-201, 6-18-207, 6-15-501, and 6-15-502

California

Compulsory school ages: 6 to 18 (by December 2)

Homeschoolers may qualify as a private school by filing an annual affidavit with the State Superintendent of Public Instruction (through the local county Office of Education) between October 1 and 15. Parent must be "capable of teaching" and maintain an attendance register, but there is no testing required. Alternatively, homeschoolers may have a private tutor (state-certified teacher) 175 days per year, three hours per day; no record keeping or testing is required. For the private school and tutor options, required subjects are the same as in the public schools (must be in English). Students may also study at home by enrolling in independent study programs through a public or private school, and complying with the school's requirements.

California Education Code sections 33190, 48222, 48224, and 51745-51747

Colorado

Compulsory school ages: 7 to 16 (also 6-year-olds who have been enrolled in public school in first grade or higher, unless parent withdraws child)

Homeschoolers may establish and operate a homeschool by filing a notice of intent with the local superintendent 14 or more days before starting homeschooling. Students must attend homeschool 172 days per year, averaging four hours per day, covering basic academic subjects. Parents must maintain records of attendance, immunizations, and results of testing or evaluations (required in grades 3, 5, 7, 9, and 11), and provide test/evaluation results to the school district on an annual basis. (District uses test scores or evaluations for purposes of evaluating the student's educational progress.) Alternatively, students may enroll in an independent or parochial school that allows home instruction or use a state-certified private tutor. If the parent is a licensed Colorado teacher, then the student is exempt from homeschooling requirements.

Colorado Revised Statutes 22-33-104 and 104.5

Connecticut

Compulsory school ages: 5 to 16 (5- and 6-year-olds may be exempted by parent)

Homeschoolers may establish and operate a homeschool by filing a voluntary notice of intent form with the local superintendent (not required). Instruction should cover basic academic subjects, including government at various levels. No testing or teacher qualifications, but homeschoolers maintain portfolios, also voluntary, to show that instruction has taken place.

Connecticut General Statutes Ann. 10-184 and 10-220; Public Acts 93-252 and 94-245

Delaware

Compulsory school ages: 5 (may be delayed with school authorization, if in the best interests of the child) to 16

Homeschoolers may join a homeschool association or organization, or may establish and operate a homeschool on their own, or may register with the local superintendent. Any of these options requires notifying the Department of Education of attendance, enrollment, and student ages by July 31 of each year, and follow up with a report of enrollment by last school day of September. Students must attend homeschool 180 days per year.

Delaware Code 14-2702 through 2704

Florida

Compulsory school ages: 6 (by February 1) to 16

Homeschoolers may establish and operate a homeschool by filing a notice of intent with the local superintendent within 30 days of establishing it (required just the first year), or they may qualify as part of a private school corporation (an incorporated group of homeschool families). Testing, admission, and record-keeping requirements for families that are part of a private school corporation are established by the corporation. Families who have filed a letter of intent with the local superintendent must maintain a portfolio of records which includes a reading list and samples of the student's work. Each year's portfolio must be kept for two years and be made available for inspection to the superintendent or designee upon 15 days written notice. Students must be tested or evaluated annually, and results reported to the superintendent. If the test scores or evaluation results are not satisfactory, student can be placed on a one-year probation.

Florida Statute Ann. 228.041 Definitions/34, 232.01 and 232.02

Georgia

Compulsory school ages: 7 to 16 (younger children are also required to attend if they have attended public school for more than 20 days)

Homeschoolers may establish and conduct a home study program by filing a declaration of intent with the local superintendent within 30 days of starting homeschooling (and by September 1 of following years). Basic academic subjects and 180 days of attendance (four hours per day) are required. Teaching parent must have a high school diploma or GED; any private tutors used (not required) must have a four-year degree. Parents must maintain attendance records (submitted monthly to the superintendent), write and maintain an annual progress report, and test students at the end of 3rd, 6th, 9th, and 12th grades (test scores kept by parent).

Official Code of Georgia Ann. 20-2-690 and 20-2-698

Hawaii

Compulsory school ages: 6 to 18 (by January 1)

Homeschoolers may establish and operate a homeschool based on a customized, structured, up-to-date curriculum by notifying the principal of the school student would otherwise attend before starting homeschooling (required the first year and any year student would change schools), maintaining a record of the curriculum, and testing students in grades 3, 6, 8, and 10. Annual report to principal must include the test results or an evaluation (completed by either a certified teacher or the child's parent). Alternatively, students may enroll in an alternative educational program approved by the school district superintendent, during which they will participate in testing at the same time as public school students.

Hawaii Revised Statutes 21; 21;296-12, 298-9

Idaho

Compulsory school ages: 7 to 16

Homeschoolers may provide an alternate educational experience in which the students are "otherwise comparably instructed." Students must "attend" during the same days and cover the same basic academic areas as public school students, but there is no notice, record keeping, or testing required, and no minimum teacher qualifications..

Idaho Code 33-202 and 33-203

Illinois

Compulsory school ages: 7 to 16

Homeschoolers may operate a homeschool as a private school. Instruction must be in English and must cover basic academic areas plus honesty, justice, kindness, and moral courage. There is no required notice, record keeping, or testing, and no minimum teacher qualifications (although a withdrawal letter for students who have been enrolled in public schools may be advisable).

Illinois Compiled Statutes Ann. 5/26-1

Indiana

Compulsory school ages: 7 (or from the time child is first enrolled in a school, if younger) to 18

Homeschoolers may operate a homeschool as a private school, with student attending 180 days per year. No notification required unless the state superintendent specifically requests it. Homeschoolers must maintain attendance records, but there is no required testing and no minimum teacher qualifications.

Indiana Statutes Ann. 20-8.1-3-17, 20-8.1-3-33, and 20-8.1-3-34

Iowa

Compulsory school ages: 6 (by September 15) to 16

Homeschoolers may enroll in a homeschool assistance program through a public or accredited nonpublic school, following the requirements of the program, or may provide "competent private instruction" for at least 148 days per year. The private instruction option requires filing of a "Competent Private Instruction Report Form" with the local school district every year by the first day of school (or within 14 days of leaving public school), with students attending 148 days per year. There are no minimum teacher qualifications or required subjects. By June 1 of each year, parents must submit to the local school district either standardized test results (from testing completed by May 1), a portfolio, or a report of progress from a properly accredited correspondence school. If scores or progress are below standards, child may be enrolled in school or placed under approved remediation. If a licensed teacher is involved in the homeschool (either as a supervisor, with meetings twice a quarter, or as a private tutor), there is no requirement for submitting test results or a portfolio at the end of the year.

Iowa Code 1999: 299-1 through 299-24 and Iowa Administrative Code Section 31.7 (4) d.

Kansas

Compulsory school ages: 7 to 18

Homeschoolers may operate a homeschool as a non-accredited private school "substantially equivalent to the public schools" by registering the name and address of the school with the state board of education. Although the law states that students must attend 186 days each year and teachers must be "competent," there is no requirement to report attendance and the school board has no authority to define "competence." There are also no requirements for testing. Alternatively, homeschools can be operated as satellites of accredited private schools and be subject to that school's requirements. Students can be exempted entirely from educational requirements in the high school years for religious reasons.

Kansas Statutes 72-1111 through 72-1113

Kentucky

Compulsory school ages: 6 to 16 (younger if student has graduated from high school)

Homeschools may qualify as a private school by notifying the local board of education of the names of attending students within two weeks of the start of the school year. Students must attend 1,050 hours per year, the equivalent of 175 six-hour days and receive instruction in basic subjects. There are no testing requirements or minimum teacher qualifications, and the only records required are an attendance register and scholarship records.

Kentucky Revised Statutes: 159.010, 159.030, 159.040, 159.160, and 158.050

Louisiana

Compulsory school ages: 7 to 17 (or younger, if high school graduate)

Homeschooling parents may either choose to register with the state as a homeschool (with many requirements for approval) or establish a private school in their home (a much simpler process). Homeschoolers who choose to establish and operate a homeschool (as approved by the board of education) file an application and a copy of the child's birth certificate within 15 days of starting to homeschool (and each year after that). Under this option, parents are required to show, at the end of each year, that the education offered is at least as good as that in the public schools (by test results, teacher evaluation, or portfolio review); that is, that their children are at grade level or above. If they are below grade level, and they can show that they have progressed one grade level from the previous year, they will be approved for homeschooling the following year. Otherwise, they will not. Parents bear the cost of tests, if they elect to use that method to prove that their children have progressed. Under the private school option, homeschoolers file a letter of intent to operate the private school in their home, and are thus exempted from any requirements to prove the quality of instruction.

Louisiana Revised Statutes 17:11, 17:221(A), and 17.23

Maine

Compulsory school ages: 7 to 17

Homeschoolers may establish and operate a homeschool by completing an application form and submitting a copy to the commissioner of the state Department of Education (and a copy to the local school board as a courtesy) for approval 60 days before starting to homeschool. Basic academic subjects (including Maine studies and computer proficiency during the upper grades) are required, but there are no required records and no minimum teacher qualifications. Students should attend 175 days per year, and must be tested or evaluated once a year (results to be submitted to state and local authorities). Alternatively, homeschoolers may operate a homeschool as a non-approved private school, as long as they teach at least two unrelated students, and thereby be exempt from all attendance, subject, and testing requirements. There are no minimum teacher qualifications for non-approved private schools.

Maine Revised Statute Annotated Title 20A-5001A

Maryland

Compulsory school ages: 5 to 16, with one-year exemption available for 5-year-olds

Homeschoolers may establish and operate a qualified homeschool by signing an assurance of consent form and submitting it to the local school superintendent 15 days before beginning homeschooling. Parents must maintain a portfolio showing that they are providing regular, thorough instruction, which the local superintendent will review at designated intervals (no more than three times a year). There are no minimum teacher qualifications or testing requirements, but a non-satisfactory review could result in children being placed back in public schools. Alternatively, parents may enroll students with a state-recognized correspondence school, church school, or other umbrella organization offering a homeschool program, by notifying their local superintendent (on the one-time assurance of consent form), which exempts them from any requirements for portfolio reviews or state supervision. The private organization then provides the necessary reviews and support.

Annotated Code of Maryland, chapter 22, 7-301(a)

Massachusetts

Compulsory school ages: 6 to 16

Homeschoolers may establish and operate a homeschool as approved in advance by the local school committee or superintendent. The lack of statewide standards for homeschooling gives parents a freedom to make their own cases to the local school boards, most of which now are comfortable with homeschoolers. Landmark state supreme court decisions Charles and Brunelle give the boards guidelines for what they may and may not ask for and plainly show that home schools legitimately differ from public schools. Parents should describe their educational plan (limited to listing the subjects—and possibly resources and grade levels—that will be covered) and some kind of plan for periodic evaluation (method to be mutually agreed upon by school officials and parents) with confidence in their own abilities to know what is best for their children as well as in their own academic qualifications.. Local school districts then approve the homeschool as an alternative method of education equal "in thoroughness and efficiency, and in progress made" to the public schools in the same town. If approval is denied, the district must give reasons, and parents have the opportunity to re-submit a plan that will satisfy their requirements more fully.

Massachusetts General Laws 76-1, Charles (1987) and Brunelle (1998) decisions

Michigan

Compulsory school ages: 6 to 16

Homeschoolers may establish and operate an organized home education program, being subject to the local school district's interpretation of the compulsory school attendance law. There are no requirements for notification, record keeping, or testing, and no minimum teacher qualifications under this option, but basic academic subjects must be covered. Alternatively, homeschoolers may operate a homeschool as a non-public school. As such, they notify the Department of Education and comply with teacher certification (unless claiming a religious exemption) and requirements for record keeping, enrollment, and courses of study, but there are still no testing requirements.

Michigan Revised School Code section 1561(3) and 1561(4)

Minnesota

Compulsory school ages: 7 to 18

Homeschoolers may establish and operate a homeschool by filing an annual report (listing the name, birthdate, and address of each child taught, plus teacher and immmunization information) to the superintendent of the local school district. Basic subjects must be covered (and parents must make available records that prove they are). If the teaching parent doesn't have a baccalaureate degree, homeschoolers must submit a quarterly report to the local superintendent showing the achievement of each child in the required subjects. In addition, an annual test (standardized, nationally-normed) is required (for parents' use only), and if a student does not achieve at least the 30th percentile, parents are required to obtain further evaluations to determine whether the student has learning problems. Superintendent may request one home visit per year, and more if problems are found, but the parent may decline the visit and bring teaching materials and plans to the superintendent's office instead.

Minnesota Statutes 120A.22, 120A.24 and 121A.15

Mississippi

Compulsory school ages: 6 to 17 (on or before September 1)

Homeschoolers may establish and operate a homeschool by filing a certificate of enrollment with the district's attendance officer by September 15 of each year. There are no required subjects or records or tests and no minimum teacher qualifications. The number of days of required attendance are whatever it takes to progress one grade level per year.

Mississippi Code Ann. 37-13-91

Missouri

Compulsory school ages: 7 to 16

Homeschoolers may establish and operate a homeschool by providing a notice of intent (for their own protection from truancy laws) within 30 days of beginning homeschooling and on September 1 of each year after that. Parents must maintain a record of subjects taught, activities engaged in, school work samples, and evaluations (or a credible equivalent for each of these). Students must receive 1,000 hours of instruction per year, at least 600 in the five required subjects, of which 400 are at home. There are no minimum teacher qualifications or testing requirements.

Ann. Missouri Statutes 167.031, 167.042, 167.061, 167.071, 162.996 and 167.619

Montana

Compulsory school ages: 7 (before the first day of school) to 16 (or completion of 8th grade, whichever is later)

Homeschoolers may establish and operate a homeschool by filing an annual notice of intent with the county superintendent. Parents must maintain attendance and immunization records and provide the same basic instructional program as the public schools. Students must receive 180 days of instruction (four hours per day for grades 1–3 and six for grades 4–12). There are no minimum teacher qualifications and no testing requirements, but records must be available for inspection by county superintendent.

Montana Codes 20-5-102 and 20-5-109

Nebraska

Compulsory school ages: 7 to 16

Homeschoolers may establish and operate a homeschool as a private school by filing an annual notice of intent with the state commissioner of education by August 1 (or 30 days before starting to homeschool). Private schools must provide evidence of compliance with safety regulations. They can elect to not be state-accredited (and thus be exempted from teacher certification requirements) by signing a statement that the legal requirements for accreditation either violate religious beliefs or interfere with the parents' rights to direct their children's education. Basic academic subjects are required, but the state cannot impose testing on homeschool private schools unless it also imposes testing on all other private schools. Students should receive a minimum number of hours of instruction (1,032 in elementary grades and 1,080 in high school grades), and parents must have records to prove attendance and some kind of sequentially progressive curriculum.

Nebraska Revised Statutes 79-201, 79-1601, 79-1602, 79-1701, and 85-607

Nevada

Compulsory school ages: 7 to 17

Homeschoolers must file an intent form with the local school board, in which they state that they assume full responsibility that their child will receive "equivalent instruction." First-year homeschoolers must 1) have the form also signed by a consultant (three-year homeschool veteran) or licensed teacher; 2) be a licensed teacher (in any state) for the grade level to be taught; or 3) use an approved correspondence course. After the first year (as long as parents comply with the annual requirement for written evidence of taking responsibility for their children's education, above), this requirement is waived. The intent form also requires a description of goals and objectives, a list of resources to be used to meet them, and a school calendar, to be broken down into days per month. There is no required testing. Homeschoolers may opt for "dual enrollment" to give them access to all public school courses and programs (except sports)

Nevada Revised Statute 392.070

New Hampshire

Compulsory school ages: 6 (on September 30) to 16

Homeschoolers may establish and operate a homeschool by filing a notice of intent with a non-public school principal, the state commissioner of education, or the local superintendent by the first day of school (followed by a curriculum sketch within 30 days). Instruction must cover basic academic subjects, including U.S. and New Hampshire constitutional history and art and music appreciation. Parents must submit, by July 1 of each year, standardized test results or a written evaluation by a certified teacher or some other form of progress measure approved by the participating agency above. Unsatisfactory results (or failure to report) will place the homeschooler on probation, with one year to produce another test or evaluation with satisfactory results. Homeschoolers maintain a portfolio with reading/text lists and examples of writing and other work. There are no attendance requirements or minimum teacher qualifications.

New Hampshire Revised Statutes 193-A

New Jersey

Compulsory school ages: 6 to 16

Homeschoolers may educate their children at home without formal notification, but may elect to notify school districts to protect themselves from charges of truancy. There are no requirements for attendance, testing, record keeping, notice, or teacher qualifications. The subjects covered should be comparable to public school subjects.

New Jersey Statute Ann. 18A 38-25

New Mexico

Compulsory school ages: 5 (prior to 12:01am on September 1) to the age of majority or when the student has graduated from high school (children under 8 can be excused)

Homeschoolers may establish and operate a homeschool by filing a notice of intent, a calendar of planned school days (which should match the local school district in number), and a record of (or signed objection to) immunizations with the school district. These notarized documents must be submitted within 30 days of starting homeschool and by April 1 of each year following. The home-school operator (parent) must have a high school diploma or equivalent, and maintain attendance and immunization records. Students must receive instruction in basic academic subjects and in grades 4, 6, and 8, take a standardized test, either with the school district or through Bob Jones University Press (BJUP) Testing Service. If parents elect to use BJUP, district must be notified of their intent to do so by January 15.

New Mexico Statutes Ann. 22-1-2, 22-1-2.1, and 22-2-2

New York

Compulsory school ages: 6 (by December 1) to 16 (must complete that school year), or until student finishes high school if that comes first

Homeschoolers may educate their children at home by filing an annual notice of intent with the local superintendent by July 1 or within 14 days of starting homeschooling and submitting an individualized home instruction plan. Parents must be "competent" teachers, and must keep and be willing to show attendance records to show that students are attending the equivalent of 180 days of schooling per year (900 hours per year for grades 1-6 and 990 hours a year for grades 7-12). In upper level grades, students must receive a certain number of hours of instruction in a comprehensive list of specific subjects each year, and parents must report courses, hours, and grades quarterly. Each year, parents must file test results or a written evaluation by a certified teacher, homeschool peer review panel, or other approved person (must be a test every other year in grades 4–8 and every year in grades 9–12).

Regulations of the New York State Commissioner of Education, section 100.10

North Carolina

Compulsory school ages: 7 to 16 (16 –17 year old homeschoolers who want a driver's license must be enrolled with the DNPE)

Homeschoolers may establish and operate a homeschool by filing a notice of intent with the state division of non-public education when they start. The teaching parent, who must have a high school diploma or GED, must maintain attendance and immunization records (or statement of religious exemption). The results of annual standardized tests must be kept for one year after testing. Attendance record and test results must be submitted annually to the DNPE. Students are to receive instruction in basic academic subjects and attend homeschool at least nine calendar months per year (excluding holidays and vacations), but the law doesn't specify which months. The DNPE may request a home visit, but in practice, they usually don't unless there has been a complaint.

North Carolina General Statutes, Article 39 115C-378 and 115C-547 through 115C-565

North Dakota

Compulsory school ages: 7 to 16

Homeschoolers may establish and operate a homeschool by filing an annual notice of intent with the local superintendent 14 days before starting to homeschool or within 14 days of establishing residency inside the district. Parents must have either 1) a teaching certificate; 2) a four-year college degree; or 3) a high school diploma or GED; and must be monitored by a certified teacher for the first two years (and for all grades K–3, and continuing if testing shows scores under the 50th percentile). Parents may also 4) qualify by passing the national teacher exam with at least the cut-off score. Students must take a standardized test (given by a certified teacher) in grades 3, 4, 6, 8, and 11; receive instruction in a long list of academic and practical living skills; and attend homeschool 175 days per year, four hours per day. Parents must also maintain a record of courses and academic progress (including test scores), and submit test results to the local superintendent. (Composite scores below the 30th percentile require remediation, but not necessarily a return to public school.) There are additional requirements for autistic children. Alternatively, a parent with an ND teaching certificate may operate a homeschool as an approved private school, and be exempt from the recording and testing requirements.

North Dakota Century Code 15-34.1-01 and 15-34.1-04

Ohio

Compulsory school ages: 6 to 18

Homeschoolers may establish and operate a homeschool by submitting an annual notice of intent to the local superintendent. Parents must have a high school diploma or equivalent, or work under a person with a four-year college degree (until student's test scores show proficiency or parent earns high school diploma or equivalent). With renewal notification, parents must submit standardized test results or a written narrative showing satisfactory progress or some other approved assessment. Students attend 900 hours of homeschool per year, and receive instruction in basic academic areas (including Ohio history), physical education, and first aid.

Ohio Revised Code 3301-34, 3321-03, and 3321-04

Oklahoma
Compulsory school ages: 5 to 18

Homeschoolers may establish and operate a homeschool with no formal notification and "in good faith" and provide approximately 180 days of instruction in basic academic subjects, but there are no requirements for attendance, record keeping, or testing, and no minimum teacher qualifications.

Oklahoma Statute Ann. Title 70, 10-105 (A) and (B)

Oregon
Compulsory school ages: 7 to 18 years (or upon completion of 12th grade)

Homeschoolers may establish and operate a homeschool by notifying their education service district in writing when they start. (No notification is needed for following years unless the family moves to a new district.) Students must receive instruction in the same subjects as public schools (primarily in English), attend the same number of days/hours, and take an approved comprehensive test in grades

3, 5, 8, and 10 (administered by a qualified neutral person); additionally, if the student was withdrawn from public school, the first test must be taken within 18 months of withdrawal. Test scores are submitted only if requested by the education service district, but if the scores fall below the 15th percentile, the student enters a period of probation with more testing requirements. Oregon sets no minimum teacher qualifications and requires no record keeping.

Oregon Revised Statutes 339.010, 339.030, and 339.035

Pennsylvania

Compulsory school ages: 8 (or when the child enters school, if younger) to 17

Homeschoolers may establish and operate a homeschool by filing a notarized affidavit with the local superintendent before starting homeschooling (and by August 1 in following years). Parents must have a high school diploma (or equivalent), and maintain and submit annually a portfolio for each student (with materials used, work done, annual evaluation, and standardized test results for required grades). Students must be tested in grades 3, 5, and 8; attend homeschool 180 days per year (900 hours for elementary and 990 hours for secondary); and receive instruction in a list of basic academic areas (including Pennsylvania history), plus art, music, and fire prevention. The written evaluation must be completed by June 30 of each year. Alternatively, parents may operate the homeschool as an extension or satellite of a private school (whose principal must file a notarized affidavit with the Department of Education). Another alternative is for parents to use a paid, teacher-certified, private tutor, whose credentials (and criminal history record) must be filed with the local superintendent. Both these alternatives exempt parents from minimum teacher qualifications, testing, and record keeping, except for whatever the private school or tutor requires.

Pennsylvania Statute Ann. Title 24, 13-1326 and 13-1327

Rhode Island

Compulsory school ages: 6 (on or before December 31) to 16

Homeschoolers may establish and operate a homeschool by getting it approved by the local school board. Local support groups who know the "climate" can help to design a program that will be considered "substantially equal" to that of the public schools by the local school board. Students should receive instruction in the same academic subjects as the public schools, including Rhode Island history and, in high school, the Rhode Island constitution. There are no minimum teacher qualifications, but parents must maintain an attendance register, and, depending on the school district's requirements, will need to submit an acceptable form of evaluation, which may include report cards or standardized tests.

Rhode Island General Laws 16-19-1

South Carolina

Compulsory school ages: 5 (before September 1) to 17 (earlier if graduated from high school); 5-year-olds may be excused from kindergarten with submission of written notice to the school district

Homeschoolers may establish and operate a homeschool as approved by the local school board. Parents must have a high school diploma (or GED)

and maintain records of subjects taught and activities engaged in, a portfolio of the student's work, and academic evaluations. Students must attend homeschool for 180 days per year (at least four hours per day) and receive instruction in basic academic areas. Twice yearly, parents must submit a progress report to the school district, including attendance records and evaluations in each of the required subjects. Students must also participate in the annual statewide testing program and the Basic Skills Assessment Program. Depending on the school district, homeschoolers may find it easier to join the South Carolina Association of Independent Home Schools and comply with their paperwork and accountability options (which will exempt them from keeping state-required records, testing, and submitting progress reports to the school district); or to join an equivalent homeschool association with at least 50 members (and still maintain the state-required records but be exempted from testing requirements).

Code of Laws of South Carolina Ann. 59-65-10, 40, 45, and 47

South Dakota

Compulsory school ages: 6 (by September 1) to 16; children under age 7 may be excused

Homeschoolers may establish and operate a homeschool by having an "Application for Excuse of Attendance" approved by the local school board. Anybody (not just parents) may instruct students, as long as no more than 22 children are being taught at the same location. There are no minimum teacher qualifications, but the state Department of Education may investigate to see if students are being taught adequately in the minimum subjects of language arts and math, and parents should be prepared to show attendance records and proof of academic progress. Students must be tested in the same grades as public school students (4, 8, and 11). Test scores are kept on file at the public school the student would have attended, and must show satisfactory progress or certificate of excuse for attendance may not be renewed.

South Dakota Codified Law 13-27-2, 13-27-3, and 13-27-7

Tennessee

Compulsory school ages: 6 (earlier if child has enrolled in any public, private, or parochial school for more than six weeks) to 17; 6-year-olds may be excused for one semester or one year with application to principal

Homeschoolers may establish and operate a homeschool by submitting a notice of intent to the local superintendent by August 1 of each school year. Parents must have a high school diploma or GED for teaching grades K–8 and a college degree (or an exemption) for teaching grades 9–12. Attendance records (showing 180 days per year, four hours per day) must be submitted to the local superintendent at the end of the school year and kept available for inspection at other times. Students must receive instruction in basic academics and either college preparatory or general subjects in high school grades, but there are no required subjects for grades K–8. Students must take a standardized test in grades 5, 7, and 9, which shall be given by a person designated by the commissioner of education or a testing service approved by the local school district. If the homeschool is operated in association with a church-related school, the requirements for attendance, subjects to be studied, and record keeping are waived except as prescribed by the church school, and minimum teacher qualifications are reduced to none for grades K–8 and a high school diploma (or GED) for grades 9–12. Students in grades 9–12 must still be registered with the local school district, and must be tested in the same way the local school district tests students at their grade level. For any required tests, results are sent to the district. If students fail to meet minimum standards for two years in a row, they must be enrolled in a public or private school.

Tennessee Code 49-6-3001, 49-6-3050, and 49-50-801

Texas

Compulsory school ages: 6 (or younger, if previously enrolled in first grade) to 17 (until the end of that academic year)

Homeschoolers may establish and operate a homeschool as a private school, which exempts them from any state or local oversight. Homeschools must be run in a bona fide manner and use a written curriculum (video or computer courses qualify) that covers basic specified academic subjects, and parents must cooperate with reasonable requests to verify that they are doing so.

Texas Education Code sections 21.032 through 21.040

Utah

Compulsory school ages: 6 to 18

Homeschoolers may request an exemption from compulsory attendance from the local school district. Applications to homeschool should show that attendance will be substantially the same as public schools and students will be instructed in the required basic academic areas (consult a list before preparing application). There are no minimum teacher qualifications, but the local school board can consider the basic educative ability of the teacher. There is no testing required. Also, if a group of homeschool families sets themselves up as a private school, none of the requirements for attendance, subjects, record keeping, or notification apply. The families are instead accountable to the private school organization.

Utah Code Ann. 53A-11-1012

Vermont

Compulsory school ages: 7 to 16

Homeschoolers may establish and operate a homeschool by filing a written notice of enrollment with the commissioner of education any time after March 1 for the subsequent year, along with information about how subject areas will be covered and any required assessments from the previous year. If the homeschool is deemed inadequate, enrollment may be disallowed (but only after a hearing). For allowed enrollments, students must attend 175 days per year and receive instruction in basic academic areas, including Vermont government and fine arts. There are no record-keeping requirements or minimum teacher qualifications. Parents must submit annually either: 1) a written assessment by a certified (or approved Vermont independent school) teacher; 2) a report from a commercial curriculum publisher, parents, or student's instructor, together with a portfolio; or 3) results of an acceptably administered standardized test.

Vermont Statute Ann. Title 16, sections 1121, 16(11), 166b, and 906

Virginia

Compulsory school ages: 5 (on or before September 30) to 18; 5-year-olds can be excused

Homeschoolers may establish and operate a homeschool by filing an annual notice of intent with the local superintendent by August 31, or as soon as practicable if starting mid-year. A teaching parent must have a four-year college degree, be a certified teacher, use an approved correspondence course, or submit acceptable curriculum and otherwise be proven able to teach. Students must attend the same number of days as public schools and receive instruction in required academic subjects. No records are required, but parents must submit results of a standardized test or other assessment every year by August 1 to the local superintendent. To continue homeschooling, student must achieve at least the 40th percentile on the test or be shown to be achieving an adequate level of educational progress on the assessment. Under certain conditions, homeschool may be exempt from some or all of these conditions (except the notification requirement) under the religious exemption statute, and if the homeschool uses a certified private tutor, there are no requirements for attendance, record keeping, or annual testing/assessment.

Virginia Code 22.1-254 and 22.1-254.1

Washington

Compulsory school ages: 8 to 18 (or 15 if regularly employed or at a level of education equivalent to graduation or determined by district superintendent to be reasonably proficient at 9th-grade level)

Homeschoolers may establish and operate a homeschool by filing an annual notice of intent with the local superintendent by September 15 or within two weeks of the start of any public school quarter. Parents must 1) have completed a year of college credit or an approved homeschool course; 2) be supervised by a certified teacher; or 3) be deemed qualified by the local superintendent. In grades 1–3, students must attend a total of 2,700 hours over the three-year period; in grades 4–6, 2,970 hours over the three-year period; in grades 7–8, a total of 1,980 hours; and in grades 9–12, 4,320 hours over the four-year period, but since there is no mechanism for reporting attendance, this requirement is liberally construed. Parents must provide instruction in basic required academic areas (including Washington State history in high school), have students tested (by a state-approved standardized test) or evaluated (by a certified teacher) annually, and maintain test/evaluation results and immunization records. The tests/evaluations are for the parents' use only and are never submitted to officials. Alternatively, the homeschool may be operated as an extension of a private school, under the supervision of a certified teacher employed by the private school, and be exempt from notification, record keeping, and testing requirements except as required by the private school.

Revised Code of Washington 28A.200.010, 28A.200.020, 28A.195.010, and 28A.225.010

West Virginia

Compulsory school ages: 6 (before September 1, or upon enrollment in public kindergarten) to 16

Homeschoolers may establish and operate a homeschool by filing a notice of intent with the local superintendent before starting to homeschool (giving two weeks' notice if withdrawing student from a public school). The teaching parent must have a high school diploma or proof of formal education at least four years higher than all students being taught. Students must receive instruction in basic required subjects, but there are no attendance or record-keeping requirements.

Parents must have students' progress assessed annually by: 1) administering an acceptable standardized test; 2) having students evaluated by a certified teacher (portfolio review); or 3) assessing progress by another means agreeable to both parents and county superintendent. Parents may not test their own children. Test scores or evaluation results are shown to the county superintendent by June 30 each year; if scores are below the 40th percentile two years in a row, homeschooling will no longer satisfy the compulsory school requirements. Alternatively, parents may seek local school board approval to operate a homeschool. In such cases, the local superintendent and school board determine whether the teacher is qualified to teach, and also determine what records, reports, tests, visits, or meetings they might require. In some counties, this would be an easier option; in others, harder.

West Virginia Code 18-18-1

Wisconsin

Compulsory school ages: 6 (by September 1) to 18

Establish and operate a "home-based private educational program" by filing a statement of enrollment with the state Department of Education by October 15 of each year. There are no record-keeping or testing requirements and no minimum teacher qualifications. Parents must provide at least 875 hours of instruction per year (equivalent to 175 five-hour days), and students must receive "a sequentially progressive curriculum of fundamental instruction" in basic required subject areas.

Wisconsin Statutes and Annotations 115.001(3g), 115.30(3), 118.15(1), and 118.165(1)

Wyoming

Compulsory school ages: 7 (before September 15) to 16 (earlier, if student has completed 10th grade)

Homeschoolers may establish and operate a homeschool by submitting to the local school board a curriculum plan to show that a "basic academic educational program" is being provided, and being approved to teach. There are no minimum teacher qualifications and no testing requirements. Parents should maintain records showing that they are teaching the required number of days and actually using the proposed curriculum. Students should attend homeschool 175 days per year and receive sequentially progressive, fundamental instruction in basic required subjects.

Wyoming Statutes 21-4-101

District of Columbia

Compulsory school ages: 5 (by December 31) to 18

Homeschools provide "private instruction" during the period that public schools are in session. No teacher qualifications, testing, or record keeping is required. Notification is required only if the child is being withdrawn from public schools.

District of Columbia Code 31-401 and 402

A

The *Unofficial Guide*™ Reader Questionnaire

If you would like to express your opinion about homeschooling or this guide, please complete this questionnaire and mail it to:

The *Unofficial Guide*™ Reader Questionnaire
IDG Lifestyle Group
1633 Broadway, floor 7
New York, NY 10019-6785

Gender: ___ M ___ F

Age: ___ Under 30 ___ 31–40 ___ 41–50
___ Over 50

Education: ___ High school ___ College
___ Graduate/Professional

What is your occupation?

_____

How did you hear about this guide?
___ Friend or relative
___ Newspaper, magazine, or Internet
___ Radio or TV
___ Recommended at bookstore
___ Recommended by librarian
___ Picked it up on my own
___ Familiar with the *Unofficial Guide*™ travel series

Did you go to the bookstore specifically for a book on homeschooling? Yes ___ No ___

Have you used any other *Unofficial Guides*™?
Yes ___ No ___

If Yes, which ones?

_____
_____
_____

What other book(s) on homeschooling have you purchased?_____

_____

_____

Was this book:
___ more helpful than other(s)
___ less helpful than other(s)

Do you think this book was worth its price?
Yes ___   No ___

Did this book cover all topics related to homeschooling adequately?
Yes ___   No ___

Please explain your answer:

_____

_____

_____

Were there any specific sections in this book that were of particular help to you?   Yes ___   No ___

Please explain your answer:

_____

_____

_____

On a scale of 1 to 10, with 10 being the best rating, how would you rate this guide? ___

What other titles would you like to see published in the *Unofficial Guide*™ series?

_____

_____

Are Unofficial Guides™ **readily available in your area?**   Yes ___   No ___

Other comments:

_____

_____

_____

_____

Get the inside scoop...with the *Unofficial Guides*™!

Health and Fitness

The Unofficial Guide to Alternative Medicine
ISBN: 0-02-862526-9 Price: $15.95

The Unofficial Guide to Conquering Impotence
ISBN: 0-02-862870-5 Price: $15.95

The Unofficial Guide to Coping with Menopause
ISBN: 0-02-862694-x Price: $15.95

The Unofficial Guide to Cosmetic Surgery
ISBN: 0-02-862522-6 Price: $15.95

The Unofficial Guide to Dieting Safely
ISBN: 0-02-862521-8 Price: $15.95

The Unofficial Guide to Having a Baby
ISBN: 0-02-862695-8 Price: $15.95

The Unofficial Guide to Living with Diabetes
ISBN: 0-02-862919-1 Price: $15.95

The Unofficial Guide to Overcoming Arthritis
ISBN: 0-02-862714-8 Price: $15.95

The Unofficial Guide to Overcoming Infertility
ISBN: 0-02-862916-7 Price: $15.95

Career Planning

The Unofficial Guide to Acing the Interview
ISBN: 0-02-862924-8 Price: $15.95

The Unofficial Guide to Earning What You Deserve
ISBN: 0-02-862523-4 Price: $15.95

The Unofficial Guide to Hiring and Firing People
ISBN: 0-02-862523-4 Price: $15.95

Business and Personal Finance

The Unofficial Guide to Investing
ISBN: 0-02-862458-0 Price: $15.95

The Unofficial Guide to Investing in Mutual Funds
ISBN: 0-02-862920-5 Price: $15.95

The Unofficial Guide to Managing Your Personal Finances
ISBN: 0-02-862921-3 Price: $15.95

The Unofficial Guide to Starting a Small Business
ISBN: 0-02-862525-0 Price: $15.95

Home and Automotive

The Unofficial Guide to Buying a Home
ISBN: 0-02-862461-0 Price: $15.95

The Unofficial Guide to Buying or Leasing a Car
ISBN: 0-02-862524-2 Price: $15.95

The Unofficial Guide to Hiring Contractors
ISBN: 0-02-862460-2 Price: $15.95

Family and Relationships

The Unofficial Guide to Childcare
ISBN: 0-02-862457-2 Price: $15.95

The Unofficial Guide to Dating Again
ISBN: 0-02-862454-8 Price: $15.95

The Unofficial Guide to Divorce
ISBN: 0-02-862455-6 Price: $15.95

The Unofficial Guide to Eldercare
ISBN: 0-02-862456-4 Price: $15.95

The Unofficial Guide to Planning Your Wedding
ISBN: 0-02-862459-9 Price: $15.95

Hobbies and Recreation

The Unofficial Guide to Finding Rare Antiques
ISBN: 0-02-862922-1 Price: $15.95

The Unofficial Guide to Casino Gambling
ISBN: 0-02-862917-5 Price: $15.95

All books in the *Unofficial Guide*™ series are available at your local bookseller.